AF556112

The Foundations of New India

By K. M. PANIKKAR

India and the Indian Ocean
Asia and Western Dominance
The Founding of the Kashmir State
The Two Chinas
The Afro-Asian States

THE FOUNDATIONS OF NEW INDIA

K.M. Panikkar

First Published 1963
First LG Edition 2019

ISBN 978–93–83723–54–6 (Hb)

Published by
LG PUBLISHERS DISTRIBUTORS
49, Street No. 14, Pratap Nagar,
Mayur Vihar Phase I, Delhi 110091
lgpdist@gmail.com

Printed at
Sapra Brothers, Noida

CONTENTS

PART I

INDIA'S INHERITANCE

Part I

The Challenge and the Response

CHAPTER I

The Challenge and the Response

I

The emergence of India as an independent nation is, it will be conceded by all, a fact of more than ordinary significance. For over one hundred and fifty years Britain had dominated the sub-continent. Even in areas where it did not directly rule, Britain's authority was supreme. Thus, it came face to face with another civilization over every aspect of which it exercised a dominant influence for a very considerable period.

The encounter between India and Britain is something which is without parallel in history. The impact of Islam, starting with the invasions of Mohammed Ghori, lasted for a longer period and in a measure is a continuing fact. But it has not had the same fundamental significance as the contact that India had with England. The dominance that Islam exercised in many parts of India was mainly political and military. Except for sporadic efforts at conversion, there was no attempt to challenge the religion, philosophy or social life of the Hindus. Their laws were left untouched. The Islamic state did not enforce an educational system. In fact Hindus and Muslims lived as parallel societies. This does not mean that they did not influence each other; but that the institutions, beliefs and social structure of Hinduism were not interfered with and their assumptions challenged by the Muslims who for a time formed the dominant community.

Nowhere in the world, in fact, was there ever the kind of encounter which Hinduism and the West had in India. Such major encounters elsewhere had led either to the displacement of civilizations or of peoples. The most outstanding instances in the old world are those of Persia and Egypt. Both were ancient and historic civilizations, but, faced with the power of Islam, they lost their identity in a greater Islamic civilization. No doubt old Iranian influence has persisted and may be said to be a continuing influence in Persia. In Egypt, the displacement has been more complete. Neither the Pharaonic nor the Greco-Roman civilization of ancient times can claim to be represented in Egyptian life today. Egyptian civilization during the last 1,200 years is predominantly Arabic and Muslim. Similar is the case with the great civilizations which had flowered under Roman and Christian influences in Africa on the southern littoral of the Mediterranean. Today they are Islamic with hardly any important cultural roots in their pre-Islamic past.

Mexico and Peru, the two great empires where the pre-Columbian Americans had developed remarkably high civilizations provide other striking examples of displacements of culture. In both these empires, the dominant Christian civilization of Spain replaced the indigenous cultures to such an extent that though in Mexico the population is still predominantly non-European, the memory of Aztec and other cultures is only through the study of history and archaeology. In Peru the remarkable social and economic structure that the Incas created totally disappeared within a short time after the Spanish conquest. Today, though one may speak of an Andean renaissance, it does not base itself on indigenous roots as the breach created by the Spanish has been too complete for an identification with the past. These are instances of the total displacement of culture.

A case which is sometimes instanced as being parallel to the encounter between India and Britain is that of China and the West. But the differences between the two are fundamental and their experiences provide no parallel at all. Unlike India, China was never occupied by a Western power. A central government of China existed all the time and, consequently, though that government was often powerless and dependent on foreign support, Western penetration outside the Treaty ports and the settlements constituted no challenge to the Chinese way of life. The administration of the country outside a few settlements was in the hands of the Chinese. There was no comprehensive education system organized by a foreign government and controlled mainly by foreigners. No foreign legal system and judicial machinery were imposed on the Chinese people (outside the concessions) till practically the last days of the Kuomintang government. Till the downfall of the Manchus in 1911–12, the Chinese looked upon the Europeans as uncivilized barbarians whose unrighteous power they were forced to acknowledge. In the period after the first Revolution, 'Westernism' no doubt had a vogue but conditions had after the first Great War changed in Europe itself, and other doctrines and ideologies began to challenge the postulates of Western civilization. Consequently, the impact of the West on China assumed a different aspect.

The conquest and occupation of India by Britain were important in that they gave the country a system which ensured peace, united the whole area again under a single administration and brought the civilization and culture of India into direct and intimate contact with the forces which were then changing the face of Europe. The century of peace between the battle of Waterloo and the first Great European War was the period of India's closest contact with Europe. It was also the period which witnessed in Europe the fruition of the ideas of the French Revolution, and the consequent reordering of society.

The great misfortune of the maritime age, so far as India and the other Asian nations were concerned, lay in the fact that for over 300 years the blockade of Asia had prevented a free penetration of culture. All sea routes were closed except for commercial traffic. While thousands of Europeans visited India and the East in search of trade, for purposes of administration, military occupation or missionary work, from India there was no movement westwards till the latter half of the nineteenth century. To the people of Asia Europe was a closed book in the sixteenth, seventeenth and eighteenth centuries.

The significance of this fact will be appreciated only when we realize the revolutionary transformation that Europe was undergoing by leaps and bounds during these three centuries, the growth of democracy in the Netherlands, the rise of Protestantism and the Counter-Reformation, the emergence of England and France as Great Powers and the Industrial Revolution. In fact that was the period when Europe gained the lead over India and China, when her technology became definitely superior to that of the East, when her social, economic and political forces underwent an expansion which generated forces sufficient to hold Asia in fee. The fact that the Asian countries were unable to appreciate the changes that were taking place in Europe resulted directly from the rigour of the da Gaman blockade which continued to be effective till the beginning of the nineteenth century.

The visit of Raja Ram Mohan Roy to Europe in 1830 was therefore from the point of view of Asia no less important than the arrival of Vasco da Gama in India. It was the first step in India's Discovery of Europe. From that time, at first a trickle, then a constant stream of visitors flowed into England which by the end of the century assumed proportions of major social significance for India. Indian students were studying at Oxford, Cambridge and Edinburgh in considerable numbers during the last decades of the nineteenth century. Leaders of Indian thought, businessmen, industrial magnates and even religious preachers came in close contact with what was taking place not only in England, but in Europe generally. The mingling of culture which was to give India its special character had already begun.

II

Ever since the dawn of history, till the arrival of Europeans in the Indian Ocean, Indian interests had laid predominantly on the sea.[1] For over a thousand years, Indian communities which had established themselves in Malaya, Sumatra and the Islands of the Pacific had the mastery of maritime communications to the Far East. With the countries on the coast of the Arabian sea, with the African littoral, with the Red Sea and Egypt, India maintained the closest political and economic relations. It may be noticed that when the seriousness of the Portuguese threat was recognized, the alliance that the Zamorin of Calicut negotiated to fight the European fleet was with the Sultan of Egypt and not with the Vijayanagar Empire across his borders.

For nearly 700 years there was a steady flow of missionaries and teachers from India into the Far East which came to an end only by about the end of the eleventh century. After the period of the Muslim invasions, the North Indian kingdoms and the Bahmini States in the Deccan maintained the closest contacts with Persia and the Middle East. In fact it may be justly claimed that culturally and from the point of view of trade India was,

[1] Panikkar, *India and the Indian Ocean*, Allen & Unwin Ltd.

before the da Gaman period, the centre of a maritime system which extended from Egypt to Canton.

Vasco da Gama's eruption into the East and Albuquerque's political system enforcing a Portuguese monopoly of sea traffic destroyed this old continental order. India was isolated from the rest of her neighbours in the Far East after the effective establishment of European naval power and from neighbours in the Middle East after the British conquest. Essentially, what the withdrawal of Britain from India meant is the restoration of India to her position in the centre of a South Asian continental system. The very existence of an independent state in the Indian peninsula with interests centred in Asia and with an economic structure which necessitates close association with its Eastern neighbours, especially Burma, Siam, Malaya and Japan, alters the political face of Asia. Undoubtedly the British-Indian system also was the centre of a political order in the same region, but its influence, though based on Indian territory and the resources available there, was purely British. Also, that influence was imperial, which reduced its associated or neighbouring countries either to the status of colonies, as in the case of Burma and Malaya, or to that of protectorates as in the case of the States of the Arabian littoral and in a measure the independent kingdoms of Siam, Nepal and Afghanistan, all of which obtained recognition of their absolute freedom only when British authority began to break down in India after the first Great War. The new state system which the withdrawal of Britain and the independence of India bring into existence in South Asia is a comity of free nations bound together by common interests, and endeavouring to develop a common Asian culture.

III

By themselves these factors would entitle the changes introduced by the independence of India to be considered a major revolution. But, more important, as it is likely to be more permanent, is the significance of this event in terms of culture. For what New India represents is not merely the establishment of a new Asian State, but the emergence of a new civilization.

The inheritance that India has stepped into is only partly Hindu and Indian. The inheritance from the West is no less important in many fields. Modern India does not live under the laws of Manu. Its mental background and equipment, though largely influenced by the persistence of Indian tradition, have been moulded into their present shape by over a hundred years of Western education extending practically to every field of mental activity. Its social ideals are not what Hindu society had for long cherished, but those assimilated from the West and derived predominantly from the doctrines of the French Revolution, and to a lesser, though to an increasing, extent from the teachings of Marx and the lessons of the Soviet experiment. Even the religious beliefs of Hinduism have been transformed substantially during the course of the last 100 years. In fact it will be no exaggeration to say that the New Indian State represents traditions, ideals and principles which are the results of an effective but imperfect synthesis between the East and the West.

The quality of civilization, as Mr R. H. Tawney has stated,[1] depends on the transmission, less of physical qualities than of a complex structure of habits, knowledge and beliefs. Modern India has inherited along with its own four thousand years of history and the habits, thoughts and beliefs coming down through ages, a not inconsiderable measure of ideals, knowledge and thought rooted in European history. It is not only through direct inheritance that these have now become a part of Indian tradition. It is to a large extent through the modifications that these ideas have forced on the thoughts, habits and beliefs of the Indian people themselves that Europe has passed into India.

The social reformation in Hindu society, the emancipation of the untouchable classes, the profoundly significant purification of Hinduism, all of which are of greater and more permanent significance than even the emergence of India as an independent State, are the outward reflections of that Western inheritance. The organization of the democratic State, its secular character, the structure of its institutions and the political principles underlying them are also essentially European in their inspiration.

The tradition of India has always been one of synthesis. Her geographical position perhaps helped her to develop a singular ability to absorb the culture of others and assimilate it without losing her own identity. It is the synthesis of the Aryan and the

[1] Tawney, R. H., *Religion and the Rise of Capitalism.*

Dravidian that laid the basis of Hindu civilization. The unity of India in her primary institutions—the village, the family, the broad legal conceptions of property—was the outcome of that synthesis. The great Gandhara school of art has definite and identifiable Greek characteristics, and the collaboration between the Greeks of Bactria and the Indian borderlands is seen also in the notable advances of astronomy and mathematics in the Gupta era. The prolonged contact with Islam had, as we know, profound significance for every aspect of Indian life, religion, literature, art and social organization and economic structure. This co-operative attitude with what comes from outside enabled India, during the last 150 years of contact with the West, to accept as her own and assimilate the knowledge and thought of Europe to an extent which has enabled her to adjust herself to the new world without undergoing a violent revolution. A meeting ground of the East and the West at least from the time of Alexander, claiming spiritual kinship with both, India was historically well fitted for evolving a new society based on the synthesis of Europe and Asia.

An Anglo-Indian administrator, Lord Meston, compared the influence of the West on India to a river flowing into the sea.[1] 'There has been nothing, or very little,' he says 'of clash between her own ancient culture and the alien culture imported from the West, no violent conflict of ideas or methods, no forcible replacement of one social system by another. The more fitting metaphor would be that of a stream of new thought and practice flowing into the sea of India's traditions and life. We can trace, for a time at least, the distinctive colour of the river, spreading out over the surface of the sea; but, as we have often cause to reflect in India, how little can we tell of its influence in the ocean depth beneath.'

While it is possible to exaggerate the influence of the West on India, the view that holds that the changes which have resulted from the contact between India and Europe have only touched the fringes of society, or merely added a veneer to it, is basically wrong, primarily because it does not take into account the transformations that have taken place and the forces that have been set in motion inside the apparent calmness of Indian life.

It is not true that there has been no clash between India's culture and the culture of the West. It is also not true that there

[1] Introduction to P. J. O'Malley's *Moslem India and the West* (OUP).

have been no violent conflicts of ideas and methods. What is true is that these clashes and conflicts have been carried on inside Hinduism and away from the view of India's alien masters. They have not led to violence in the physical sense, of forcible breaking down of institutions, of orthodoxy and heterodoxy fighting open battles, leading to loss of life. But compulsion through the sense of danger to national existence, through the growth of moral opinion, through the threat of large-scale conversions to Islam and Christianity, there was in all the major changes that have altered what at one time were considered the special characteristics of Hindu civilization, e.g. the caste system, the joint family, the segregation of untouchables, early marriage of women, etc.

Observant Indian leaders have at all times recognized and given credit to this transformation of ancient Indian cultures as being essentially the result of Western impacts. Mr Gopal Krishna Gokhale, the greatest statesman of his time in India, and a profound student of social changes, declared at the Universal Races Conference in London in 1911[1] that, 'whereas the contact of the West with other countries had only been external in India, the West had so to say entered into the very bone and marrow of the East'.

No one realized this with greater force or bewailed it more than the champions of orthodoxy who were reduced to the position of impotent spectators when the institutions to which they attached religious sanction and which they revered as 'eternal' were one after the other quietly given up, publicly denounced or legally destroyed; for instance when the Civil Marriage Act cut at the very roots of caste, when the joint family slowly decayed and gave way, when the temples were thrown open to the untouchables and widows were permitted to remarry.

But, it may be emphasized, India is no home of a *mestizo* civilization, a new way of life foreign to the soil, or unrelated to its past, a mere borrowed thing, which however showy and brilliant is alien to the genius of its people. Unlike some of the new communities of Latin America, where a predominantly *mestizo* population has taken over bodily the culture, attitude and way of life of Europe and has attempted to reproduce on its soil a civilization which has but little in common with the traditions of the indigenous races, modern India continues to be essentially Indian,

[1] Quoted in O'Malley.

certain of her own individuality, drawing spiritual inspiration and sustenance from her own past. Europe has added to it richness, has given her, as other influences in the past have given her, a new vitality and a new vision, and has helped her to reorganize herself by assimilating ideas, principles and purposes which were necessary for her transformation into a modern society

The characteristic of the *mestizo* life on the other hand, has been the submergence and the loss of identity of civilizations and their displacement by an outside way of life. This has been well expressed by a distinguished Spanish writer: 'Think of a whole continent effectively assimilated to a European civilization and life without sacrificing the native population in the process, nor leaving it outside of it, so far as it depended on the newcomers, of an absorption into the ways of Europe which enabled European forms of life to pass into the hands of people as far from Europe as the Aztecs of Mexico, the Incas of Peru and even the Tagalog of the Philippines (the only truly Europeanised Asiatics by the way); consider that as early as the sixteenth century the Indies had contributed to our Atlantic world a school of painting in Cuzco and a dance, the Chaconne, which Bach thought worthy of his music: gauge the spiritual tradition Spain has left from Manila to Santo Damingo, from California to Tierra del Fuego . . . that Spanish buildings grace the whole continent and that the language remains alive with the ways of thinking it breeds . . .'[1]

It is undoubtedly true that Spain left behind in the continent that she ruled over for 300 years a civilization which reproduced in some measure the characteristics of Europe. The Amerindians and *mestizos* contributed no doubt to this transplanted culture. Even in the century that followed the conquest we have such distinguished names as Juan Santa Cruz, Ayala and Diego de Castno—an Inca of Peru—all pure-blooded Amerindians making significant contributions to *Spanish* culture. The mixed community produced such notable figures as Garcilaso Inca de Vega, Don Bartelome' de Alba, Cristobel de Medina. But the greatness of Spanish-American contribution to European life came not from these, but from men like Balbuena and Ruiz de Alarcon and Leon de Huanco who were Spaniards born and brought up in America.

[1] Salvador de Madariaga, *The Rise of the Spanish Empire*, Hollis and Carter Ltd., 1947, p. 134.

The parallel to these in English literature are the Thackerays, Kiplings and many other Englishmen born and brought up in India. True, India also produced its *mestizo* literature. The poems of Toru Dutt, Manmohan Ghose, Sarojini Naidu, Harindranath Chattopadhyaya and others will in time be considered a curious and exotic chapter in English literature. But even they, while using English as their medium, wrote as Indians and not as men and women who had adopted Europe as their spiritual home as the *mestizo* writers did. No doubt in Spanish-American literature today there is an intense quality of nationalism, a desire to get away from the traditions of the old world and even a tendency in some States to emphasize the pre-Spanish culture, and go back to ancient Amerindian traditions. But the Spanish conquistadors, and the Church which continued the work on the spiritual plane, seem to have accomplished their work of destruction well enough to prevent any such reversion to earlier traditions.

The characteristics of the *mestizo* who formed the basis of the Spanish-American civilization is thus described by Salvador de Madariaga.[1]

'The *mestizo* carries within him . . . all the virtues and the vices of the Spaniard. But he does not carry them in their natural and spontaneous state. All these features in him live constantly under the inner opposition from his other self, the Indian, object and often victim of them. The Indian in him is subservient and faithful to that white who has conquered him; ready to flatter him and to shape himself and truth and the world to please the white, and he is proud of his own native blood and history, which in Mexico and Peru have given rise to two great well-ordered Empires; he is aloof, contemptuous of the white intruders who came to occupy the land in which he the Indian is rooted. . . The tension within the soul of the *mestizo* between the two strains of men living together under his skin in the closest intimacy could not be more acute.'

In brief the *mestizo* civilization is based on a perpetual but living contradiction of which we have a minor illustration in India in the history of the Anglo-Indians during the British rule. With the Anglo-Indian, the conflict was even more pronounced, as his

[1] Madariaga, *The Fall of the Spanish Empire*, Hollis and Carter, Ltd. 1947, pp. 103–4.

economic position was insecure and his number too small to count seriously in the shaping of India's spiritual or cultural destiny. The *mestizo* in India was merely an insignificant outer fringe, unwanted by the West and unreconciled to the East, cherishing his European heritage, but unable to capitalize it.[1] But India itself remained outside this conflict. As we shall try to show, the 450 years of contact with and 150 years of direct domination by European culture had the effect only of renovating, vitalizing and strengthening Indian tradition in many important spheres. India welcomed, accepted and assimilated much which she considered useful, or as being of permanent value. But it was as one civilization strong in its convictions of greatness and faith in its own values, testing and taking to itself something which it could transform and adopt as its own.

To the casual observer who sees only the external forms, the change in India would seem to be but little. The East has outwardly remained unperturbed and the strange and fantastic things which seem so inexplicable to the European, the sacredness of the cow, the funeral ghats at Benares, the fakirs and wandering mendicants to whom all pay exaggerated reverence, the crudeness of worship among many sects which seem to flourish today as much as they did at any time in the past. India seems to them a country of contrasts. And yet this is only a superficial view. The new civilization which Modern India represents is an undoubted fact, and the survivals which obscure it in some respects are but the evidence of its continuity, of its having grown naturally and without effort from the old trunk.

A visitor from the eighteenth century, an observant statesman, say of the Maratha court of the eighteenth century, if he visited India today would no doubt have cause for joy and sorrow and also for surprise. He would be overjoyed that foreign rule against which his people had fought for over 100 years had definitely come to an end in India, and the sacred places on the Ganges for the liberation of which his armies had fought vainly were at last under Hindu control. He would be glad that transport was so easy and well regulated and that he could perform by car, plane or railway the pilgrimages to which he was accustomed in the past. He would also be glad to see the same immense concourse of

[1] For a psychological study of the *mestizo* problem in India, see John Masters novel, *Bhowani Junction*.

people at Nasik, Benares, Hardwar and Prayag. The familiar sights of fakirs, sanyasis and yogis would gladden his heart. But his sorrow would be unbounded when he realized that the worshippers included not only the orthodox castes, but the *avarnas* or the untouchables, that the ceremonies of pollution were not being observed. He would be shocked to see women move about freely in the streets, dressed no doubt in the manner familiar to him, but conducting themselves in ways which he could not but disapprove. He would probably hear one of them haranguing a crowd or see a group of girl volunteers helping old women pilgrims. He would be disappointed at the lack of respect shown to a man of his position. He would be surprised when he was told that the great Princes of India had ceased to rule, though on reflection he might recall that his own government had in the time of its expansion dispossessed not a few: but an India without ruling princes would still be a source of surprise to him. Being a man of scholarship and cultivation, the growth of his own Marathi language and the revival of Sanskrit studies would please his heart, while the familiarity of the educated classes with English would seem strange.

What would interest him perhaps most, apart from the material amenities of life and the easy methods of transportation, would be the great cities, so different and yet so similar to Poona, Delhi, Agra and other capitals that he had known, with their pomp and pageantry, and strangest of all, most perplexing would be the Government under which he would have to live. A country without a king would seem to be wholly unnatural to him; and the idea of *Aryavarta* without an emperor, or Chatrapati and ruled not only from Delhi, but from lesser centres, by men claiming their authority from an Assembly of people would seem to him to be against the natural order of things. And yet for all these changes, he would not fail to recognize the people as his own, their Gods as his own and the spirit of the country essentially the same as that which had reared him. He would see that a *Yuga* had changed, an era had ended and another had begun.

Indeed what has happened in India is a revolution. The fact that the transfer of political power was peacefully effected does not detract from the revolutionary character either of the struggle, or the qualititative character of the change which both the struggle and the transfer brought about. The purpose of our present study is to discover the elements that constitute the substance of that Revolution, the factors that have moulded it and given to Indian life its present form and content, the doctrines that give strength and guidance to it, the connection of the new age with the past and with Europe, the characteristics that differentiate the era and give it its ideals, its temper and its outlook. The political institutions through which the unity of India has been achieved, the structure of its new society and its economic foundations must naturally also enter into the study of this question. No less important an aspect and perhaps the one with which the world is at present vitally concerned is its position in regard to the other revolutionary changes in the areas near her, more especially in China and in the countries of South-East Asia, where a rival philosophy is seeking to solve problems similar to those of India by methods which involve a definite break with the past. These then are the subjects of our enquiry.

CHAPTER II

The Hindu Reformation

I

The Union of India as an independent state has now (1962) been in existence for fifteen years. During this period, it has worked a democratic constitution, undertaken large schemes of economic development, upheld civil liberties and embarked on radical social reforms, maintaining at the same time peace and stability within its territories. That India was able to do this is a matter of surprise to most people. The political, social and communal divisions of India, the tensions between the different groups, the claims of rival communities and the demands of the princes had figured so prominently in the thirty years that preceded this independence that only the most optimistic friends of India could have anticipated so peaceful and progressive an evolution. And yet a close student of affairs who was familiar with the developments in India during the preceding hundred years could not but have been struck by many factors which should have helped him to realize that a revolution had been taking place beneath the surface of Indian society. It is these developments, some arising out of the inner compulsions of Indian society, others resulting from the external forces which the contact with Britain had given rise to, that have laid the foundations of India's new life.

The movement that culminated in the emergence of India as an independent nation had three main aspects, inter-related in their action, deriving inspiration from common sources, but separated in their areas of operation. These may be briefly described as the creation of a spiritual background for political action, a renovation of social foundations and an intellectual ferment creating and expressing a broader and more universal humanism as the basis of India's new life.

THE HINDU REFORMATION

The Hindu reformation of the nineteenth century is one of the great movements of the age which by its massiveness and far-reaching significance takes its place with the most vital developments of modern history.[1] As it was a slow process and took place under the cover of British authority and was not always obvious to the outsider, it has so far escaped serious attention. A further reason why, in spite of its tremendous import, it passed practically unnoticed is that, by its very nature, it was an internal movement which did not touch or influence outside events. But India's independence and emergence into the modern world would hardly have been possible without the slow but radical adjustments that took place within the fold of Hinduism during a period of over 100 years.

In order fully to appreciate this movement it is necessary to understand what the position of Hinduism was in the beginning of the nineteenth century. Six hundred years of Islamic authority over the Indo-Gangetic plains from Delhi to Calcutta had left Hinduism in a state of depression. It was the religion of a subject race, looked down upon with contempt by the Muslims as idolatry. It enjoyed no prestige and for many centuries its practice had only been tolerated under considerable disadvantage in many areas. It had no central direction, no organization and hardly any leadership. When the British took over the rulership of northern India Hinduism, for the first time in 600 years, stood on a plane of equality with Islam. But a new and even more dangerous portent appeared on the stage. The missionaries, feeling that there was almost a virgin field here in a society which appeared to be on the point of dissolution, took up the work of conversion. Islam, though it proselytized by fits and starts, had no separate machinery for carrying its message to the people. The Christian missionaries were different. They used no physical force, which Islam did not hesitate to do at intervals and in limited areas. But they came armed with propaganda. At first it was scurrilous invective and we have the Governor General (Lord Minto) himself in the first decade of the nineteenth century ordering the confiscation of Christian propaganda leaflets on the ground that 'without argu-

[1] There is no single book dealing with the Hindu Reformation of the nineteenth century. Romain Rolland's *Prophets of Modern India* deals fairly comprehensively with Ramakrishna and Vivekananda. C. F. Andrew's early book *Indian Renaissance* is interesting but sketchy.

ments of any kind they were filled with hell fire and still hotter fire denounced against a whole race of men merely for believing in the religion which they were taught by their fathers and mothers and the truth of which it is simply impossible it should have entered into their minds to doubt'.

But more subtle weapons were at hand. The missionaries were the first to start educational institutions on Western lines and, as from time immemorial the Hindus had paid almost superstitious veneration to learning and as, further, Western education seemed to offer chances of advancement, they flocked to these colleges. These institutions were primarily meant as centres for the spreading of the Christian gospel and in the early years of the nineteenth century the chances appeared to be favourable for a widespread acceptance of Christianity among the upper classes of Bengali Hindus.

The reaction was not long in coming, for the most distinguished mind of the age, who was greatly attracted by the message of Christianity, deliberately rejected Christ after considerable spiritual adventure and turned instead to a reformation of Hinduism.

Ram Mohan Roy[1] (1772–1833) may be called the father of the Hindu Reformation. Born into a Brahmin family, Ram Mohan was brought up as a strict Hindu, but educated as all Hindus who hoped to enter public service had perforce to be at that time, in an Islamic culture. He was a deep student of Arabic and Persian when he entered the East India Company's service where also he rose to some distinction. During this period he took to the study of English which opened to him the whole range of Western liberal thought. It was the time when the mellowed glow of the Great European Enlightenment had cast on European intellectual life an amazing serenity and sense of certainty. The light of Holbach, Condorcet, Diderot and the great Encyclopaedists had not died down and the dawn of the great nineteenth-century thinkers, especially Bentham and the Utilitarians in England, which was destined to have so powerful an influence in the development of ideas in India had not begun.

What Ram Mohan witnessed around him in India was a scene of utter devastation and ruin. The old order of Muslim rule had

[1] *Life of Ram Mohan Roy*, by Miss Willet. There is a recent biography by Igbal Singh, *Ram Mohan's Collected Works*, Panini Press, Allahabad.

disappeared overnight leaving behind it chaos in every walk of life. Hinduism in Bengal, once the centre of a devotional Vaishnava religion of great vitality, had sunk to a very low level of superstition, extravagance and immorality. A seeker after truth, Ram Mohan had turned to the new religion which the missionaries were preaching. He studied Hebrew and Greek to understand Christianity better. But his scholarship was taking him at the same time to the well of European liberalism. Ram Mohan Roy was in a sense the last of the Encyclopaedists. Thus he came to reject Christ, while accepting the wide humanism of European thought, its ethics and its general approach to the problems of life. His book *The Precepts of Jesus, the guide to peace and happiness*[1] is an interpretation of Christianity in this new light, a reply to the missionaries rather than a call to Indians.

While Ram Mohan thus rejected the Christian claims he realized that Hinduism had to be reinterpreted. That interpretation he attempted in the Brahmo Samaj,[2] a new reformed sect of Hinduism which he founded. The Samaj was not in its essence a Christian dilution of Hinduism, as has often been said, but a synthesis of the doctrines of the European Enlightenment with the philosophical views of the Upanishads. As a religion Brahmo Samaj was based firmly on the Vedanta of genuine Hindu tradition, but its outlook on life was neither Christian, nor Hindu, but European, and derived its inspiration from the intellectual movements of the eighteenth century.

Thus it may be said that as early as 1820 India had come into the direct current of European thought and had begun to participate in the fruits of Europeans' intellectual quest. The Brahmo Samaj lived up to this ideal. Its social message was Westernization meant to purge Hinduism of the customs and superstitions with which it was overlaid, to raise the status of women, to bridge the yawning gulf between popular and higher Hinduism, to fight relentlessly against caste, social taboos, polygamy and other well entrenched abuses. To the educated Hindu who felt unsettled in mind by the attack of the missionaries, the Brahmo Samaj provided the way out.

The Brahmo tradition has become so much a part of the Indian way of life now that one is inclined to overlook its distinctive

[1] *Collected Works*, Panini Press, Allahabad.

[2] See *The History of Brahmo Samaj*, by Suinath Sashu.

contribution. It does not lie primarily in the fact that it enabled Hinduism to withstand the onslaught of the missionaries, but in its introduction of a modern approach to Indian problems. India started on her long adventure in building up a new civilization as a synthesis between the East and the West in the eighteen twenties and in that sense Ram Mohan is the forerunner of new India. It has been well stated that 'he embodies the new spirit, its freedom of enquiry, its thirst for science, its large human sympathy, its pure and sifted ethics along with its reverent but not uncritical regard for the past and prudent disinclination towards revolt'.

The spirit of reform was entering Hinduism from other sources also. In 1835 the Government of India declared that 'the great object of the British Government ought to be the promotion of European literature and science among the natives of India', and embarked on a policy of Western education, the effects of which will be considered separately. It was the devout hope of Macaulay, who was the protagonist of the scheme, and of many others, that the diffusion of the New Learning among the higher classes would see the dissolution of Hinduism and the widespread acceptance of Christianity. In a letter to his father, Macaulay prophesied as follows: 'It is my firm belief that if our plans of education are followed up, there will not be a single idolator among the respectable classes of Bengal thirty years hence. And this will be effected without any efforts to proselytize; without the smallest interference with religious liberty, merely by the natural operation of knowledge and reflection'.[1] The missionaries were also of the same view, and they entered the educational field with enthusiasm, providing schools and colleges in many parts of India, where education in the Christian Bible was compulsory for Hindu students. The middle classes accepted Western education with avidity and willingly studied Christian scriptures, but neither the dissolution of Hindu society so hopefully predicted nor the conversion of the intellectuals so devoutly hoped for showed any signs of materialization. On the other hand, Hinduism assimilated the new learning, and the effects were soon visible all over India in a revival of a universalized religion based on the higher teachings of Hinduism itself.

It is necessary to remember that though the Hindu religion has

[1] Quoted in Majumdar's *Glimpses of Bengal in the Nineteenth Century*, Firma Mukhopadhya, Calcutta, 1960, p. 32.

innumerable cults and sects, the philosophic background of all of them—including Buddhism—is the Vedanta. The doctrine of the Vedanta is contained in three authoritative texts—which are not scriptures—the Brahma Sutras, the Upanishads and the Gita. Every orthodox sect in India derives its authority directly from these and the protagonists of each new religious sect have to demonstrate how their teachings flowed directly from these three sources. Thus it was that Sankara, the reformer of Hinduism in the eighth century, had to write his commentaries on all the three. Ramanuja, Madhwa and other advocates of new schools had to follow the same path. It was to the doctrines of the Vedanta as embodied in the Upanishads that Ram Mohan Roy turned when he also felt the need of a new religious interpretation.

The demand of new India was not for a new sect: it was for a universal religion acceptable to all Hindus. The first effort to provide such a basis was by Dayananda Saraswati who saw in the Vedas the revealed word of God and felt that, as the Vedas were accepted by all who claimed to be Hindus, a religion based on the Vedas should have universal appeal in India. The Muslims had a revealed book, the Holy Qoran. The Christians had the Bible, and Swami Dayananda felt that the amorphous and indefinable nature of Hinduism which exposed it to so much weakness could be remedied by providing the Hindus also with a revealed book. This seemed to him all the more the right path since the Vedas gave no authority to the usages and superstitions that had come to be accepted by the masses as Hinduism. There was no sanction in the Vedas for caste, for the prohibition of the remarriage of widows, for untouchability, for the taboos on food and the other characteristics of popular Hinduism which had been seized upon by the missionaries in their campaign and were being widely rejected by the Hindu intelligentsia.

Swami Dayananda in his *Satyaratha Prakash*,[1] or the Light of True Meaning, made a brave and ingenious attempt to see in the Vedas all that the Christians and the Muslims were claiming to be the bases of their religions—universal brotherhood and a direct and non-metaphysical approach to God and a free society.

His Arya Samaj,[2] however successful as a militant organization for the protection of Hinduism from the onslaughts of Islam and

[1] *Satyaratha Prakash* is in Hindu, I have not come across any English translation.

[2] See Lajpat Rai, *Arya Samaj*, London, 1921.

Christianity, never appealed to the Hindus outside the Punjab. The reasons were simple. The attempt to go back to the Vedas involved a denial of the Hindu culture of the last 3,000 years, a refusal to see any good in the puranic religion, in the variegated traditions which had enriched Hindu thought in the middle ages, all of which the Arya Samajists rejected without hesitation and attacked without reservation. Secondly, the Vedic religion had long ago ceased to be related to the religious experience of Hindus. The Gita had poured scorn on Vedic sacrifices, and held up the *Veda-vada-ratas* (those who delight to argue on the basis of the Vedas) to contempt. The exclusiveness of the Arya Samaj, amounting to the intolerance of other religious practices, though but a reflection of its prolonged fight against the proselytizing faiths and therefore essentially defensive, was also against the tradition of Hinduism which held firmly to the doctrine that the Gita preached, 'men worship in different ways, I give them the fruits appropriate to their worship'.

The Hindu does not deny the truth of any religion, or reject the validity of another's religious experience. But the Arya Samajists, at least in their polemical days, were rigidly exclusive. The movement, therefore, did not spread to other parts of India and its influence was limited mainly to the Delhi and Punjab areas.

The urge of educated Hindus to find a common denominator for their various sects, which neither of these movements provided, was for a time fulfilled by the activities of the Theosophical Society of which Col. Olcott, the American, and Madame Blavatsky, the Russian, were the founders. Educated Hindus all over the country turned to the Theosophical Society, which introduced into India the organization and propagandist methods of European religious activity. Its interpretation of Hinduism followed the more orthodox lines, and many of its Indian leaders like Dr Bhagwan Das of Benares and Sir S. Subramania Aiyar of Madras were also leaders of Hindu orthodoxy. Its social doctrines, however, were progressive and more important, and it cut through the sectarian lines of Indian religious organization.

Theosophic Hinduism was an all-India movement and it profoundly affected the outlook of the new generation. When Mrs Annie Besant, the extremely gifted, persuasive and dynamic personality who had already attained wide renown, became the President of the Society, its propaganda for a reformed universal

Hinduism became more marked and was carried on incessantly through schools, colleges, lectures and popular literature. Mrs Besant had become steeped in Indian culture. Her popular approach was Vedantic, as her translation of the Gita would testify.

The Vedantic reformation which was thus in the air found its most widely accepted exponent in Swami Vivekananda. Vivekananda was a Western-educated Bengali who came under the influence of Ramakrishna, a God-realized mystic whose personality had made a deep impression on the Bengali society of his day. Vivekananda was fired by a desire to revive Hinduism and purify its religious and social teachings. He toured the length and breadth of India spreading the gospel of Vedanta. A prolonged visit to America and a tour in England inflamed his patriotism, his desire to rejuvenate Hindu society and to give Hinduism a social purpose. His fervent declaration that he did not 'believe in a religion that does not wipe out the widows' tears or bring a piece of bread to the orphan's mouth' expresses clearly the changed temper of Hinduism. His own mission he described as follows. Answering the question 'what do you consider to be the function of your movement as regards India', the Swami said: 'To find the common bases of Hinduism and to awaken the national consciousness to them.' That common basis he found in the Vedanta which he interpreted in popular phraseology and preached untiringly all over India.

'All the philosophers of India who are orthodox have to acknowledge the authority of the Vedanta and all our present-day religions, however crude some of them may appear to be, however inexplicable some of their purposes may seem, one who understands them and studies them can trace them back to the ideas of the Upanishads. So deeply have these Upanishads sunk into our race that those of you who study the symbology of the crudest religion of the Hindus will be astonished to find sometimes figurative expressions of the Upanishads. Great spiritual and philosophical ideas in the Upanishads are today with us, converted into household worship in the form of symbols. Thus the various symbols now used by us, all come from the Vedanta, because in the Vedanta they are used as figures.'[1]

[1] *Collected Works of Swami Vivekananda*— 7 volumes, Advaitasram, Almora. Vol. III, p. 121.

Again: 'Thus the Vedanta, whether we know it or not, has penetrated all the sects in India and what we call Hinduism, this mighty banyan tree, with its immense and almost infinite ramifications, has been throughout interpenetrated by the influence of the Vedanta. Whether we are conscious of it *or not*, we think the Vedanta, we live in the Vedanta, we breathe the Vedanta and we die in the Vedanta and every Hindu does that.'[1]

He not only preached this gospel but trained up a body of missionaries, men of education, pure life and religious zeal to carry the message to the villages.

There were innumerable other sanyasis and learned men who though belonging to no particular sect were preaching the same principles all over India. In fact the revival of Vedanta in Hindu thought at the end of the nineteenth and in the first two decades of the twentieth century constitutes a religious movement of national significance. It was at the end of this period that Aurobindo gave what may be called the classic exposition of the entire Vedanta doctrine in his *Essays on the Gita* and later in his *Life Divine*. By this, Vedanta may be said to have been restored to its place as the common background of all Hindu religious thought.

The unifying doctrine was the Vedanta, but the abstract conceptions of this philosophical approach could only appeal to the élite. Popular Hinduism continued in the old way, sectarian, devotional and based on daily rituals. But it also underwent extraordinary changes. The gnarled branches of this ancient tree either fell away by themselves or were chopped off by legislative action promoted by the reformers. Child marriage, which many Hindu communities considered as an essential part of their religion, was abolished by law, through the insistence of popular agitation. The remarriage of widows was permitted. Social disabilities based on caste vanished by themselves and the occupational basis of caste-communities was weakened. Temples were thrown open to the untouchables and in the most orthodox province of Madras Hindu religious endowments were placed under the control of public bodies. The movement for the regeneration of the depressed classes assumed a national character and their participation in social political life became a major factor in the last days of British rule. Popular Hinduism had a

[1] *Collected Works of Swami Vivekananda*, p. 323.

more vigorous life than it ever had during the past few centuries, but it had in the course of 100 years changed its character and temper, though it had kept much of its form.

The major difficulty of Hinduism which had made it a wild jungle growth of widely varying customs, usages and superstitions was its lack of a machinery of reform and unification.

The institutions of Hinduism, which in a large measure became identified with the religion itself, were the results of certain historical factors. They were upheld by *law* and not by religion. Vivekananda put the point well when he wrote: 'Beginning from Buddha down to Ram Mohan Roy, every one made the mistake of holding caste to be a religious institution. . . . But in spite of all the ravings of the priests, caste is simply a crystallized social institution, which after doing its service is now filling the atmosphere of India with stench'.

The caste organization, the joint family, the rights of inheritance and the relationships arising out of them, which in the main were the special features of Hindu society, were social and legal and not religious institutions. They could not claim divine origin or religious sanction, and were upheld by man-made laws and not by any church or priesthood. It is a truism to say that legislation of today meets the social needs of yesterday and, unavoidably, law as a conservative force lags one step behind social necessities. When the great codes of Hindu Law were evolved, no doubt they represented the social forces of the time, but soon they had become antiquated. The succession of authoritative commentaries would show that the urge for modification was widely felt, and in the absence of a legislative authority, the method of a progressive interpretation by commentators in each succeeding generation was the only one available to Hindu thinkers.

The immutability of Hindu law and customs was never a principle with the authors of the great codes or their commentators. In fact the monumental volumes of Dr Kane's *History of Dharma Sastra* would demonstrate clearly that in every age social thinkers tried to adjust Hindu institutions to the requirements of the time. If the laws are changeable it follows that the institutions which are based on such laws are equally changeable. The great weakness of Hindu society was not that the laws had remained immutable, but that the changes introduced have been spasmodic, local and dependent to a large extent on the ingenuity of individual commentators. They were not in any sense a continuous renovation of legal principles, not a legislative approximation to changing conditions.

The reason for this lack of direction of social ideals and the failure to prevent the growth of anti-social customs was undoubtedly the loss of political power. Not only was India as a whole ever under a single sovereign authority, but even the political unity of North India which existed with occasional breaks from the time of the Mauryas (320 BC to that of Harsha (AD 647) was broken up by the political conditions of the eighth century and lost for a period of 600 years after the Muslim invasions at the end of the twelfth century. As a result, the Hindu community continued to be governed by institutions moulded by laws which were codified over 2,000 years ago and which were out of date even when they were codified.

The Muslim State had no legislative machinery, and when for the first time India was united under the British and the entire Hindu community lived under a common administration, the authorities of the East India Company after a first effort at social reform withdrew, under the pretext of religious neutrality, from activities which they thought might cause popular upheaval. Perhaps it was a wise step, as the motive force of large-scale social reforms must come from the people themselves and legislation can only give statutory sanction to principles which have already gained wide acceptance. The reformation of the Hindu religion was therefore an essential prerequisite of social legislation.

It was only after the first Great War that the legislating State came into existence in India. Under the scheme of partial self-government (Dyarchy) introduced in 1921, there was established a central legislative authority with a majority of non-official elected Indians, which was competent to change the laws of Hindu society and to enforce obedience to such laws through the length and breadth of British India. In the provinces the direction of government passed in a large measure to elected legislatures. The legislative achievements of the Central and Provincial governments in the field of social reform have been fundamental, though they did not go anywhere as far as public opinion demanded. The Civil Marriage Act and the Age of Consent Act (raising the marriageable age of girls to 14) were among the more important pieces of legislation which the Central Indian Legislative Assembly enacted.

The Civil Marriage Act validated marriages between men and women of different castes of Hinduism. It struck at the very root of the orthodox brahminical conception of caste, and annulled the laws of Manu and the other orthodox codes of Hinduism. The 'immutable law' prohibiting *varna-samkara*, or the mixture of castes, ceased by this single piece of legislation to be legal or enforceable through the length and breadth of India. The Age of Consent Act was equally revolutionary. It was the custom for over 2,000 years at least for some sections of high caste people to have girls married before the age of puberty. There was not only long tradition behind the custom, but it was considered compulsory at least for Brahmins in the light of certain authoritative texts. The Indian legislature made this custom, which had so much religious authority behind it, illegal and the performance of such marriage a penal offence.

That the legislating State of Independent India would not permit the social anarchy of Hinduism was clear from the beginning but it was not contemplated that it would from the very start make the modernization of Indian society one of its primary objectives. The new legislature, even before it took up the consolidation of political gains, formulated as an essential part of the constitution a comprehensive system of fundamental rights enforceable by law. This provided for the absolute abolition of untouchability and made its practice in any form an offence punishable by law.

Women were given equal status, and it was laid down as a Directive Principle of state policy that the object of government shall be to secure and protect a 'social order in which justice, social, economic and political shall inform all the institutions of national life'. The new parliament elected on adult franchise took up the questions of social legislation in a comprehensive manner. The marriage laws of the Hindus were thoroughly overhauled and made uniform all over India. While orthodox Hinduism had prescribed sacramental marriages, there were many other widely differing systems prevailing in different parts of India. These varied from the polyandrous marriage customs prevalent among the Indo-Tibetan tribes of the Himalayas to the completely secular system prevalent among the matrilineal communities of the South. A uniform marriage law, enforcing monogamy, permitting divorce under certain conditions, was one of the major legislative achievements of the new parliament. By another piece of legislation Hindu succession laws have been made uniform, providing among other things for a share in the ancestral property to the daughter, thus cutting at the very root of the Hindu conception of the joint family. These may well be claimed to be the consummation of a hundred years of effort to organize Hindu society on a modern basis.

In summary it may be said that new India has started on a wide programme of social adjustment, the object of which is to transform Hindu society from an amorphous mass into an integrated community, capable of absorbing the ideals of modern democratic life. In order to do this it was necessary to separate religion from social institutions and also to reform the religious beliefs, so as to provide a common background to the community and create in them a sense of solidarity. This was the achievement of the Hindu reformation which acting through many channels and deriving its inspiration from many sources, national and foreign, revived the higher religious truths of Hinduism and provided the Hindu people with a sense of unity and an urge for social welfare. The modern State which succeeded the British administration had the ground ready and prepared for them, for the victory of social reform had already been won in the public mind even before the legislators gave it statutory recognition.

II A NEW MESSAGE IN AN OLD SCRIPTURE

The Hindu Reformation briefly outlined in the preceding chapter was indeed a significant fact, but it would have remained basically a religious movement but for the rediscovery of the Bhagavad Gita[1] as the political and social gospel of Hindu India. The urgent need was to endow the Hindu people as a whole with a new ethic and a message for social action and to discover a dynamic doctrine which, while providing Hindus with modern social ideals, would enable them to transform their society. A doctrine which

[1] The best translation of the Gita in English from the layman's point of view is Sir Edwin Arnold's poetic version. There are numerous other excellent translations with commentaries, including one by Dr Radhakrishnan, Allen & Unwin, Ltd. London; Telang's Edition in the *Sacred Books of the East* (Oxford) is authoritative.

would give the sanction of orthodoxy to modern ideas was what Hinduism required. This is what the Gita did. It provided a new ethic: it enabled new social ideals to be formulated without apparently violating orthodoxy; it allowed the philosophy of the Hindus, so long considered to be contemplative and world-denying, to be interpreted as a dynamic doctrine for action for the welfare of the world. In fact it gave to modern India a scripture which, at once orthodox and universally accepted, was also, so to say, a handbook of revolution.

The Bhagavad Gita or the Lord's Song is a religious text embedded in the great national epic, the Mahabharata. Held in veneration by all sects professing Hinduism, it had as early as the sixth century AD come to be regarded as one of the most authoritative expressions of Hindu thought. It was commented upon by the great philosopher Sankaracharya in the eighth century AD to provide support for his doctrine of renunciation. Protagonists of different sects had appealed to it through interpretations and commentaries for authority for their special ideas. How this text, which for over 1,500 years had acquired the undisputed position of a religious scripture to which every polemical writer or apologist appealed for authority in support of his special brand of thought, became the political *vade-mecum* of modern India is one of the strangest developments in history. And yet undoubtedly it came to have supreme importance in providing inspiration for modern India's political action, so much so that the British government at one time even seriously considered the question of proscribing it. The clearest evidence of the comprehensive character of its influence lies in the fact that every leading personality, from the first prophet of revolutionary nationalism Bal Gangadhar Tilak to Radhakrishnan, and many political leaders including Mahatma Gandhi and Rajagopalachari, felt it necessary to write new commentaries on this ancient text in terms of the political and social life of modern India. The extraordinary influence of the Gita on the spiritual and social life of India may also be judged from the strange phenomenon of many hundreds of popular books published all over India in the regional languages explaining this or that aspect of the text in terms of today's problems.

Before we discuss the new political and social ideas that have come to be associated with the Gita in recent times, it is necessary to clear one misunderstanding. The Gita is primarily religious in its teaching. It is a supremely sacred text of Hindu religion and it is thus that the Gita is still looked upon by the Hindus. But it is not in that sense that it emerged as the scripture of modern India but as a text providing a new ethical, social and political message suited to the needs of today.

What provided the dynamic for this new message was the Gita's uncompromising emphasis on action, its definition of the ideal man as one who with a mind which has attained equability and serves society without desiring selfish ends, solely for the benefit of the world. Hindus had been told by all who claimed to know, especially by Western thinkers, that their religion was world-denying, that they were fatalists, that their scriptures did not teach them any social obligations, in fact Hindu religion with its doctrines of *Maya*, *Karma* and individual deliverance could not have a social purpose as its highest ideal was renunciation of the world. The Hindus themselves had come to believe this and could find no reply to the claim made by the West that progress could not be reconciled with Hinduism, with its belief in caste and its emphasis on other-worldly doctrines. It therefore came as a revelation to them when orthodox scholars and thinkers began to affirm that the Gita contained not only a call for social action but that it emphasized man's duty in the world and the necessity of adjusting social relationships to suit the times.

This revolutionary interpretation was primarily the work of Bal Gangadhar Tilak, the father of Indian Nationalism. Tilak was a Mahratta Brahmin who had from his early age dedicated himself to India's freedom. A profound scholar of Sanskrit and a writer and a thinker of high quality, Tilak, whose orthodoxy no one could question not only as a Chitpavan Brahmin but as a practising Hindu, first discovered in the Gita scriptural authority for his programme of activism in politics. 'Arise and fight the battle of Dharma' is the recurrent call of Krishna in the Gita. Unrelenting war against oppression and unrighteousness is the opening message of the Gita. In the commentaries and interpretations accepted as authoritative by the different philosophic schools beginning with Sankara, it was not this aspect, but either the devotional or the renunciatory ideal preached in the later parts that was emphasized. The special contribution of Tilak was to re-emphasize the context of the Gita and to draw attention to the positive energism which the earlier portion of the Gita preached. *Gita Rahasya*[1] or the Secret of the Gita, in which he expounded with a wealth of scholarship and with unimpeachable orthodoxy this revolutionary view, is a remarkable book. It makes no allusion to politics and yet it is clear that the call to rise and fight as interpreted by Tilak is not in relation to the epic struggle between the Kurus and the Pandavas but has direct reference to the political situation in India. Though it is not difficult to understand the nationalist implications of the Gita in its call to awake and arise, the social, ethical and revolutionary doctrines which modern India discovered in this sacred text can be understood only after detailed explanation.

The activitist teachings which the Gita is said to contain are addressed to the ordinary people.[2] They are based on three conceptions which are not found in other Hindu scriptures. These are the ideal of *Sthitiprajna* or the person of equable mind, the doctrine of *Nishkama karma* or action without personal desire or attachment, and the principle of *Loka samgraha* or welfare of the world towards which all action should be directed. As these three constitute the ideals of Hindu activism, which inspires New India, they deserve to be considered in greater detail.

Loka samgraha or the welfare of the world as the motive and object of all action is the special contribution of the Gita to Hindu religious and social thought. It follows naturally from the doctrine of unattached action which is the central theme of Krishna's teaching. If action is to be selfless and is to be without reference to the fruits thereof (in relation to the actor) then the question naturally arises, why should any one persist in a course of action? The old theories of *Yajna* or sacrifice provided a simple answer: action is to please the gods and to derive worldly benefits through them. Since that was not *Nishkama karma* or action without reference to the results for the actor, the Gita rejected it and supplied the answer that the object of all action should be *Loka samgraha* or the welfare of the world.

[1] The *Gita Rahasya* is in Marathi. The English translation published from Bombay in two volumes is competent but not too good.

[2] The Gita is in three parts: the first part deals with *Karmayoga* or the yoga of action—addressed it is said to the ordinary man—*Jnana yoga* or the yoga of knowledge, addressed to those of high intellectual evolution, and *Bhakti yoga* or the yoga of devotion, addressed to the spiritually evolved. The latter two yogas may no doubt be considered superior and the Gita itself considers *Bhakti yoga* to be the ultimate way, *but for the world in general*, with which we are concerned, the yoga recommended is the *yoga of action.*

The social theory behind the *Loka samgraha* doctrine of the Gita is most important. The conception of a world order which it is the duty of the individual to uphold by dedicating his activity towards that end, runs all through the teachings of the Gita. The earlier Vedic religion had no such conception. Nor did the later thinkers who built up the comprehensive structure of Upanishadic thought devote any attention to social development. The Hindu doctrine of society as a caste organization (*Chaturvarnya*, the four orders) developed independently of religious thought, and is not connected with the spiritual teachings of the Upanishads. For the first time the Gita gives a social content to religion and emphasizes the welfare of the world as the purpose of all action. The doctrine of sacrifice is thus given a wholly different meaning by Krishna.

The Gita's view of society, as indeed of the Hindu thinkers in general, is a hierarchical organization based on functions and qualities. It upholds a doctrine of harmonies. In Hindu practice this ideal of social solidarity had crystallized into that strange and all-pervading organization with which Hinduism itself came to be identified—the system of caste. Whatever its origin, caste led in time to a fragmentation of society, each fragment walled off and kept isolated from the other. But the doctrine behind the conception of the four castes or the fourfold division of society, was simple enough, though in fact this division of *Chaturvarnya* was never more than a theorization of social thinkers. The *Chaturvarnya* postulated a *body social*, and the anology of the limbs of the body found expression in the doctrine of Brahmins being born from the head, the Kshattriyas from the arms, the Vaisyas from the thighs and the Sudras from the feet of the creator. This symbolism is so much a part of Hindu tradition that the word *bahuja* (born from the arms) is a common synonym for the Kshatriya or the warrior cast as *padaja* (born from the feet) is for the Sudra.

This conception of the fourfold order of society was a rationalization and had no relation at any time to the facts of caste. As Sir Aurobindo, the most authoritative modern commentator of the Gita, has put it: 'In point of fact,' he says, 'the verses of the Gita have no bearing on the existing caste system because it is very different from the ancient ideal of *Chaturvarna*, the four clear-cut orders of the Aryan community, and in no way corresponds with the description of the Gita. Agriculture, cattle-keeping and trade of every kind are said here to be the work of the Vaishya; but in the later system, the majority of those concerned in trade and in cattle-keeping and artisans, small craftsmen and others are actually classed as Sudras—where they are not put altogether out of the pale—and with some exceptions the merchant class alone, and that not everywhere, ranked as Vaishya. Agriculture, Government and service are the professions of all classes from the Brahmin down to the Sudra. And if the economic divisions of function have been confounded beyond any possibility of rectification, the law of the *Guna* or quality (as declared by the Gita) is still less a part of the later system. There, all is rigid custom, *acara*, with no reference to the need of the individual nature. If again we take the religious side of the contention advanced by the advocates of the caste system, we can certainly fasten no such absurd idea on the Gita as that it is a law of a man's nature that he shall follow, without regard to his personal bent and capacities, the profession of his parents or his immediate or distant ancestors, the son of a milkman be a milkman, the son of a doctor a doctor, the descendants of shoemakers remain shoemakers to the end of measurable time, still less that by doing so, the unintelligent and mechanical repetition of the law of another's nature without regard to his own individual call and qualities, a man automatically furthers his own perfection and arrives at spiritual freedom.'[1]

In fact there is nothing in common between the caste system and *Chaturvarnya*. *Chaturvarnya* or the fourfold order of society is a doctrine of social solidarity. Caste—the essential principle of which is division based on birth—is the very opposite, a doctrine of fragmentation.

An even more significant teaching in the Gita is its doctrine of the rejuvenation of society. Krishna declares 'Whenever and wherever Dharma decays and unrighteousness prospers, I shall be born in successive ages for the purpose of destroying evildoers and re-establishing the supremacy of the moral law'.

The Gita foresees the inevitable decay of all institutions and the necessity at different times of revolutionary changes to restore the harmony of life. While the Gita emphasizes that there are permanent social values, it does not give support to the doctrine that what exists is always the best and that change in itself is something to be resisted. It goes much beyond this. It emphasizes

[1] Sri Aurobindo, *Essays on the Gita* (published originally from Pondicherry), second series, p. 329.

that social institutions are liable to decay and petrification when the original values are lost sight of and social chaos follows as a result of which the purposes behind social organization begin to be misunderstood or misinterpreted. At such times, qualitative change or revolution according to the Gita is a divinely ordained process.

This sublimation of the doctrine of change is one of the major contributions of the Gita to modern India.

To a static society held down by custom and tradition and suffocated by the accretions of ages, the teaching that change is divinely ordained when society has decayed came as a life-giving revelation. There it was provided in the most authoritative text that Dharma requires to be restated in every age and society must be reorganized to suit new needs. No stronger weapon could have been put in the hands of those who desired to reshape Indian society and give it purpose and vitality. The old doctrine of *avatars* found a new meaning, for in the past the text of *yada yadahi* (whenever Dharma decays I shall be reborn) was interpreted literally as a promise of God to take human shape to set matters right. Like many other teachings of Hinduism it was perverted into a doctrine for the acceptance of the present on the plea that when it suits God He will be born into the world and change things by His direct action. It became therefore in the hands of sectarian teachers another argument for passivity.

The new doctrine of the yoga of action gave this text an extended content and a new significance which infused into the Indian mind a religious fervour enabling it not only to give vigour to political action but transform Hinduism itself from a static social organization to an intensely vital and dynamic force.

The revolutionary dynamic of this triple conception of *Sthitiprajna*, the man of the equable mind, of *Loka samgraha*, welfare of the world, and of *Brahma Yajna*, action dedicated to God, lay hidden for a thousand years owing to the dominance of the renunciatory creed of which Sankara was the champion. As we have seen, the earlier religious thinkers only used the Gita to support their own previously enunciated religious doctrines and paid no attention to the social ethic of Krishna's teachings or to its political implications. The depression into which Hindu society fell during the period when the Gangetic valley was under the authority of the Muslim Rulers helped the doctrine of renunciation by the widespread escapism to which orthodoxy had sunk. It is thus only in the nineteenth century that the Gita emerged as a gospel preaching the ideal of the *Karma yoga*—of selfless action in this world for the benefit of this world.

The new interpretation gave to India what it was looking for, an authority in Hinduism for what the educated mind had accepted as necessary. The reformist thinkers of modern India were, to begin with, impressed by the social purpose and wide humanism of Christianity, and the earliest spiritual stirrings of educated India were towards a dilution of Hindu religion with Christian thought which was best exemplified by the Brahmo Samaj in its first phase.

Tilak's exposition of the more activist doctrines of the Gita struck the intelligentsia with the force of a new message because they were dealt with objectively and in a truly orthodox tradition without any reference to political controversies. But the meaning was clear enough because of the author's background and the social and political conditions of India. Bal Gangadhar Tilak had been sentenced to two long terms of imprisonment. He was the accepted leader of the more extreme nationalist party in India who considered it their duty 'to arise and fight' foreign rule. To Tilak therefore India was the *DharmaKshetra*—the Field of Righteousness—and the inactivity which seemed to have gripped India was but a reflection of the unmanliness that Arjuna felt on the field of battle. The Gita helped Arjuna to get rid of his dejection. The same purpose it can now fulfil on this new Field of Righteousness. To Tilak it was clear that it was only through the message of the Gita that India could save herself.

The social and religious background also helped to give the message of the Gita a new importance. The end of the century witnessed the apogee of missionary activity in India. The attack on Hinduism was from all sides: the injustices of the caste system. the alleged lack of social purposes in Hindu teachings, its world-denying character, etc. The Gita as newly interpreted provided a conclusive answer to all these charges.

If activism was what Tilak emphasized, it is the *Sthitiprajna* doctrine—that of selfless service—that Gandhiji taught by his commentary on the Gita. Gandhi's exposition of the Gita was not a learned one. It was not a work of objective scholarship like that of Tilak, or of inspired interpretation like that of Aurobindo.

Gandhiji believed in selfless action for the good of the world and he found that doctrine stated with unambiguous lucidity and authority in the Gita. He was in fact the embodiment of the Gita ideal of the equable mind devoted to action meant for the benefit of all—the *Sthitiprajna* who unmoved by anger or by fear had his feet planted firmly in the world and directed all his action to the benefit of the world. He was the true *Karma yogin* and his commentary on the Gita is therefore a statement of his personal credo.

Gandhiji's special contribution to the integral teachings of the Gita is not selfless action for the welfare of the world but the emphasis on the means. There was a suggestion in Tilak's *Gita Rahasya* that the *Karma yogin's* action, as it was dedicated to God, was above moral laws so long as the object was clearly understood to be the common weal. It is this unexpressed doctrine of Tilak that Gandhiji sought to set right by his commentary on the Gita and the practical interpretation he gave to it through his own life.

To Gandhiji it was not sufficient that the ideal should be *Loka samgraha* or the welfare of all. It was even more important that the means should be ethically right. For action to be *Brahma Yajna* or sacrifice or dedication to God, it must be pure and uncontaminated not merely by selfishness but by anything which injures others. His doctrine of *ahimsa* or non-violence was therefore *not* the creed of pacifism or a denial of force, but an emphasis that the force of action should not be such as to injure the true nature of another's law of life—of the *Swadharma* of the opponent.

It was the Mahatma's conviction that foreign rule, i.e. the imposition of an alien way of life and thought, was not merely sinful because it was an attack on the Dharma of the ruled but it was even more against the Dharma of the ruler. That is why all through the twenty-eight years of his fight against British rule and even when he denounced that rule as satanic, he claimed to be a true friend of the British, as they now accept him to have been. The very denunciation of British rule to be satanic is the clue to his approach and can in its full significance be understood only in terms of the Gita doctrine of *Swadharma*, or the law of one's own nature.

The most comprehensive interpretation of the Gita, in the sense of being the most integrated in its spiritual values, is the one by

Sri Aurobindo. The background of the author is important. Brought up from an early age in England and educated in the European classical tradition with a training in Greek and Latin, Aurobindo appeared on the Indian political stage as the advocate of a violent revolution. He was the inspirer of the terrorist movement and was arrested in connection with the Alipore bomb case. But he underwent a spiritual transformation during his incarceration in the Bankipore jail, and it was a new Aurobindo that settled down to a life of rigorous austerities, study and contemplation in Pondicherry, then the capital of French India. From that time for a period of forty years he was one of India's great spiritual teachers. His final teachings are embodied in a great work entitled *Life Divine*, but the work which has had the greatest influence in shaping the thought of modern India is his *Essays on the Gita.* Published originally over a period of four years in a magazine entitled the *Arya*, edited by him, this new interpretation won immediate recognition as a masterly exposition of the permanent truths of the Gita in the context of modern life and in the language of modern thought.

Aurobindo's commentary is primarily a work of religion, but in view of the author's training and background it has had a wide social significance. It emphasized the ethical nature of the Gita's teachings, tore down mercilessly the obscurantist interpretation that polemical writers had given to its social message and for the first time helped the Indian public to understand its teachings in terms of life's problems.

The Gita has thus become the scripture of the new age, the main foundation on which its ethic, its social doctrines and even its political action depends. Its message is carried daily to the common man in a thousand new popular versions, as the number of books on the subject published every year in every language amply testifies. It is the inspiration and guide, and no one can claim to understand the developments which are taking place in India who has no appreciation of this fundamental fact.

It will thus be seen that, as a result of the operation of these many forces, Hindu religion had by the time of independence acquired a truly national character. It had reorganized itself on an all-India basis. Its general body of doctrines had received a nation-wide acceptance; its social institutions had begun to reflect the sense of community.

How is it that so important a movement affecting 360,000,000 people either escaped attention or when it did receive attention was underestimated? Political observers were misled by the emphasis laid on the recovery of independence and by the drama of the political struggle which Mr Gandhi had inaugurated. Besides, the externals of Hindu religion always repelled European observers, to whom the worship of Kali and the homage paid to the symbol of Siva represented the infamous. They preferred to shut their eyes. Foreign observers who studied Hinduism seriously were the champions of their own faiths, who brought their preconceived ideas of religion to bear on Hinduism and were therefore misled into generalizations wide of the mark. They were bewildered by the difference between the external form and the internal significance of many aspects of popular religion. The variety of its creeds seemed to them confusing. Hinduism appeared to the outsider only a number of disintegrating sects which stood in the way of the unification of the Hindu people. It was held to encourage masses of men in idle ways of false asceticism and self-torture, to deny by its caste system the brotherhood of man. In its higher form it appeared to the outsider to be anti-social. The Hindu movement was therefore generally estimated by the Christian observer more as a desperate struggle of a reactionary paganism to maintain its hold on the ignorant through an appeal to nationalism, and for this reason they were led to underestimate it. Today the most casual observer can see that without the reformation of Hinduism on a broad basis Indian independence would not have been possible.

CHAPTER III

The Christian Tradition

Modern India is not exclusively Hindu in tradition or inspiration though in view of the predominance of Hindu population and its continuity through history it is but natural that the most widely accepted way of life is Hindu and it is the Hindu culture that gives to Indian life its special characteristics. But the contribution of other religions—notably Christianity and Islam—through their own adherents and indirectly through their reaction on Hinduism are also highly significant in the development of modern Indian tradition.

This is especially true of Christianity. Christianity in India has a history extending to over 1,900 years, for the ancient tradition witnessed as early as AD 192 by Pantaenus of Alexandria about the existence of a Christian community in India, following, as it was widely believed, the apostolic activities of St Thomas, has now been accepted by the Catholic Church. In any case it is undeniable that the Christian tradition in India is a very old one. Its contribution to culture was however local. With the arrival of the Portuguese the situation changed a little. The Portuguese were active in the mission field and especially from the time of St Francis Xavier attempted large-scale conversion of the lower classes on the coastal areas of Western India. But the influence of such activities on Hindu life was negligible. In the nineteenth century, however, the Church in England took up this work with zeal, concentrating on proselytization among the aborginal tribes and backward classes and seeking through educational, medical and other social work to influence the higher classes. Their work in the field of conversions has been on the whole sterile for after 150 years of ceaseless activity it has not made any serious dent on Hinduism.

The reason for this failure is not far to seek. Mahatma Gandhi in his autobiography has recorded how, as a young boy, he was shocked by the virulent attack of a missionary preacher on everything that pertained to Hinduism. Also, the insistence of the early missionaries on a clean breakaway from the family relationships and the surroundings of the Hindus, though it prevented those whom they were able to convert from going back, made it impossible for the Christian message to reach any but a small section. It may be remembered that the missionary who came out to India to preach the gospel of Christ was also the representative of an alien civilization which was identified with the governing classes and thus he often unconsciously assumed airs of superiority.[1]

An equally important reason was the ignorance of the early missionaries in matters relating to Hindu religion. It appeared to them that it should be sufficient to tell the educated Hindu that God could not have three eyes, and goddesses represented as having eight hands were obviously impossible. What the missionary of those early days did not realize was that even an uneducated villager had a satisfactory understanding of what those images, which appeared so grotesque to an alien, stood for, and he did not make the mistake of thinking that the image represented the physical form of the Deity, as the missionary in his simple way was inclined to assume.

It is true that many missionaries now try to understand sympathetically the religious ideas of Hinduism and some have even written learned books on the subject. The vituperative period of missionary effort has passed, but even now the curious and primitive belief in the exclusive possession of truth which the preachers of Christianity parade falls jarringly on the ears of the Hindus, who had at all times fervently believed and have been taught to believe by their sacred books that all paths lead to the same God.

If the effort of the missionaries failed in the field of religion in other spheres their work has had notable success. Especially their educational institutions introduced a new spirit of understanding, a better appreciation of life in the community and gave an added impetus to a rethinking of values: men like Dr William Miller of

[1] For a detailed discussion on the subject, see the Author's *Asia and Western Dominance*, London, Allen & Unwin Ltd., 1953.

the Madras Christian College, C. F. Andrews[1] of St Stephen's College in Delhi and numerous less-known personalities all over India helped to bring up generations of students to whom the dedicated lives of their teachers became shining examples of service.

In the field of social service also the foreign missions have a fine record of achievement. The inspiration of many activities, notably of the advocates of social reform both in their desire to raise the moral standards of the people and in their narrow philistinism and intolerance, can be traced directly to the missionaries. The agitation against the practice of dedicating women to the temples (Devadasis), the movement for freeing widows from the rigorous and often inhuman code of restrictions enforced against them, the revolt against child marriage—in fact most of the activities, the declared object of which was to rid Hindu society of abuses—had their origin in the influence of missionary teaching. The same influences were responsible for the attitude of the reformers towards Indian dancing, which, following the missionary lead, was roundly denounced as being immoral, for the denial of values in Indian sculpture, which was written down as crude exhibitions of monstrosities of many heads and hands, for the rejection of the classical literature of the Puranas as encouragement to superstition. In short, the social reformers, who based themselves on the missionary approach to India, while they prepared the ground for the purification of Hindu life were, generally speaking, out of sympathy with the mind of India and therefore had but little influence with the masses.

The one field where missionary activity had a positive result was in relation to the untouchables and the aboriginal tribes. These large communities, numbering over 60,000,000 people all over India, were from time immemorial outside the pale of Hindu society. Hindu society at one time recognized but few civil rights in regard to the untouchables. They were condemned to the meanest type of labour and were denied approaches to public institutions like schools, roads and wells.

The missionaries saw a unique opportunity here. When their failure with the higher classes became more and more evident they diverted their activities to the conversion of the untouchables and lower castes. Their success in the way of conversions was only

[1] *C. F. Andrews: a biography*, by Sykes and Chaturvedi, London, Allen & Unwin Ltd., 1949.

moderate, mainly because the untouchables themselves, strange as it may seem, were deeply attached to Hinduism. But the call of Christianity had other results. The Christian convert from untouchability rose in social level. The missionaries were able to ensure that the social disabilities of Hinduism were not enforced against the convert. He was also given the facilities of education in mission schools and often was provided with employment. Though the convert from among untouchables was himself an unhappy man, as his own community rejected him, and the other Christians did not accept him, except where large numbers of the same community had been converted, the difference in social conditions was sufficiently glaring to create widespread discontent among the depressed classes who had remained within the Hindu fold. The seed of discontent thus planted led to the upsurge of the depressed classes, which was one of the most significant movements of the two decades preceding the establishment of independence.

Other factors, such as the growth of urban labour, the awakening of the 'lower orders' everywhere following the Russian Revolution, Mahatma Gandhi's flaming zeal for the cause of these 'children of God', contributed greatly to the success of the movement for the uplift of the untouchables. But its original source was the preaching of the Christian missionary and the discontent created among the untouchables by the continued disabilities of those who remained Hindus and the social rise of others who had been converted to Christianity. Nothing however so clearly emphasizes the rejection of the converts by the community than the fact that the leadership of the movement of the untouchables remained exclusively in the hands of those who had remained within the fold. Dr Bhim Rao Ambedkar, who organized and led the Scheduled Caste Federation and was the most outstanding personality that the community has produced in modern times, though he denounced Hinduism in unmeasured terms in the days of his political fight, lived to introduce the Hindu Code in Parliament, later in life married a Brahmin social worker and finally opted not for Christianity but for Buddhism. Mr Jagjivan Ram, the leader of the nationalist section of the erstwhile untouchable classes, who as Minister for Labour in the first National Government was responsible for far-reaching legislation to improve the condition of labouring classes, has always been an orthodox Hindu and most others who devoted themselves to the cause of these communities have remained within the Hindu fold. All the same, the revolt against Hindu social customs which they led fearlessly and with zeal originated primarily in the activities of the missionaries.

Perhaps the most important contribution of Christianity, though indirect, was the sense of communal solidarity that it gave to Hinduism. The Hindus, in their long history, had never been a community. They were a loose confederation of many caste-communities, of which the integrated unit was the 'sub-caste' (sub because it is supposed to be affiliated to one of the four divisions of society). There were many thousands of sub-castes and a Hindu's marriage, social relationships and loyalties were normally limited to these groups. The idea that the Hindus formed a single community was remarkable by its absence.[1]

It is the attack of the Christian missionaries on Hinduism as a whole that first created among educated classes the idea of such a community. The organization of the Christian communities, the solidarity of their social institutions, and the growth of Christian churches worked as examples. Though many things contributed towards the growth of this feeling among the Hindus—notably the desire for national unity and the communal movement among the Muslims—its origins undoubtedly lie in the defensive attitude towards the Christian attack. The 150 years of rivalry with the Christian religion which was backed by the prestige of the ruling race, and the visible success of 'the Christian nations' helped the divided, disorganized and mutually exclusive sections of Hinduism to feel and act like a community. It is this necessity for defence that gave to Vivekananda and others the chance to appeal for a consolidation of Hindu religious thought, for the social reform societies to carry on their activities and for orthodox Hindu leaders everywhere to organize schools and colleges, and for Pandit Malaviya and his followers to establish the great Benares Hindu University.

In the earlier years when Hinduism was examining its own doctrines and institutions, it was Protestantism that was most active in the realm of missionary effort. The doctrines of Protestantism, which made direct appeal to the scriptures and denied the necessity of mediation between God and man and placed all men on an equal footing before God, helped the Hindus to

[1] See the author's, *Hinduism at Cross Roads*, Asia Publishing House, 3rd edition, 1960.

understand their own religion. It was the Protestant view of religion that urged Ram Mohan Roy first to study the Christian scriptures in Greek and Aramaic and then forced him to search the Upanishads directly for the discovery of religious truths. The externalization of religion did not have the sanction of the higher religious thinkers of Hinduism and the Protestant view therefore seemed to conform to Indian practices. Also, the study of English literature, history and thought which dominated the Hindu mind for over a century (this will be discussed later) represented a predominantly Protestant tradition. The history of English liberties has always been identified by English writers themselves with the growth of Protestantism and thus indirectly, through the wide acceptance of English political ideals and the deep penetration of English literature, Protestantism lent its colour and temper to the modern Hindu mind.

Christianity directly contributed but little to the growth of nationalist feeling. The earlier generation of high caste converts, Kalipada Mukherji, Michael Madhusudan Dutt and Raja Harnam Singh remained nationally minded Indians even after their acceptance of Christianity: but with the growing estrangement between the British Government, to which Christians as a community looked for encouragement, and the nationalist movement whose avowed object was to recover India's freedom the Christian community found itself placed in a very difficult dilemma.

The break came with the upsurge of national sentiment which followed the first Great War. Kanakarayan Paul's famous article 'Watchman, what of the night' may be considered the first call to the community to realize the strength and weight of the new forces. Paul, a devout Christian, was also an ardent champion of the cultural traditions of India. The alienation of the Christian community from the rich inheritance of India's past was a matter of grave concern to him. As the Secretary General of the YMCA in India he was instrumental in publishing, under Christian auspices, a series of very valuable general studies, entitled the 'Heritage of India'. Written by Christian scholars, but with deep understanding and general sympathy, this series of books, which dealt with every aspect of India's cultural tradition, helped the Indian Christians to break away from the influence of the narrow missionary attitude of looking down upon everything which was Indian. And yet it is remarkable that the first great non-co-operation movement of Mr

Gandhi (1920–3) failed to move the community, and only one Christian of any standing joined the national struggle and he, George Joseph, was one of the authentic 'St Thomas' Christians of India and not a convert of the missionaries. But the change had come, and in the later phases of the struggle an increasing number of Christians began to identify themselves with the national movement.

There is another aspect of Christian activity which had important repercussions, and that is the work of the missionaries among the aboriginal tribes. The dwellers in the mountains and the jungles, these aboriginal inhabitants of India, though a forgotten people, maintained in their mountain fastnesses their own primitive ways of life. As a result of continuous encroachment over centuries they have been pressed further and further back into the jungles and lived in what might not unjustly be called natural reservations. Though sections of them living nearer to settled villages had become Hinduized, the communities as a whole had succeeded in maintaining their primitive identity. Their ways of life had not materially changed from what Bana had described in Harsha Charita in the seventh century, or Somadeva in many tales of the Ocean of Stories. They had been neglected alike by the Hindus and the Muslims. The Christian missionaries saw in these neglected millions a unique field for their activity. They met with some success there but their greatest success was in arousing Hindu conscience and sense of moral responsibility in this matter.

The missionary effort among the scheduled tribes in the interior of India, e.g. the Santals in Bihar, the Maria Gonds in Madhya Pradesh, etc., was on the whole beneficial, but the same cannot be said of their activities among the tribes in the border regions. The dream of an independent Christian tribal area separate from India seemed to have haunted their minds in the wilder areas of Assam, where some of the British officials also encouraged such views as a method of weakening the national movement. Apart however from this attitude of general unfriendliness to India in border areas, the work of the missionaries among the aboriginal tribes may be said to have created a tradition of social service which modern India has inherited. If the Indian Constitution includes special provisions for the welfare of tribal communities and *adi-vasis* (aboriginal inhabitants) and if the Centre and the states are making concerted efforts to bring them up to the general level of India, much of the credit for such activities must be given to the missionary.

In estimating the contribution of Christianity to modern India, there has generally been a tendency to confuse it with the influence of the West. No doubt the two were often intermixed, but the secular traditions of the West which influenced India through her contact with Britain could hardly be claimed as part of the Christian contribution. They are, therefore, dealt with separately.

CHAPTER IV

Islam

The nationalism of Islam[1] is basically more dynamic than that of Hinduism. The pride of empire, the unity of its religion, the solidarity and brotherhood of Muslim people and their determination not to remain subject to any alien authority led to an early integration of Islamic opinion in India. The fact that the circumstances which followed the Great Rebellion of 1857 made it necessary for Islam to make a temporary alliance with the British to recover lost ground, should not lead the observer to forget the fact that even in the period of their greatest helplessness Muslims looked forward to their independence of both the British and the Hindus. The numerical superiority and the unexpectedly quick recovery of the latter gave them sufficient grounds for alarm. The organization of Islam in India was, therefore, frankly communal, and its outlook was governed by the single fact of ensuring to the Islamic nation in India its independence and authority.

The Muslims at all times everywhere have been an integrated community separate from others. Though during the period of Muslim authority over large areas in northern India there was close political contact between Muslims and Hindus, it was broadly speaking on the basis of the Rulers and the Ruled. It is true that under the British at different times the communities came together for political action but they remained separate entities, 'the two eyes of India' as Syed Ahmed had declared. The most notable instance of such an alliance was during the agitation relating to the Khaliphat, when after the first Great War Britain and her allies proposed to the Turks peace terms which seemed to

[1] On the whole of this subject in relation to India see Prof. Cantwell Smith *Islam in the Modern World*, Chapter relating to India.

limit the authority of the sovereign Khalif. An agitation was started in India under the leadership of Manlana Mohammed Ali for ensuring the independence of the Commander of the Faithful. Under the leadership of Mahatma Gandhi the Congress after 1920 extended full support to the Muslim claim and for a period of four years the Muslim agitation against the Western nations and particularly against Britain became identified with the Congress. But after 1924 the communities again fell apart and the support for the Indian national movement was limited to a small group of nationalist Muslims.

As separately organized communities living lives of their own, though neighbours, the influence they exerted on each other was not fundamental. The great principles of Islam did not affect Hinduism as a whole, though here and there minor sects came into existence as a result of their influence on each other. The social structure of Hinduism remained almost unaffected by 700 years of association with Islam. Even so far as untouchability was concerned, though there were in some places quite large-scale conversions to Islam, the very fact that at the end of Muslim authority in North India the so-called untouchable communities numbered many millions would prove clearly the absence of Islamic influence on the social structure of Hinduism.

Till the establishment of British authority the Muslims had felt no rivalry towards the Hindus. They were so well established in their political authority with visible symbols of superiority in Delhi and the great provincial capitals that there was no occasion for them to feel any kind of jealousy. But after the Mutiny the situation showed a change. The Hindu revival which was the marked feature of the second half of the nineteenth century made them realize that not only had India ceased to be a *Dar-ul-Islam*, or an Islamic country, but that the Hindus whom they had looked down upon till then were fast leaving them behind. Indeed it led to an attitude of hostility towards the Hindu community. The organization of the Congress showed that the Hindus had developed a new political conscience and the Muslim leaders of the time thought that they recognized in it a great political danger. On the eve of the third session of the Indian National Congress in Madras Sir Syed Ahmed declared at a public meeting in Lucknow 'If you accept that the country should groan under the yoke of Bengali rule and its people lick the Bengali's shoes, then, in the name of

God! jump into the train, sit down and be off to Madras'.[1] That the awakening of Hinduism would lead to the growth of separatism among the Muslims was clear from the beginning.

The British authorities, suspicious of the growing Hindu nationalism, encouraged this separatism. It is unnecessary to discuss the origins of separate electorates, communal proportion in all appointments, even in the army, the distinction between provinces on the basis of communal majority, the conflict between Urdu and Hindi, between the Persian script and the Nagari script, going down to music before mosques and to slaughter-houses. The importance of the communal nationalism of the Muslims so far as India was concerned lay not so much in the partition of India, and the creation of the new Muslim State of Pakistan, but in its repercussions on Hinduism. The militant spirit of Islam led to the organization of the Arya Samaj in the Punjab which, for the first time since Guru Govind Singh organized the Sikhs for a similar purpose, created a sense of organized militancy in Hinduism. The Arya Samajists were fanatically monotheist and egalitarian, as they saw in these two qualities the strength of Islam. They embarked on a programme of proselytization and also took back into the fold of Hinduism those who had been converted to other religions. While it undoubtedly introduced acerbity into the communal politics of the Punjab, the Arya Samaj, by adopting the methods of Islam and adding to them the social purpose of the Christians, became the percursor of the sense of community which was soon to pervade the general body of Hinduism.

The Muslim communal organizations brought into existence their counterparts among the Hindus. The Hindu Mahasabha was the reply of the Hindus to the Muslim League. Though never very strong organizationally, its activities helped to create a Hindu feeling, which with the growing intransigence of Muslim politics, permeated deeply even the Congress. The National Congress held firmly to its ideal of a non-communal and an all-embracing political organization, open to every class of Indian without regard to religion or sect. Through all the difficult days of communal animosity it successfully adhered to this doctrine which was soon to blossom into the idea of the Secular State.

[1] Quoted in R. C. Majumdar's *Three Phases of India's Struggle for Freedom*, p. 20. Bharatiya vidja Bhavam, Bombay 1960

But though the Congress held to its non-communal credo, its predominantly Hindu membership was not impervious to the influence of communal politics. The criticism that the Muslim League levelled at the Congress that there was no essential difference between it and the Hindu Maha Sabha, though unjust to its leaders and those who moulded its policy, had a large element of truth in regard to the rank and file. Communal politics had become so much a part of Indian life that those who were not continuously on guard against it fell victims to its insidious poison. The influence of the Hindu Maha Sabha was not therefore to be judged by the strength of its membership or the influence of its leaders. In fact the religious nationalism of Islam made the Hindus community-conscious and in this sense it was a source of great strength to Hinduism also.

The majority of the newspapers of India were frankly communal. The Muslim press, with a few exceptions, existed solely for championing the interests of the community. The Congress had no press of its own and the nationalist press, which was Hindu in composition, reflected largely the communal interests even while fighting the battles of nationalism. This was unavoidable. The result of this continuous warfare of words was a strengthening of the community-consciousness on both sides. The *Rashtriya Swayam Sevak Sangh* (RSS, the organization of militant Hindu youth) which at one time threatened the foundations of the new State was the direct child of this temper.

The acceptance of the two-nation theory and Pakistan's declared intention of establishing a State based on Islamic principles had the effect of encouraging the growth of a school of political thought among the Hindus, known as *Hindu pada padishahi*, a State based on the supremacy of the Hindus. Though this doctrine had originated in the early days of the revolutionary movement in the first decade of the twentieth century, it gained political influence only after the growth of Islamic separation. The most prominent advocate of this theory, Vinayak Savarkar, was an old-time revolutionary who had served a sentence of transportation for life in the penal colony of the Andaman islands. He looked back to the glory of the period of Mahratta ascendancy (1717–1785) when a State based on orthodox Hinduism ruled over the major portion of the Indian sub-continent. He had, with singular consistency, advocated this doctrine of an exclusive Hindu State, but had not found much support among the masses of Hindus who were content to follow the more liberal ideals of a composite, secular state of which the Mahatma was the champion.

But the growth of the idea of the Islamic State gave Savarkar the opportunity for which he was waiting. Especially among the virile races of the Maharastra, who had fought and destroyed the Moghul Empire, he found a ready hearing. The RSS spread its tentacles into the rural areas and organized a volunteer corps which numbered many hundreds of thousands. When on August 16, 1946, the Great Killing of Hindus took place in Calcutta, the RSS was ready for retaliation. The bloody vicious circle of large-scale retaliation, by both communities, by the Hindus in Bihar and Gurmuktesar and by the Muslims in Rawalpindi, Multan and many other areas in the Punjab and North-West Frontier Province, and which reduced the great city of Bombay to a state of mad fury for many months, was in effect a fight between the Muslim national guards and the RSS. The Congress watched this menacing growth with a sense of impotent despair and it took Mr Gandhi many months of hard labour and two fasts to restore a sense of sanity to the Hindu community. The Hindu militants considered him their chief enemy.

The establishment of Pakistan naturally reduced the Muslims in India to the position of a national minority, numerically important, culturally valuable, with a great part to play in the evolution of New India—but still a minority which has to depend on the goodwill of the majority and adjust itself to the changed conditions of a nation State. The Muslims in India number over 45,000,000. They have an educated leadership, which has contributed to the nationalism of India's new secular society. The separate electorates which under the British gave expression to the theory of two nations and divided the Hindus from the Muslims has now been given up, with the approval of the Muslims themselves. The communal ratio of appointments which helped to keep alive this separation has also been surrendered. The Muslims have now become, for the first time after the British assumed authority, Indians professing Islam, no doubt a separate community but all the same identified in their political and economic interests with the rest of India.

Islam's main contribution to new India is the fact that it is its presence which makes India a multi-racial state. Though in number they are no more than ten per cent, they constitute a parallel society everywhere. From the Himalayas to Cape Comorin, there is no area where the Muslim presence is not felt. Also, they are much more than a religious minority. Their culture and way of life are everywhere different from those of the Hindus and other communities around them. Unlike the Christians who, though they profess a different religion, are not in their way of life different from the Hindus, the Muslims, whether in the South in Kerala or in Kashmir, represent a culture of their own. It is this major fact which gives to new India its special political characteristic and compels it to uphold its secular character.

CHAPTER V

The British Heritage

The British or Western share in the traditions of modern India extends over many fields. Apart from what may be called superficial approximation which inevitably results when one culture dominates another, which need not be considered here, the impact of Britain has acted both as a catalytic transforming Indian ways and traditions, and as a new contribution assimilated by the intellectual classes and entering through them into the life of the nation. Where it has acted as a catalytic, as for example in the reorganization of Hindu life, in providing new impetus in the fields of literary and other artistic creation, in generating new social urges, the inheritance has been more indirect though no less real and will be dealt with in the sections dealing with these developments in Indian life.

The major contributions of Britain in India's new life relates to the spheres of ideas and organization. In the sphere of ideas must be included new ways of thinking and criticism, the cultivation of science and a scientific approach to problems and the transplantation and acclimatization of political and social ideals. In the sphere of organization must be included the introduction of large-scale industries, the creation of political institutions and the development of civic life. It is in these matters that modern India shows a breach with the past. No doubt without direct British rule the ideas which we now trace to the British would have penetrated India, but it is doubtful if we look at the experience of other countries, whether they would have been assimilated in the same way as India has done, and become part and parcel of her traditions. Equally in organizational matters, some of these would have been adopted as other newly independent countries are now doing but the success with which India has adopted both political and economic institutions shows the strength of the tradition implanted in India as a result of the Indo-British impact.

The most important contribution of Britain to India's new tradition is a spirit of criticism. It is not that in India's long history there were no periods when a spirit of criticism was flourishing. The Buddha, for example, was an embodiment of the spirit of criticism. No aspect of Indian life escaped his eagle eye. But in recent ages such a critical approach had altogether disappeared from among the Hindus. In the Muslim period great reformers like Guru Nanak reflected the earlier spirit of the Buddha, but it was as a result of the impact of Islam and did not go beyond limited religious circles. The spirit of criticism and what may be called an attitude of questioning towards inherited institutions however irrational was not active among the intellectual classes in the period immediately preceding British rule. What was in the *Smritis* or sacred books could not be questioned. The ultimate authority for the validity of all opinions was a reference to the Vedas. Even the reformers had to go back to the ancient texts to justify their ideas.

The spirit of criticism revived in India under the influence of the West. The very bases of Hindu institutions came under examination. Even where irrational institutions like caste, untouchability or the inferior status of women were defended, it was significant that such justification was no longer on the basis of old texts but in the very language of new thought.

This new method of approach and these new ways of thinking which began in the early decades of the nineteenth century developed unchallenged to the end of British rule in India. Originally it was confined to a small group who had come under the direct influence of European ideas. But with the spread of English education all over the country and with the process of infiltration which made the regional Indian languages the vehicles of these ideas they spread to ever-widening circles.

What is even more significant than the growth of these advanced opinions is the fact, which we have already traced in an earlier section, of how every one of the social institutions to which the Hindu people had attached importance in the past and which the outside world had come to consider as the special characteristics of Hinduism had been quietly given up or reformed beyond recognition. The primacy of the Brahmins and their special claim to reverence, accepted at all times and never questioned except by reforming religious sects, became for example the *raison d'être* of a popular political movement in Madras and the Maharastra. The fight against untouchability, which also was an institution of respectable antiquity, became a nationwide political issue. In fact there was no aspect of Hindu society which was not subjected to popular criticism. It should also be added that reaction, though in retreat and unable to influence intellectual classes, did not cease fighting till the very end.

It is not only in relation to social institutions and pseudo-religious beliefs that this attitude of criticism was to be seen. The Hindus have a literature beginning with the Vedas (circa 1500 BC). It is thus the longest living literary tradition since, unlike other ancient literatures, the hymns of the Vedas are still repeated all over India and as literature they are translated and studied in all modern Indian languages. This great literature in Sanskrit, Pali and Prakrit was at all times studied with reverence and treasured as something unique, as indeed it is. It is not less intensively studied now, but the approach to it has become different. The blind admiration for anything clothed in Sanskrit has given place to a critical appreciation; so much so that D. L. Roy, the Bengali dramatist, even ventured to tilt his lance against Kalidasa, universally recognized as the greatest of Indian poets and dramatists.

The critical attitude towards Sanskrit literature is best reflected in the prevalent tendencies in regional languages. A century ago dramatical literature in these languages was modelled on Sanskrit. In poetry the conventions of Sanskrit were followed. Today the literary opinion in regional languages is highly critical of Sanskrit forms and both in poetry and prose follow the lead of the West. The most significant creative activity which one sees in modern India is in the realm of short story, novel and drama. The inspiration—at least in regard to form—for these comes from English, French and Russian.

Not very different is the position in regard to painting, sculpture and other arts. When after a period of lifeless imitation Indian artistic activity revived, it leant heavily on past traditions. The mural paintings of Ajanta became the model and inspiration for the revived school of Indian painting. Here again, after a short period of revivalism the critical spirit began to manifest itself and the modern school does hesitate to borrow their techniques from the popular schools of the past or from the modernist masters of Paris and Mexico.

The critical outlook has indeed become a dominant feature of India and it is one of the basic contributions of Britain to modern India.

No less important is the creation of widespread interest in science and technology. The spirit of scientific enquiry had ceased to operate in India by about the eighth century AD. It was an intellectual Dark Age that shrouded India till the middle of the nineteenth century. Thus, though Indians were in contact with sciences and technology at least at second-hand through the merchants who traded with them, they showed no curiosity or interest in any of the advanced machines, instruments and techniques used by the Europeans. Even in respect of artillery there was never any attempt to master the processes of manufacture or learn its secrets. In this matter the Indian approach was very different from that of the Japanese. From the time of the very first contacts the Japanese were curious about the sources of European power and there was always a group of intellectuals—known as the Rangkusha Circle—which was patiently trying to master western sciences. Though the contact with the West was much more widespread, no such interest seems to have developed among Indian intellectuals. There was no Indian counterpart of the Japanese Rangkusha.

Strangely enough, though Europe and India had been in close contact for centuries, there was no Discovery of Europe by India till the latter half of the nineteenth century. Thus the Indians were strangers to the great scientific discoveries of the seventeenth, eighteenth and the earlier half of the nineteenth century and the economic and industrial revolution which followed them. It must also be said that the British system of education in the nineteenth century did not encourage scientific studies or develop scientific curiosity in India. A few institutions for developing certain lower levels of technology were no doubt started, but the great universities following the tradition of Oxford and Cambridge concentrated on humanities. But India had in the meantime discovered Europe, especially Britain, and come to recognize wherein the strength of the West lay. The demand for scientific and technological education became insistent with the growth of the nationalist movement. The first major step taken in that direction was the establishment of the Indian Institute of Science at Bangalore as a result of the munificence of the far-sighted industrialist Sir Jamshedji Tata. In fact Indian capital, which by the end of the nineteenth century had become dominant in the cotton industry in Bombay, began to realize that without a firm basis in modern science India would never be able to catch up with the West in economic production. After the Reforms of 1919 which gave to the middle classes in India considerable voice in shaping policy, the development of scientific studies received great encouragement. By the time of independence India had become science-minded and anxious to participate in advanced researches carried on in all important spheres of knowledge. A very significant achievement of India in the first few years of independence has been the establishment of a network of national laboratories all over the country under the direct authority of the central government.

Also in the field of technology India has been making heroic efforts to catch up with the West. In fact this attitude of enthusiastic acceptance of the scientific approach and this determined endeavour not only to master the secrets of modern science but to participate to the greatest extent possible in the work of advancing scientific knowledge has been one of the special characteristics of modern India. While her own freedom from prejudice has been to a large extent responsible for this open attitude to science, there is no doubt that this new-found enthusiasm is one of the results of her contacts with the West. It is perhaps an indirect reaction, not something directly encouraged by Britain. It is based on India's own desire to catch up with developments in Europe and America.

The future historian will undoubtedly consider the introduction and acclimation of new political ideals as one of the most far-reaching results of India's prolonged relationship with Europe. There are three different aspects of this question which deserve consideration if the full significance of Britain's impact is to be understood. The first relates to the conception of nationalism as a binding factor of political organization. India's unity in the past was based on a conception of *Swadharma* or of culture and religion and except as a matter of conquest involved no sense of a politically united India. The Muslims, no doubt, had a conception of a single India, theoretically under the Sultans and Padshahs of Delhi, for the throne of Delhi was considered by them to involve the sovereignty of India. This much should be said to their credit that they had at least the theory of a united Indian state. This was so much a conviction with them that when Seringapatam was captured by Wellesley in 1799 from Tipu Sultan, the first thing that the representative of the Nizam of Hyderabad did was to have the *Kutbah* read in the local mosque in the name of the shadow emperor of Delhi, thereby, it would seem, setting right a great wrong done by the independent Sultan in denying the authority of the Emperor of Delhi over the territories of Mysore. How strong this feeling was may again be seen from the fact that at the time of the Mutiny, though the leaders of that movement were claimants to independent states, they resuscitated the shadow of imperial power as an act of homage to the unity of India.

This conception of political unity was broadly speaking an Islamic conception. With the breakdown of the Empire of Delhi a new ideology was required, if India's political unity was to be realized. The new doctrine of nationalism which had become the accepted creed of the West provided India with the ideology it required to gain a new sense of unity.

Nationalism is based on a unity of culture—a common tradition of shared history. There was undoubtedly a broad unity of culture based on Hindu religion, Sanskrit and Sanskrit literature, art, architecture, conceptions of social organization and family law, among the Hindus who constituted the vast majority of the population of undivided India. But it was equally clear that this unity based on culture did not extend to the Muslims who, though a minority of twenty-five per cent on an all-India basis, constituted a majority in some provinces. That the culture of the Muslims differs basically from the culture of the Hindus is obvious. Nor did their 700 years of contact produce either a common culture or modify Hindu institutions to such an extent as to blur the differences between the two communities. In fact on the basis of culture and religion there were two different nationalisms in India. Long before Mr Mohammed Ali Jinnah and Mohammed Iqbal, Syed Ahmed had, according to Richard Symonds, declared that the 'Hindus and Muslims form two separate political entities with separate outlook and conflicting interests'.[1] At the beginning of British rule in India the Muslims were a nation while the Hindus were an inchoate mass of people slowly trying to achieve self-realization based on their common religion and culture.

So far as shared history was concerned, it was obvious that between the Hindus and the Muslims a great gulf existed. Except during the period of British authority when both shared the experience of political subjection the Hindus and Muslims were, so to say, on the opposite sides of history. Hindu historical memories were of Muslim invasions, conquests, demolition of temples and political humiliations. Muslim histories were on the other hand chronicles of empire and domination for a considerable time. To the Hindus, even in the absence of a sound historical tradition, the heroes were Rana Kumbha, Rana Pratap, Shivaji and others who resisted Muslim authority. Even minor personalities who organized local resistance were elevated to the position of popular heroes. On the other hand, to the Muslims the great historical figures were those who upheld the tradition of Islam and who governed according to the strict ideas of the Islamic state.

Muslim nationalism had a developed historiography behind it; but the Hindus, though they had a considerable historical tradition embodied in the Puranas, *Kavyas* and other forms of literature, had not developed history as a separate branch of knowledge. Nothing was therefore known of Indian history before the advent of the Muslims, which was a major fact which stood in the way of the emergence of a conception of Hindu nationhood. British historians in the early period accepted the Muslim view of Indian history as may be seen from Elliot and Dawson's strange volumes of the *Chronicles of Islamic Kingdoms* which they style the 'History of India told by her own historians'. Of the two thousand years of Indian history before Islam entered India, the early historians of India know nothing because there was, as we said, no developed Hindu historiography. James Mill, who wrote the first great *History of India*, was convinced that the Hindus had no history before the Muslims and they were always in the same abject condition as that in which the British found them in Bengal in the eighteenth century. Elphinstone's *History of India* deals with pre-Muslim India in a few pages.

[1] R. Symonds, *The Making of Pakistan*, pp. 30–31.

The creation of a Hindu historiography and the recovery of India's great past constitute the most spectacular, as also the first fundamental contribution of European scholarship to India. In the century that passed between the acceptance of the identification of Sandrocottus of Alexander's history with Chandra Gupta Maurya and the discovery of the Indus valley civilization lies the great romance of the rediscovery of India's past and the creation of a national self-image for the Hindus as one of the creative civilizing peoples of the world with a continuous history of 3,000 years. The works of scholars like Princep Bothilingk, of excavators and archaeologists like Alexander Cunningham and Marshall, of students of literature, religion and culture like Sir William Jones, Max Muller and A. B. Keith opened up to the astonished eyes of Indians themselves a continuous history of political, social and cultural activity which was not inferior to that of other contemporary civilizations. Also, European scholars working in Central Asia, China and South-East Asia recovered the astonishing history of ancient Indian cultural expansion which established Hinduized kingdoms and empires in the Pamirs, in Malaya, in the Indonesian archipelago, and the fertile valleys of the Mekong.

All this reconstruction of India's past and the translation and popularization of great Indian philosophical and religious classics was the work almost exclusively of European scholars: English, German, French, Swedish, Russian, in fact scholars from every part of Europe. It was only in the last decades of the nineteenth century that Indian scholarship began to participate effectively in this work. The foundation of the Asiatic Society of Bengal by Sir William Jones, poet, scholar and judge, the decipherment of the Asokan inscriptions, opening up the vista of ancient history from records preserved in stone, metals and coins, the discovery of Ankor Vat in the overgrown jungles of Cambodia, the exploration of Central Asian caves by Stein, Pelliot and others, and finally the excavations at Mohenjodaro—these are but the most sensational events of a truly thrilling story of the rediscovery of a lost intellectual world through the disinterested work of foreign scholars. Nor should one forget to mention the massive achievements of men in the different Universities of Europe and later of America—Oxford, Cambridge, Paris, Heidelberg, Leyden, Harvard—who through love of learning translated, interpreted and published the vast literature which lay buried in Sanskrit and Pali, thereby opening up not only to the West but to the new middle classes in India itself an immense and almost unknown realm of religious thought and artistic achievement.

The question may legitimately be asked whether there would have been an Indian nationalism if this recovery of India's past and the consequent creation of an Indian national image had not been achieved through the work of European scholars. The answer to this question is clear. There would undoubtedly have developed national movements in India, but not on the basis of only two nations dominantly Hindu and Muslim but of many regional states, the Marathas, the Andhras, the Bengalis and others. Without a Hindu ideology, picturing the Hindu people as one, which Western scholarship and historiography enabled Hindus to create and develop, the alternative would have been the growth of regional nationalism based on recent and still remembered histories. India in fact would have been balkanized into numerous states each cherishing a nationalism of its own and not recognizing the common nationhood.

Britain thus helped to create and develop two nationalisms in India. Of these, the Islamic was a pre-existing fact, and Britain in the early days recognized it as such and treated it as being basically and irreconcilably hostile to its authority. Recognizing the strength of this Islamic national feeling and foreseeing no danger from the rise of a Hindu nationalism, the early British authorities not only favoured the Hindus but in a measure identified themselves with Hindu opinion. A strange example of this was the proclamation of the Governor General Lord Ellenborough—after the Afghan War of 1842—in which he announced to the Hindus, 'Our victorious army bears the gates of the temple of Somnath in triumph from Afghanistan and the despoiled tomb of Sultan Mahmud looks upon the ruins of Ghaznee. The insult of 800 years is avenged'. Though this strange claim is paralleled only by Herodotus' idea that the Persian king invaded Greece in order to avenge the insult to Troy, the proclamation is significant as showing how in the days before the development of Indian nationalism, the British authorities were inclined to support the Hindu point of view.

It is also significant from this point of view that the original foundation of the Indian National Congress had the support of a section of British officials. It is only when it was realized that the Congress was likely to foster an all-India nationalism which would one day challenge British authority that the authorities turned to the Muslims, who had by this time recognized their weakness and were prepared to be the loyal supporters of British rule. The encouragement of a separate Muslim nationalism—a pre-existing factor of great historical strength—was from the point of the British only a counterpoise to the rising claims of the Hindus, who in the name of their newfound nationhood were with slow but certain steps advancing towards a claim for political independence. This dual nationalism finally found its realization in the creation of two nation-states—India and Pakistan.

Another significant aspect of the British contribution to Indian tradition is in the realm of political ideas and institutions. The Indian tradition in the past, from that of the Nandas to the Moghuls and the Marathas, was imperial, that of a political organization of non-participating obedience. It was based on the separation of the ruler from the ruled, the *raja* from the *praja*, the emperor from his subjects. The British practice was not different. More than that, it emphasized the alien character of the rulers and the difference in their colour and race. But the political doctrine they taught and by hesitating steps tried to introduce, first through municipal and district councils and later through legislatures, local and central, was that of representative government, that is, 'a community of participating wills' where the distinction between the ruler and the ruled ceased and decisions were the result of discussion and debate. The British Government never put the doctrine completely into practice as the theory conflicted with their racial and imperial interests. But they helped to get the theory firmly planted in India and further provided at lower levels opportunities for practical training in the work of democratic government.

Apart from effecting this fundamental transformation in political ideas, the British connection was also responsible for the wide acceptance of liberalism as the political creed of India. What is really significant in the political life of India after independence has been the strength of the liberal tradition: the insistence on civil liberties, the supremacy of law, government by public debate and moral suasion, elections based on universal franchise and the extension of the conception of political community to the entire nation. In fact, surprisingly enough, in spite of the socialist bias in their economic policies, both the Government of India and the main opposition parties (excepting of course the Communists) have their feet firmly planted in the soil of liberalism.

That civilization can through human effort be made to move in a certain direction is the faith of liberalism. That it should be made to move in such a way as to ensure social justice, liberty, equality and other freedoms is the essential feature of liberal policy. These two basic ideas of liberalism may be contested, as indeed they are, by important schools of thought, the first as being no more than a faith without adequate evidence from the historical experience of man and the second, the realization of equality, being capable of achievement only through a complete and revolutionary reconstruction of economic life under proletarian dictatorship. Such partisan views notwithstanding, the new liberalism, adjusting itself to the social forces of the day and reconciling itself to the changed conception of the state, will continue to be the source of inspiration and the guiding light for the great majority of mankind outside the communist countries. And even when it is overtaken and superseded, as all ideas must necessarily be, its basic principles will have become transformed and assimilated into the general traditions of civilization.

The British contribution to the institutions under which India is living is no less significant. Elected parliament, assemblies and councils are undoubtedly reproductions of British counterparts. Their procedures, forms and modes of conducting business are based on British precedents. That they are now developing their own conventions is no argument against the accepted fact of the institutions themselves being rooted firmly in British traditions.

The judicial system which prevails in India is no less dominantly British in tradition. India had an elaborate system of law and procedure at least from the time of Manu. It had also a system of popular judicial administration based on the *panchayats* or village councils. The history of the British judicial system in India need not concern us here. Suffice it to say that, after trying a dual system of British law and procedure for Europeans and Indians living in certain areas and of traditional Indian laws and procedure for Indians generally, the British Government finally gave effect to a uniform system of justice and law enforcement under High Courts established by the Crown. Also the system provided for appeals to the judicial committee of the Privy Council in England, thereby placing the administration of justice in India under the supervision of the Privy Council. How greatly this last privilege was valued and how much it helped to shape judicial traditions in India is well brought out by the fact that Motilal Nehru, the leader of the Swarajist party in Parliament and one of the great figures in the non-co-operation movement, in Parliament spoke openly against the proposal to abolish appeals from Indian high courts to the Privy Council before independence was achieved.

Not only is the legal system under which India lives today the result predominantly of British legislation in India, but the evaluation of evidence, the civil and criminal procedures, and the whole approach of judges and lawyers to the administration of justice are taken over from British practice. British rule has left an immense and impressive corpus of legislation in India, covering practically every field of life—excepting, broadly, social relationships where Hindu and Mohammedan law, modified by occasional reforming acts, were allowed to function. That they have become assimilated with Indian life today is a fact which no one denies. No doubt there is a demand for the reform of the law and the judiciary—only to the extent of simplifying the more elaborate procedures and making the administration cheaper and less rigid. The British legal and judicial traditions continue to be the basis of India's modern life.

One other aspect of India's public life deserves to be emphasized as being derived from British traditions: and that is municipal administration. There were at all times large towns and cities in India and we have evidence of *Nagara Srestins* (heads of merchants' guilds in towns). *Nagaradhykshas* (heads of city administration), of organizations of self-governing trades and professions under their own heads. We have also descriptions of city life, for example in Vatsyayana's *Kama Sutra* where the author discusses the kind of life appropriate to a *nagarika* or a city dweller—his accommodation, food, amusements, etc. What Britain created in India was therefore neither a city tradition nor a city life, but civil government under municipal authorities. When Bombay came under the British crown as a part of the dowry of Catherine of Braganza, Charles II endowed it with a municipal charter placing it on the same footing as 'our borough of Greenwich'. Wherever the British Company acquired actual direct authority as in Madras or later in Calcutta, they introduced the elaborate machinery of their municipal institutions. Gradually when India came under their direct authority a modified system of municipal government was introduced. Today every city in India has its municipality or corporation and a vigorous civic life based on adult franchise. The administration of cities and towns is the concern of the citizens and this system which has become an essential part of our life is directly inherited from the municipal tradition of Britain.

Christopher Dawson in the *Making of Europe* has emphasized how, when other institutions of Rome broke down in the areas which had been Romanized in the time of her greatness, the towns and cities created by Rome upheld the traditions inherited from her. Such a breakdown of civilization as happened in Western Europe after the fall of Rome is altogether unlikely in respect of a country like India whose civilization and social structure are essentially based on her own traditions, and yet if there is a weakening of the factors which new India has inherited from Britain and the West, civic life in the larger cities will perhaps be the one European institution to survive.

In the economic field the dominance of the European tradition may be seen in the organization of large-scale industries with funds subscribed by the public but under private management. India had at all times been an industrial country, but her industry though widespread was of the handicraft type. Its financial organization was either individual proprietorship or joint family partnership. In the case of major industrial activity like mining, State ownership was the rule, as may be seen from Kautalya's Arthasastra. In India there was always considerable accumulation of capital in private hands. This however was mainly invested in trade and commerce and not in industrial undertaking which being on a handicraft and cottage basis did not require much investment.

What Britain did was to demonstrate how large-scale production could be organized, financed and marketed. The East India Company itself was the prototype of a commercial organization on the largest scale. What was significant was not only the size and character of the operations of the Company but the financial structure which was based on stock raised from the public. This system of tapping the wealth available with the general public for commercial and industrial enterprises under the direction of a group of entrepreneurs was something which Western Europe had discovered and perfected. With the abolition of the Company's monopoly private British enterprise began to enter the field in India. British companies began to operate in purely industrial fields. Soon their organizations and methods were taken over by Indians who ventured into large-scale industry in Bombay and Calcutta in competition with British interests. The organization, financial structure and techniques of the new industrial system which gradually began to develop under Indian leadership were copied from Europe and followed British traditions.

We have now indicated briefly the main elements of the Western contribution to the traditions of modern India. There is however one fundamental and overriding fact in this connection which remains to be discussed, and that is the acceptance by India of the twin doctrines of change and progress. The accepted idea in India was of a fixed order of things—*Sanatana Dharma*, an eternal system of values from which there can only be degeneration. *Sanatana Dharma* or the Eternal Law of Righteousness is still a popular word with the Hindus but today even those who preach it confine it strictly to religious values. That social organization and relationships and the material set-up of life must change according to changing conditions is now accepted by all. There is no orthodoxy in reading by an oil lamp when electricity is available; nor is there any particular value involved in eating with one's fingers and not with knives and forks. That social structure will reflect changes in economic conditions is now the accepted view today.

With this doctrine of change is connected the complementary idea of progress. The Hindus, more than perhaps other people, believed that movement in time meant regressions for societies—the very opposite of the doctrine of progress. They postulated a gradual and steady decline of man through four ages beginning with the Golden Age of *Satya Yuga* or the Age of Truth and coming down to *Kali Yuga*—the Age of Evil. This was the accepted belief in India as indeed it was with the West also in medieval times.

Modern India was slow to accept the doctrine of progress in social life. Ram Mohan Roy pleaded for the improvement of the condition of women, not on the basis that it was progress but that it was a restoration of the conditions which existed before. Swami Dayananda—the founder of the Arya Samaj—attacked caste, it may be noted, on the ground that it had no authority in the Vedas. The first great thinker who forcibly preached a doctrine of change in social matters was Swami Vivekananda and since his time the opposition to the doctrine that society requires adjustment with changing times and that morals and dogmas have also to be critically examined in each generation has ceased to command general acceptance.

A belief in progress, a forward-looking attitude, acceptance of change when change is found to be necessary, these are the most far-reaching contributions of the West to the ideals of modern India; and it is with the help of these that she is building her new society.

PART II

THE SOCIAL STRUCTURE

CHAPTER VI

THE SOCIAL STRUCTURE
The New Society

CHAPTER VI

The New Society

The invasion of the mercantile economy of Europe produced vast, though unseen, changes in the power relationship of classes in all Asian countries. In India, on which the main brunt of this new invasion fell, the effect of the new economy which was introduced at the great trading centres of Surat, Bombay, Pondicherry, Madras and Calcutta began to be felt on a national scale by the middle of the eighteenth century. Contemporary records speak of crowds of Indian merchants and businessmen from all parts of the country thronging to the Company's buildings to work as brokers and agents, as upcountry salesmen and as contractors. Gujerati Hindus, Parsis, Marwadis from distant Rajputana, Chettis from Ramnad and a miscellaneous crowd of Armenians, Baghdadi Jews and Kutchis and Khoja Memons throve under the shade of European mercantilism and grew in time to be a *compradore* class depending on the protection of the foreigner and allied with him in exploiting the people of the country.

Of the community of merchant princes, who were closely connected with the EastIndia Company, Jagat Seth who arranged for the defeat of Sirajud Dowla at Plassy and Omi Chand, through whom Clive conducted the negotiations were the most prominent representatives. These powerful groups financed the wars of the potentates struggling for mastery all over the peninsula, conducted negotiations, effectively manipulated factions at different courts and generally exercised political power behind the façade of Kings, Maharajas and Nawabs.

With the change in the character of the East India Company and its assumption of governmental responsibilities, new classes again began to struggle for mastery. The old governing classes of the Moghul Empire were essentially military and aristocratic.

These classes lost their importance and fell completely into the background. Though they continued to stay in their decayed palaces and to be received by the officials of the Company with the condescensions due to fallen dignity, these Rajas and Nawabs ceased in a generation to have any political significance. These classes had also provided the leadership in war in earlier times. The Company's armies required from India only sepoys and a few junior officers and the avenue of military distinction was also closed to them. From all but the lower grade of administrative posts, Indians of all classes were excluded after Lord Cornwallis's reforms at the end of the eighteenth century; and even for these junior posts it soon became necessary to possess a competent knowledge of English.

The nobility and the administrative classes thus became the Great Disinherited in the first quarter of the nineteenth century and gradually the vacuum was filled by the new classes which came into being to meet the needs of the new rulers. From the early days of their authority, the Company had developed an elaborate and complicated judicial system, of Sadar and Dewani Adalats and their subordinate courts to which all who lived within their jurisdiction had access. This system necessitated the growth of a body of lawyers who understood the complexities of the administrative machinery and also the subtleties of the processes of law administered by the Company.

After the Great Rebellion when the Crown took over the direct Government (1858) the High Courts of judicature modelled on the Courts in England came into existence. The great codes of civil and criminal law with their complementary system of procedure and evidence, which undoubtedly constitute the most enduring as well as the most magnificent achievement of British rule in India, gave additional opportunities for Indian talent. As other major avenues were at that time closed to them, the legal profession began to attract the most ambitious brains in the country. A *noblesse de la robe*, learned, eloquent and ambitious, anxious to take over the leadership of society soon began to make its influence felt. Among the leaders of the country who met to establish the Indian National Congress in 1885, all but a few businessmen and journalists were lawyers who had achieved undoubted eminence in the profession. Of the Presidents of the Congress during the first fifteen years ten were lawyers.

The social ideas of this class, which provided the dynamism to all movements in India at the time were, broadly speaking, moulded by their legal education. The Rule of Law was to them the basis of all society. They visualized India as a replica of England, an industrialized and commercial society with a limited democratic government. Their nationalism at that stage did not go beyond a gradual participation in the administration of the country, in the civil services and in the judiciary and the establishment of a parliamentary system, so that Indian opinion might be associated with the government. They were, generally speaking, advocates of social reform, though after a preliminary and ineffectual attempt to include it in the platform of the Congress which had to be given up mainly as a result of opposition from the Madras group, always more orthodox than others, a compromise was reached by the organization of a parallel social reform conference which was to meet at the same place and on the same dates as the Congress.

Side by side with the development of this powerful class of lawyers, may be mentioned the journalists, who came to the fore as early as the first half of the nineteenth century. Calcutta boasted of no less than 200 papers and journals, mostly in Bengali, before 1885. In the period that followed the Great Rebellion, the development of journalism was rapid. The first resolution at the meeting of the Congress in 1885 was moved by Mr G. Subramanya Iyer, the editor of the *Hindu* of Madras.

The broad middle classes which began to develop around the learned professions were strengthened by the growth of a new class of industrialists and merchants to whom the changed conditions in India had provided an unparallelled opportunity. The country was united: peace reigned over its length and breadth. A uniform and stable currency replaced the numerous coins of varying value which had hampered trade. Postal and telegraph communications were easy and railways connected the major centres of activity. An immense demand for goods was the immediate result and Indian merchants in consequence entered on an era of prosperity. The American Civil War witnessed the first great impetus to industry on modern lines and the cotton mills of Bombay and Ahmedabad were the outcome of this demand. Soon Indian merchants realized that with a foreign government in authority they could not make much headway, as at this time the authorities in Whitehall and their representati es in Calcutta made no secret of their policy of strengthening and encouraging only British industry and trade in India. The growing commercial classes, industrialists and financing houses therefore effected a merger with the educated classes, then struggling to consolidate their position under the leadership of the learned professions.

Dadabhai Naoroji, for long known as the grand old man of India, Liberal Member of the British Parliament, and twice President of the National Congress, was himself a pioneer in trade in earlier life. D. E. Wacha, also a president of the Congress and for many years its organizational chief, was connected with the textile industry, while other liberal stalwarts like Sir Cowasi Jehangir and Sir Manakji Dadabhai were leading men in the industrial life of the nation. The close association of the great captains of industry like the Tatas and the Birlas with the nationalist movement was but the logical outcome of the alliance between the struggling Indian capital and the middle classes on a nationalist platform which the early days of the Congress had initiated.

By the end of the century a great middle class with a general unity of vision, a competent leadership and a body of social ideas had come into existence. Liberalism was their creed: self-government and economic freedom their political objective, the regeneration of India, organized as a progressive, forward-looking community accepting freely from the West its sciences and its New Learning, was the great ideal they placed before themselves. The rise of the National Congress to undisputed pre-eminence showed their awareness to the moral and material possibilities opening before them, and when the British Government began to yield increasingly to their demand for participation in the higher administration it was the middle classes that stepped in. They had for 100 years manned with efficiency, skill and probity the provincial services which were becoming increasingly important. During the entire period of British authority, they had manned all but the highest ranks of India's complex and pervading revenue and police administration and the subordinate judiciary, and had provided sufficient technical personnel to share effectively in the work of such departments as engineering, forestry and irrigation. In spite of the handicap of the competitive examination for the Indian Civil Service taking place in London, a considerable number had also begun to penetrate into the superior services. When with the Minto–Morley reforms of 1908–9 Indian leaders were taken into the central and provincial Cabinets, it was the middle classes that provided the men who were able to acquit themselves well in the difficult task of co-operating with the British civil servants in the government of the country.

It was the forward-looking reforms of Lord Ripon, establishing a system of elected local self-government in India at as early a date as 1882–3, that provided the first political opening to the ambitions of the middle classes and gave them a valuable training ground in administration. It is noteworthy that Sir Phiroze Shah Mehta, the first outstanding leader of the Congress, Dr T. M. Nair and Sir Thyagaraya Chetty who were the leaders of the great social democratic movement of Madras, Sardar Vallabhbhai Patel and Pandit Jawaharlal Nehru—not to speak of lesser men—all had their first administrative experience in the municipalities of their respective areas. It would not be too much to say that this timely reform of Lord Ripon gave the first constructive bent to Indian political activity and, while providing the middle classes with a sphere in which to prove their talents, also accustomed the people to the leadership of the new classes.

The landed aristocracy and the ruling classes of the past, in spite of belated attempts by the British authorities to encourage them to come forward, were unable to share in this work. They were liberally provided with offices, titles and dignities by the Government which noted with increasing alarm the growth of the middle classes who made no pretence of any loyalty to the British rulers. But in spite of large-scale official patronage, the older aristocracy was manifestly unfit to shoulder leadership in modern India. They had not participated in the intellectual revolution that had taken place: they had not adjusted themselves to the new life with which India was throbbing.

In the cultural renaissance of India, the landed aristocracy had no share. The only notable exception to this is the Tagore family, whose varied contributions to the development of Indian culture give it a unique place in modern Indian history. But apart from the Tagores the aristocracy had been singularly barren of talent. In the biographies of representative Indians of the nineteenth century that Mr G. Parameswaran Pillai collected and published, only one name from the ruling classes finds a place. If the list was extended to the twentieth century, the only name which is likely to be included is that of Sayaji Rao Gaekwar, the Maharaja of Baroda, whose leadership in many fields—education, social reform, industrial development—entitled him to be ranked among the great men of his time in India.

The social ideas of the new middle classes represented the broad liberalism of nineteenth-century England. They were essentially the products of the New Learning which Macaulay's system of education had introduced. A generation before Macaulay won his battle against the Orientalists, Elphinstone had noted (1822): 'Many natives have begun to discover curiosity and interest about the form of their government as well as its proceedings together with a strong spirit of reform as applied to the science, religion and morals of their nation. . . . Bengalees talking about liberty, and philanthropy and declaiming against the efforts of the Tories to crush the infant liberty of the press . . . is a wonderful advance'. The basis of Macaulay's education was instruction in English language, literature and history. Macaulay himself had laid down as the object of his educational policy the doctrine of inculcating into Indian minds the science and learning of the West. He conceived his scheme as an instrument for a rapid policy of Europeanizing the thought of Indians. Keshab Chandra Sen, the great leader of Westernization in the period following the Mutiny, had declared: 'We have been conquered by the British: we live under the British. We must follow British ideas'.

To the educated Indians of the nineteenth century, the English language was a treasured possession. They prided themselves on the mastery of the language. Much as we may feel amused by this strange attachment to a foreign language, and look upon it as many European observers did as evidence of degeneracy, it should not be forgotten that the English language was the only window open to the new classes through which to see Europe and the new world and the sole medium through which they derived their political, social and economic ideas. Besides, English was at that time the language of liberty and it is no wonder that the Indian intelligentsia held fast to it and prided in their mastery of the language. The language of revolt had always a place of high honour in English literature and the love of liberty was undoubtedly implanted into Indian minds by the study of English literature.

As for English history, it appeared to Indians, as it doubtless did to many contemporary thinking minds everywhere, the broadening of freedom from precedent to precedent. It was interpreted as enshrining the principle of the inevitability of popular rule, and the natural decline of autocratic authority in the modern age. The contrast between an England governed by a parliament based on popular sovereignty and an India governed under the authority of the same parliament, by an alien bureaucracy which denied the right of the people and restricted their liberties, was glaring. To the middle classes of India in the nineteenth century such action was 'Un-British' and their appeal was always to the libertarian traditions of England, against the autocracy of its agents in India.

If their political attitude was governed by what they considered to be the genuine traditions of England, their ideas of government were based on the liberal traditions of Mill. Mill's tracts on Liberty and on Representative Government were their political scriptures and the liberalism of the Victorian age, even after its vogue had diminished in England, continued unshaken in its hold on the Indian middle-class mind, and may even now be considered one of the major strands in Indian political thought.

The main reason for this acceptance of the values of liberalism, though they are now under heavy attack, is the fact that India escaped the direct consequences of the two great wars which submerged liberalism in Europe and ushered in the era of economic democracy. Also, the attention of Indian leadership was concentrated on the achievement of freedom, and the Congress movement, as a result, was not moved as much by political doctrines as by a desire to attain the single object of eliminating British authority. The National Congress was an army fighting by peaceful means for the liberation of India, and it put forward no serious political programme for a long time beyond the attainment of independence. Mr Gandhi's emphasis as stated before was on the purity of means. The instrument which he fashioned was mass action, and to that extent it was against the accepted liberal tradition of India. But the main doctrines of liberalism—freedom of the individual, belief in legislation as a process of betterment, moral suasion as the basis of political action, separation of religious matters from the range of the State—these continued to be deeply rooted in the Indian mind.

The middle class in India, though it performed a historic function with ability and wisdom, had numerous weaknesses which rendered its action ineffective in many spheres of national life. In the first place it had a distrust of the masses and of the common man. The democracy it visualized was a government by the educated upper classes, the new aristocracy of intellect and wealth. As Sir Ramesh Chandra Mitra stated in his welcome address to the Congress in 1896: 'The educated Community represented the brain and conscience of the country and were the legitimate spokesmen of the illiterate masses, the natural custodian of their interests. To hold otherwise would be to presuppose that a foreign administration in the service knows more about the wants of the masses than their educated countrymen. It is true in all ages that those who think must govern those who toil: and could it be that the natural order of things was reversed in this country?'

Burke, the champion of aristocratic liberalism, was their sage, and they could neither visualize nor adjust themselves to the doctrine of mass action which the Mahatma advocated and the poor man's paradise which he wished to see established in India. The ryots, or peasants in the field, and workers in the town meant nothing to them; untouchability was a blot on Hinduism and they were anxious to see it removed, but the idea of political rights for the depressed classes or their economic regeneration did not appeal to them. The urgency that Mr Gandhi gave to this problem seemed to them sheer madness, while his idea of making the villages the bases of national revival seemed to them altogether impracticable. In fact their ideas being derivative, and reflecting the thought of the comfortable age of Victorian England, when political thinkers outside the small group of revolutionaries were assailed by no kind of doubt, they were unable to understand the special problems of India on which neither lead nor light was available in the scriptures of their school.

An even more fundamental weakness of the new society was its isolation from the rest of the community. They were in a sense strangers in their own land. Many of them were so intoxicated with the new wine of the West that they were ashamed of their own past and in most cases were ignorant of things Indian. While they discoursed fluently about literary movements of Europe and took considerable pains to understand the intellectual trends in Europe, the general outlook of the class was one of indifference to things

Indian and a contempt for India's past. This attitude cut them off from the masses, with whom in any case they had no bond of spiritual or intellectual sympathy. Besides, the new middle class was essentially urban and the problems of the rural masses did not interest it seriously. The New Society lived in a world of its own, identified India with itself and became immersed in intellectual and political problems unconnected with the interests of the vast masses whom they claimed to represent.

To the lawyers who provided leadership for this new society, the masses meant the mob, an illegal body in the view of those trained in legal processes. On this question their attitude was not essentially different from that of the British bureaucracy, who loved the dumb masses as they provided the 'raw material' for the administrative work on which they prided themselves. An examination of the resolutions passed year after year at the sessions of the National Congress from its first meeting in 1885 to the emergence of the Mahatma in 1920 would show how little the masses of India came into the consideration of the new classes. Their main concern in the first years was for simultaneous competitive examinations in India and in England for the civil services, so that a greater proportion of the superior services might be obtained by the educated classes in India. Other problems which seemed to them to require urgent reform, were the separation of executive and judicial functions, which in effect meant the exclusion of the civil services from judicial posts and the reservation of judgeships in the High Courts to those recruited from the bar or from subordinate judicial services; and the introduction of a larger elected element in the provincial and central legislatures, again openings for the middle classes.

A third weakness also indicated the limitation of the new classes as a whole. Their economic conceptions were of the vaguest kind, and were coloured by the doctrine of a permanent drain of India's resources for the benefit of England. There is no doubt that the economic policy of the British administration in India never seriously lost sight of the permanent interests of British industry and commerce. It is equally true that British shipping, industry and commerce had a stranglehold on the economic life of India in the period between 1870 and 1914. Indian industrialism was only in its initial stages and was confined to the textile factories of Bombay and Ahmedabad. But the new middle classes had no conception of major economic policies, and the merchants and industrialists who were associated with the Congress had not gained sufficient experience to venture forth into new regions. Thus while liberal India sighed vaguely for industrialization and continuously appealed to the Government for facilities for technical education, they had not yet begun to visualize a planned economy for India, or an exploitation of India's national wealth for the benefit of her own people.

It is also a factor which should be remembered in our evaluation of this class that the political henchmen of the British also came from among them. From the earliest days of the British and French companies there were the Nandkumars and Anandaranga Pillais who were prepared to put their political talents at the service of the new Rulers. The middle classes followed this tradition, and the long list of honours awarded to public men twice a year was the clearest evidence of the moral weakness of the New Society in its relations with the British Government. It should not however be considered that all who thus co-operated with the Government were quislings. Not a few among them, for instance Satyendra Sinha (the first Lord Sinha of Raipur), Sir Sankaran Nair and Sir Tej Bahadur Sapru, combined distinguished service to the British Crown in India with steadfast loyalty to the national cause, but as a whole it can be said that the politics of the middle classes before Mr Gandhi's appearance on the Indian political stage were governed by appointments and disappointments.

This weakness of ambitious leadership, which in the circumstances suffered deeply from a feeling of frustration, was recognized by men like G. K. Gokhale and Pheroze Shah Mehta. It was the realization of this fact which led Gokhale to found the famous Servants of India Society, a body of dedicated workers who undertook not to seek or accept Government appointments and agreed further to devote their lives to the service of the country on nominal emoluments. Thus the discipline of *Ashram* life in politics which was to count for so much under the leadership of Gandhi was first introduced by Gokhale. There was however one essential difference. Gokhale visualized politics as a vocation for experts, and it was one of the conditions of membership in the Servants of India Society that an entrant should devote himself to five years of intensive study of Indian problems with special reference to some aspect of his own choice.

The strength and weakness of the middle classes in their liberal period will be more clearly understood if we study the character and achievements of some of their representative personalities in the period between 1870 and 1920. We may take as representatives of this age, which produced a large number of remarkable men, Keshab Chandra Sen, the social reformer and religious leader, and Surendranath Bannerji, one of the leaders of the earlier Congress, both from Bengal, Pheroze Shah Mehta and G. K. Gokhale from Bombay.

Keshab Chandra Sen[1] was born of a non-Brahmin family and was attracted early in life (1857) to the reformist teachings of the Brahmo Samaj, which then at the height of its prestige was seriously attempting to organize educated Bengali society on a Western model. He came into great prominence as the champion of Westernization and the leader of the group which fought with zeal and vigour against the Hinduizing tendencies which began to assert themselves, and which found a leader in Maharshi, Tagore, the father of the poet Rabindranath Tagore. The Maharshi or the 'great sage', who had joined the movement in 1843, was the real organizer of the Brahmo Samaj, for the new church had been left in a loose and disorganized condition by Ram Mohan Roy. But the Maharshi in spite of his reforming tendencies remained a staunch Vedantist, attached to the higher doctrines of Hinduism. At this stage the section of the Brahmo Samaj of which Keshab was the head almost broke away from Hinduism and showed tendencies of approximation with Unitarian Christians on whose pulpit Keshab appeared on a number of occasions. But later in life the reformer seems to have mellowed, especially after he came under the influence of Sri Ramakrishna, and while remaining an advocate of social reforms to the very end, became more reconciled to Hindu ways of thought.

Keshab Chandra Sen was a man of flaming zeal and his motto may be summed up in the words of Voltaire, 'Écrasez l'infâme'. To him the Hindu social institutions, especially caste, enforced widowhood, worship of cows, etc., represented the infamous. English middle-class society, with its self-assured calm, its faith in a simple religion, its distrust of theology and speculation, seemed to him the ideal that modern India should set before

[1] See G. Parameswaram Pillai's *Representative Indians*, Chapter on Keshab, and Max Muller's *Biographical Studies*.

itself. His influence in Bengal was very considerable, though even among the Brahmos there was a growing desire for adjustment with progressive Hinduism, which led to a serious split in the new church.

Even after Keshab came under the influence of the saintly Ramakrishna and gradually drew closer to Hindu religious thought, his work for the reformation of Hindu society continued. Keshab Chandra Sen may in this way be said to represent the spiritual conflict of the age, to which most thinking Hindus of the new educated middle class were subject. The significant point in his strange history, which was but a more intensified version of the mental processes of most Hindus of his generation, was his final reconciliation with the Hindu religion.

Surendranath Bannerji[1] was of a different type. Born of a *kulin* Brahmin family of moderate means, he was one of the first Indians to enter the civil service by open competition in England. For a minor irregularity he was dismissed from the service and found his vocation in education, politics and journalism. He established the Ripon College of which he was the principal for many years. He also founded as a vehicle of political propaganda a daily newspaper in English—the *Bengali*—and edited it till he took up office.

But it was neither as an educationalist nor as a journalist that Surendranath was destined to become famous. Politics was his *metiér* and in 1867 he founded the Indian Association of Calcutta. It was meant to be the centre of an all-India movement, for Bannerji had even at that early period seen the vision of a United India. That was the era of nationalism in Europe, of Mazzini, Garibaldi and Kossuth—and Surendranath had been greatly influenced by the fervent genius of the Italian prophet. A born orator—known popularly as the 'Indian Demosthenes'—Surendranath was for thirty-five years the trumpet voice of Indian nationalism.

He was associated with the Congress movement from the beginning and was twice its president. He came into all-India fame and leadership when, following the ill-fated partition of Bengal by Lord Curzon, he organized the first movement for direct action in Indian politics and advocated a boycott of British

[1]See *Making of a Nation* by Surendranath Bannerji, OUP.

goods as a political weapon, and the encouragement of *Swadeshi* or Indian manufactured goods as its counterpart.

But in spite of his deviation into mass agitation he remained a 'moderate', a liberal, whose admiration for England was unshakeable and whose paragon in politics was Gladstone. When the Montagu–Chelmsford reform of partial self-government was introduced in 1921 he accepted office as a Minister, and the tribune of the people died as a knight and an honoured servant of the Crown.

Surendranath Bannerji was a great patriot and his amazing oratorical gifts and tireless energy in propagating the message of liberty helped greatly to create a sense of nationalism in the new classes. And yet the vision of India he had was an extremely limited one. He mirrored the ideas of the English educated men of his time, and in his thought and speech identified the country with them. Neither the worker in the city nor the peasant in the field entered into his calculations. The economic regeneration of India was no part of his programme and his published autobiography entitled *The Making of a Nation* is a testament of the liberal tradition in India, fervently nationalist but curiously blind to the forces immediately outside the narrow circle of Western-educated classes.

Sir Pheroze Shah Mehta[1] was a leader of another kind. A Parsi barrister of Bombay who had risen to the top of his profession, he was neither an orator nor a propagandist. Nor was he moved by the moral fervour of many of his contemporaries to rid India of the social and religious abuses that weakened her. But he was the strong man of his time, a man of cold, penetrating intellect and iron will, who bent others to his way of thinking and knit the otherwise disorganized moderate opinion into a single group. Early in life he established an ascendancy over the municipal government of Bombay, which he maintained to the end of his life.

Unlike most of his contemporaries, he was indifferent to the honours of office, and his great administrative talents found ample opportunities in running the Municipal Corporation of India's premier city. It was characteristic of him that he hated all ideas of mass agitation. The movement in Maharastra led by Bal Gangadhar Tilak, which through cautious steps and devious

[1] Mody, H. P., *Pheroze Shah Mehta, a biography*, Times of India Press.

paths was activating the Maratha peasantry and the workers of Bombay, found in Pheroze Shah the most determined opponent. Tilak's tactics were original. He revived the cult of Ganpati—the popular elephant-faced Remover of Obstacles—and gave it a political basis. He popularized among the Marathas the epic story of Shivaji who two and a half centuries ago had organized the national recovery of the Hindus and helped to destroy the overwhelming might of the Moghuls. He provided a philosophical and religious basis for a movement of political terrorism. All this was directly opposed to the creed of Pheroze Shah Mehta, whose staunch liberalism detected in Tilak's movements—then comprehensively known as Extremism—a grave danger to India's steady progress towards self-government. The period between 1906–15 may well be considered the fight between these two personalities, and when the rival ideologies joined issue at the Congress of Surat (1908) it was Pheroze Shah who was left the master of the field.

Gopal Krishna Gokhale[1] who was closely associated with Pheroze Shah Mehta represented all that was best in the liberal tradition. A Maharastra Brahmin, of the class that had governed the great Maratha Empire for a century preceding the establishment of British authority in India, Gokhale started his life as a teacher of mathematics. He had become a member of the Deccan Education Society founded by Mahadev Govind Ranade, the object of which was to establish national institutions for training young men for the service of the country. The members of the society had to undertake to serve it for a period of twenty years on a nominal salary of Rs. 75 a month. The compelling call of politics soon brought him into the Congress arena, where his earnestness and selfless devotion to the cause of the country made him one of the most respected figures. Elected to the Imperial Legislative Council, as the Central Legislature was then called, Gokhale though still in his thirties was recognized even by that champion of Imperialism, Lord Curzon, to be the outstanding spokesman of the Indian point of view. It was not by oratory or by appeal to liberal sentiment or by unreasonable criticism that Gokhale established his dominating position in that hostile atmosphere. It was by his mastery of facts and figures, by his understanding of the problems of government and by sweet

[1] The Rt. Honourable V. S. Srinivasa Sastri, CH, *Gopal Krishna Gokhale, a biography*, Servants of India Society, Poona.

reasonableness in persuasive argument. He was, in fact, modern India's first statesman.

Gokhale recognized that modern politics was not all agitation, and that training and intellectual equipment and selfless devotion to the cause of the people were essential if the Indian national movement was to start on a career of constructive activity. The Servants of India Society which he established in Poona (1905) with the object of training a band of political workers was a new departure in India. Its contribution during the fifty years of its existence has been astonishingly varied. In the work of organizing labour on an all-India basis it played a very notable part through N. M. Joshi, the father of Indian Trade Unionism, and at one time a senior member of the Servants of India Society. The cause of Indians abroad it made particularly its own, and Gokhale himself, and his successor Srinivasa Sastri, are now best remembered for the work they did in the interests of their countrymen in Africa. International politics has been the special field of Hridayanath Kunzru who was also the founder of the Seva Samiti of Allahabad, an association devoted to social service. The Society had always at its disposal a body of earnest workers to send to any area where famine or flood relief had to be organized. In the sphere of reclamation work among tribal classes also it achieved remarkable success.

In two very difficult fields Gokhale gave proof of his constructive statesmanship. He was the chief representative of Indian opinion who worked in close consultation with the British Government during the formative stages of the Minto–Morley reforms (1907–8) which for the first time admitted Indians to a share in the government of India and liberalized the representative institutions. He was also responsible for the negotiations with General Smuts and the South African Government which brought to a close the first stage of a struggle of Indians in that country for human rights.

The brief analysis of these leading figures of their time who were outstanding representatives of their class should help to understand both the strength and weakness of the new society. They were fervently patriotic, anxious to see India advance politically and socially and they worked steadily for that purpose. They were moved by great ideals and held firmly to the doctrines of liberalism. But they were aliens in India, strangers to their own people, and their ideas and beliefs were not shared by any but a small class of educated people. Thus, when the great flood of the Mahatma's non-co-operation movement overwhelmed them in 1919–21 they became impotent and helpless, unable to struggle against it but unwilling to be carried forward by its force.

The most vigorous reaction to the Gandhi movement came from Sir Sankaran Nair, lawyer, judge, one-time President of the Congress, member of the Central Cabinet, a sturdy patriot who had resigned his post on the issue of the measure of self-government after the first Great War. In a vigorous book entitled *Gandhi and Anarchy* he attacked the whole conception of Gandhi's non-co-operation and prophesied disaster. It was an attempt to measure revolution by the yardstick of liberal legalism—a vain protest of the middle classes against what they looked upon as the demoniac power of the masses.

The rise of the new middle classes to pre-eminence in Indian life naturally witnessed the breakdown of the theory of caste. The strength of the caste system in the past had been in its defensive power.

Ketkar has pointed out in his *History of Caste*[1] that the overthrow of the Hindu Princes and the dispersal of Hindu political power by the Muslims had led to a great increase in the prestige of the Brahmins, and with it, naturally, a great strengthening of the doctrine of caste. Hindu society was saved from dissolution during the period of Muslim invasions mainly through the strengthening of the caste controls. But with the British Government which professed neutrality in matters of religion and theoretically at least placed all religions on an equal footing, the defensive functions of caste ceased to be important. More, the theory itself came under devastating criticism by the new middle classes who had become inheritors of the doctrines of the French Revolution.

The processes by which the hold of caste on Hinduism was gradually loosened need not be discussed at length here. It is sufficient to mention that every Hindu religious leader in the nineteenth century who contributed to the modernization of Hinduism was an ardent advocate of the abolition of caste, Vivekananda no less than Ram Mohan Roy, Dayananda Saraswati no less than Gandhiji. Socially, the material setting of life in the nineteenth century in India helped more to undermine the caste

[1] Ketkar, *History of Caste* (Kegan Paul).

system than even the teaching of reformers. The industrialization of important areas, the growth of a large urban population, common public institutions like schools, hospitals and transportation rendered the rigid practice of caste regulations impossible for large sections of people. Again, the legislative activity of the State undermined many of the basic doctrines of caste. Civil marriage between different castes, prohibited by the lawgivers of Hinduism, control of Hindu religious endowments, the equality of all—the Brahmin and the Pariah alike—before the law, all these transformed caste from an effective social system into an interesting sociological survival.[1]

The most significant evidence of this change is the composition of the new classes. The new middle classes cut through all the castes from the highest Brahmin to the lowest Pariah. The intellectual leaders of the new classes were recruited from all sections without reference to the prestige of their hereditary castes. No doubt a good percentage still came from the Brahmin castes, but the more influential leaders were either non-Brahmins, or members of the Brahmin community who foreswore caste and accepted the creed of equality.

Keshab Chandra Sen, the prophet of the Brahmo Samaj, Vivekananda, the champion of new Hinduism, Aurobindo, the philosopher of new India, were all members of non-Brahmin castes, while Ram Mohan Roy, Ramakrishna and the Tagores were Brahmins who denounced the conception of caste. Even in the orthodox south, Dr T. M. Nair, the leader of the social democratic movement, Sankaran Nair and Thyagaraya Chetty rose to political eminence as doughty fighters against caste.

In the non-co-operation movement, the leadership belonged exclusively to those who had renounced their caste affiliations. Gandhiji himself was a Vaisya, while Brahmin leaders produced by the movement, such as Jawaharlal Nehru and Rajagopalachari, had in their own personal lives renounced the privileges of caste and allied themselves by marriage with others. The intellectual classes were the new Brahmins of India, an aristocracy of learning, sacrifice and service. Dr Ambedkar, the leader of the erstwhile untouchable classes, may be considered the most representative non-Brahmin of the age. A lawyer, economist and social thinker,

[1] Panikkar, *Hinduism at Cross Roads*, Asia Publishing House, Third edition, 1960.

his political activity was chiefly directed towards an awakening of the depressed classes, but his main achievement was the piloting of the new Indian Constitution which included as a 'fundamental right' a clause providing for the abolition of untouchability. The father of the Indian Constitution, it was also his privilege to introduce into the legislature the Hindu Code, a modernized consolidation of the law and custom of the Hindus.

If the new Brahmins were not selected on a hereditary basis and came from all classes, the same is true, even to a larger extent, of the new Kshatriyas, or the warrior classes—the *bahujas*, those born of the arm of God. The Indian Army was one of the major unifying forces under the British Government. Though recruited exclusively from what were known as the 'martial classes', it bore no relationship to the hereditary Kshatriya caste which had in fact vanished as an effective force long before from the Indian social scene. There were men from all castes in the Indian Army, from the Brahmins to the untouchables. Recruited mainly from rural areas, this new Kshatriya class was socially levelled upwards and formed the nucleus of a vigorous village life in the areas from which it was recruited. It was unfortunate that the British Government for political reasons confined recruitment to certain limited areas and castes, restricting this process of democratic devlopment to classes favoured by them.

The new Indian Government's policy in this matter has been of great national significance. It has thrown open the army to all classes and organized a territorial force and a cadet corps on an all-India basis. The isolation of the army from the general public which was an essential part of British military security, for fear that the army might be contaminated by nationalist sentiment, is now a thing of the past. The national character of the armed forces and their recruitment from all classes, without reference to regions, caste or class, creates a new Kshatriya tradition in India. The cultivation of uniform traits and virtues by a large body of people recruited from all over India and trained to a better way of life than is prevalent in the villages, and disciplined to think and act together, cannot but be a major factor in the social evolution of the country. The experience of social changes which service in the army introduced in the Punjab villages, which formed the main recruiting area of the old army, is being repeated on a national scale. Its social potentialities especially in the development of a vigorous, educated, and modern life in the villages are indeed unmeasurable.

Nor is it to be considered that the new classes engaged in trade, commerce and industry are drawn exclusively from the traditional caste of Vaisyas. It may be surprising to see how much of the old caste is still engaged in these professions, but the new Vaisyas—even in Hinduism—are drawn from all classes. The first Hindu millowner of Ahmedabad, Sir Chinnubhai Madhavlal Ranchordia, Baronet, was a Brahmin, and all castes have gone into industrial life and business without the prejudices of their ancient occupations.

But the real new caste of the future is the Technologist. Technology is the priestcraft of the new religion—the industrial way of life—and the technologists, from the skilled worker to the scientist, inventor and planning engineer, form a graded priesthood on whose ministrations the community depends for its life. It is the emergence of this class to social importance and power that constitutes the governing fact in the modern world, whether it be in Capitalist America or in Communist Russia.

In the Gandhian view of society, based predominantly on reconstructed and practically self-sufficient village units, the technologist did not count for much. The Mahatma's distrust of man's dependence on machinery, especially in the rural society that he visualized, precluded any emphasis on technological skill. But the years of independence have completely changed this position. With large-scale plans for the construction of numerous high-power dams, with a programme of rapid industrialization in all spheres, including such highly specialized schemes as ship-building and aircraft production, committed to a programme of mechanization of agriculture and a comprehensive development of highways, harbours and internal navigation, new India has had to enter the technological age at one bound. The establishment of great institutes of technology and the numerous institutions for industrial and scientific research marked this basic change of attitude. The British Government had itself done something in this direction. The Roorkee College of Engineering now over 100 years old was the first recognition of the importance of technology in the modern age. Other institutions followed at intervals, but the object which the Government had was limited to the provision of personnel for its own technical departments. On the transference of power India was woefully short of trained personnel to take in hand the great schemes of industrial and agricultural reconstruction which her leaders had planned and consequently they were forced to send an army of young men abroad, mainly to America and England, for such training.

All these factors contributed to a breakdown of the ancient system of caste, in both its religious and functional aspects. Though India has not yet achieved her ideal of a casteless society, the hold of caste is no longer there as a prime factor either in social organization or in political grouping. The emergence of labour as a political force and the position in national life achieved by the movement of the untouchables no less than the doctrine of social equality enshrined in the new constitution, are effective safeguards against any attempts to reinstate the doctrine of caste.

CHAPTER VII

The Awakening of the Masses

From 1920 to 1948 the Indian stage was dominated by the frail figure of Mahatma Gandhi.[1] Returning in 1915 from South Africa, where he had perfected his technique of direct action through the masses, he spent a period of five years familiarizing himself with conditions in India, tirelessly moving about from province to province and village to village and identifying himself everywhere with the peasant, the field labourer and the untouchable. In the period of discontent and political frustration that followed the first Great War, Gandhiji who had by this time come to be accepted as a Mahatma—or a great soul—announced his new programme for the immediate attainment of self-government of India. It was a curious jumble of many items, but its import was clear. It was a call to young India to cast aside all that it had so far cherished as essential for progress. Lawyers were to give up their practice, students to turn their backs on colleges and institutions maintained or supported by government, the public to withdraw their co-operation from government and generally to organize themselves in villages and towns to live a life independent of British administration. Pressure on government was to be exercised by a programme of civil disobedience, by the boycott of foreign cloth and refusal to pay taxes when the masses were organized and ready for it.

To this comprehensive policy was added a scheme known as 'constructive work', the object of which was to rehabilitate the

[1] The literature of the Gandhian movement is immense and no short bibliography will be of any use. But the following books may be consulted. *A Biography of Mahatma Gandhi* by Tendulkar, published by the Government of India, eight volumes; Nehru's *Autobiography:* Rajendra Prasad, *A History of the non-cooperation movement.*

villages. The main items of this programme were communal unity, removal of untouchability, prohibition of alcoholic drinks, the popularization of *khadi* or handspun cloth, village sanitation, new education, the rejection of *purdah* or the seclusion of women and the organization of peasant labour.

The older leadership, wedded to the doctrine of liberalism, saw in this movement a danger to everything it held sacred. Gandhiji was going back on Westernization: he was preaching civil disobedience of laws. He did not want young men to be educated in English. Clearly, in the view of the moderates, it was the type of reactionary leadership which was likely to undo the work of a century. But the country thought otherwise. From one end of India to the other, the common people were fired by an enthusiasm which the colourless creed of gradualism had failed to evoke. The masses had become revolutionary, for Gandhiji, not satisfied with providing a programme, went from village to village all over India rousing the masses to action.

The attraction of Gandhiji's movement lay in the fact that essentially it was an appeal directed not to the psychology of the new urban classes but to that of the peasant population in India's 700,000 villages. To the masses in the villages English education of the new schools and colleges meant little or nothing and the legal theories of the liberals seemed totally unreal. Gandhiji devised his programme in such a way as to combine into one single scheme the hope and ambitions of the villager, to give him a new zest for living, providing at the same time for such essential reforms as would purge village society of its evils. He added to the demand for independence the vision of a peasant who translates that independence into something in terms of his own immediate surroundings.

Gandhiji took up his residence in a village. At the Sabarmati ashram, and later at Sevagram, he attempted to reproduce his ideal, the self-sufficient village where the peasants were educated through social service and lived a community life, from which untouchability, intoxicating drinks and foreign cloth were banished. It is interesting to note that both the Mahatma and the poet Tagore had by different routes reached the same conclusion—that the future of India lay in her villages. The Sriniketan or the Institute of Rural Reconstruction was Tagore's contribution to this doctrine. Gandhiji's was on a national scale.

All his political doctrine was coloured by his vision of India as an integration of rehabilitated villages. This is what he himself has stated: 'The constructive programme is the truthful and non-violent way of winning Purna Swaraj (independence). Its wholesale fulfilment *is* complete independence. Imagine all the forty crores of people busying themselves with the whole of the constructive programme which is designed to build up the nation from the very bottom upward. Can anybody dispute the proposition that it must mean complete independence in every sense of the expression, including the ousting of foreign domination?'[1]

It is easy to see why the urban middle classes scoffed at this humdrum programme, which had none of the appeal of a revolutionary political movement. Yet the masses of India recognized the message. Gandhiji was willing and quite happy to neglect the politically minded classes for, as he expressed it, there existed 'a deep chasm' between them and the masses. The politically minded classes, by and large, rejected the new message. The Congress that accepted Gandhiji's leadership was not the same institution that a succession of very distinguished men, from W. C. Bonerji who presided at its first meeting to Lajpat Rai who presided over the special session which accepted the Gandhian doctrine, had with patient care built up and cherished for thirty-five years. To them, trained to think in terms of parliamentary procedure and to measure progress by discussion and moral persuasion, both the method of direct action which Gandhiji advocated and the reconstruction of rural life which he conceived as the basis of India's independence were dangerously reactionary. To them *khadi* meant no more than coarse cloth, and their economics revolted against Gandhiji's ideal of going back to handspinning when obviously the future lay in industrialization. To them Gandhiji's reply was simple. '*Khadi* must be taken with all its implications. It means a wholesale *Swadeshi* (of one's own country) mentality, a determination to find all the necessaries of life in India and *that through the labour and intellect* of the villagers. This means a reversal of the existing process. That is to say, that instead of half-a-dozen cities of India and Great Britain living on the exploitation and the ruin of 700,000 villages of India, the latter will be self-contained. . . . This needs a revolutionary change in the mentality and tastes of many. . . . It vitally touches the life of

[1] Forward to Constructive Programme, Navajivan Press, Ahmesubad, 1945.

every single Indian, makes him feel aglow with the possession of a power that has lain hidden within himself, and makes him proud of his identity with every drop of the ocean of Indian humanity, of its economic freedom and equality and therefore ultimately, in the poetic expression of Jawaharlal Nehru, 'the livery of India's freedom'.[1]

It is this identification with the humblest which made Gandhiji take up his residence in villages, to dress in a loincloth like the lowest labourer, and to live in untouchable colonies and houses during his visits to towns. It was his principle that all the Congress workers should so far as possible be so identified. Except during periods of active political struggle, the Congress workers were expected to live in rural areas and carry on the constructive programme. And in fact, whatever their limitations, the army of *khadi*-clad workers who devoted their lives to the betterment of Indian villages, carried on their labour of love among untouchables and fallen women, introduced into the villages new ideas of sanitation, fought social prejudices and transformed the outlook of the masses in India to a greater extent during a period of twenty-five years than anything else during India's long history.

Naturally the Gandhian movement helped to alter fundamentally the traditional class-relationships in India. The leadership of the non-co-operation was undoubtedly in the hands of urban classes. The many thousands of young men and women who marched in and out of jail and underwent unheard-of privations during a period of twenty-five years came mostly from the urban areas. It is they who sacrificed their all, gave up their studies in colleges and schools, broke the hearts of their parents and followed the hard path that the Mahatma laid down.

But there was a basic difference between them and the classes that provided the leadership in the earlier periods. The political classes of the past represented a prosperous middle class, men who had made their mark and were accepted in their own circles as leaders of society. The followers of the Gandhian movement were in the main young men and women who saw the vision of a free India and were moved by a spirit of service, for what Gandhiji asked them to do was to go into the villages and not merely preach the gospel of the new life, but *prove* it *by* their life work.

[1] See *Selections from Gandhi*, Navajiram Publishing House, 1947. This is an excellent selection of the Mahatma's opinions on different topics.

Those of the elder generation who followed him, prosperous lawyers like Motilal Nehru, C. R. Das and Rajagopalachari, had to sacrifice their all and adopt the strange new life which the Mahatma imposed on all his followers as the symbol not only of their sacrifice but of their identification with the peasants of the countryside. 'The first thing', he insisted, 'is to cultivate the mental attitude that we will not have possessions or facilities denied to millions, and the next immediate thing is to rearrange our lives as fast as possible in accordance with that mentality.' The charge that Gandhiji laid on workers whom he sent to the villages may be stated in his own words as follows:

'Our contact with them begins through their service, through the spinning wheel, but it does not end there. The spinning wheel is the centre of that service. You will find the people cheerless and fear-stricken. You will find houses in ruins. You will look in vain for any sanitary or hygienic conditions. You will find the cattle in a miserable way and yet you will see idleness stalking there. The people will tell you of the spinning wheel having been in their homes long ago, but today they will entertain no talk of it or of any other cottage industry. They can have no scope left in them. They live, for they cannot die at will. They will spin only if you spin. Even if 100 out of a population of 300 in a village spin, you assure them of an additional income. . . . "I am alone, how can I reach 700,000 villages." This is the argument that pride whispers to us.'[1]

With an army of young men and women indoctrinated in these ideals, and distributed from one end of the country to the other, and with a programme which even the illiterate peasant had no difficulty to grasp and understand, and which directly appealed to his interests and with the hope of a new age which the Mahatma was able to arouse in all, the entire atmosphere of India was changed and became charged with revolutionary tension. Gandhiji's own crusading zeal against social injustice, against the misery of the widows and the disabilities of the untouchables, his intense faith in God and the belief in moral values, and the halo which his saintly and pure life cast on all his doings, helped by an almost superhuman energy which never tired of explaining in the minutest detail every question put to him, enabled him to convey to the vast masses a new sense of dignity, independence and self-

[1] *Young India*, issue of June 2, 1927.

reliance, which stood firm against all disappointments and resisted silently, but with determination, the terror, the blandishments and the bribes of the British Government for over a quarter of a century.

It is the masses that stood by the Mahatma in his successive struggles, each one of which was followed by a wave of repression more deadly than that which preceded it.

The awakening of the masses and the shift of political emphasis from the towns to the rural areas are matters of permanent importance in the social structure of new India. The crucial problem now was to bridge the gap between the villages and the towns which an alien system of education and a mercantile economy inherited from the East India Company had forced on India. Gandhiji himself realized this and the new educational scheme which he devised and which now forms the basis of India's educational policy is an attempt to solve this question and create a basic harmony between the educated classes and the villagers. The scheme of Basic Education is outside the scope of our discussion here. It is sufficient to emphasize that, as Mr Gandhi has stated in his introduction to the Report of the Committee which drafted the detailed syllabus, 'it was a scheme of rural national education through village handicrafts'. Its object was 'to educate village children in the villages so as to draw out all their faculties through some selected village handicrafts in an atmosphere free from superimposed restrictions and interference'.[1]

In 1943 when Gandhiji came out of his last incarceration he enlarged the scope of his original idea. In his own words: 'I have been thinking hard during the detention over the possibilities of Nai Talim (new education); we must not rest content with our present achievements. We must penetrate the homes of the children. We must educate their parents. Basic education must become literally education for life'.[2]

Gandhiji had a clear vision of the social purpose behind his scheme of education. 'My plan,' he said, 'to impart primary education through the village handicrafts like spinning and carding, is thus conceived as the spearhead of a silent social revolution fraught with the most far-reaching consequences. It will provide a healthy and moral basis for relationship between the city and

[1] Introduction to the Report of the Committee on Draft Syllabus.

[2] Ibid.

the village, and thus go a long way towards eradicating some of the worst evils of the present social insecurity and poisoned relationship between the classes. It will check the progressive decay of our villages and lay the foundation of a juster social order, in which there is no unnatural division between the "haves" and "have-nots" and everybody is assured of a living wage and the right to freedom.'[1]

The most far-reaching result of the Gandhian awakening of the masses has been the enlargement of the conception of democracy. The limited social classes that the earlier nationalist movement represented thought of democracy as a government by the *élite*. It was based on the doctrine, as Ramesh Chandra Mitra had explained, of the educated classes being the trustees of the masses, of 'those who think governing those who toil'. The non-co-operation movement, by basing itself on the activity of the masses and by concentrating itself on work in the rural areas, made the new nationalism an upsurge of the people and thus enlarged the conception of democracy. Gandhiji's view of politics was from the angle of the poor and exploited peasant, dependent on an uncertain monsoon, sunk in ignorance and perpetually in the clutches of the moneylender.

Though his own solution was therefore essentially a rural democracy which turned its back on large-scale industrialization, which New India under the compulsion of circumstances was forced to abandon, she has held firmly to the basic conception of a democracy in which political power is shared by all and is not confined to the modernized upper strata. The Constitution of independent India not only provides for adult suffrage with complete equality for men and women—constituting thereby by far the largest electorate in the world—but also ensures adequate representation for the depressed classes. 'The real swaraj is the swaraj of the masses', Gandhiji had proclaimed. But it took a quarter of a century of struggle to transform the traditionally dumb masses of India into a vitally revolutionary force.

Thus it will be seen that the liberal political creed of Indian Nationalism was the work of the new middle classes whose rise

[1] Introduction to the Report of the Committee on Draft Syllabus.

was the most significant phenomenon in Indian social life before the Gandhian movement. This middle class created the National Congress, gave expression to the political ambitions of the educated sections of the community, developed a press and public opinion in India and provided leadership for the social reform movement which grew up side by side with nationalism. Their gradual eclipse during the Gandhian movement was not immediately noticed as the most prominent leaders of the non-co-operation movement, C. R. Das, Motilal Nehru, Abul Kalam Azad, Rajendra Prasad, Vallabhai Patel and others, came from these classes. But below the surface a great change was taking place. The younger leaders were not lawyers or generally men trained to liberal professions. Political activity had to spread to other classes than those from which the Congress in its earlier days recruited its members. So long as the power remained with the British this change in the class structure of the national movement did not become obvious. But with independence the situation began to change. Though national leadership continued to be in the hands of the great personalities surviving from the great struggle, Jawaharlal Nehru, Rajendra Prasad, Maulana Azad, B. C. Roy, and others, the composition of the legislatures began to show a marked change. Two tendencies were visible. The first was a shift of membership from urban to rural classes. In the past, even for rural and district constituencies, the preference was for candidates from the cities. With adult franchise and the awakening of the masses, rural interests began to assert themselves. Today in all the state legislatures there is a sizeable bloc of representatives from rural areas. The second noticeable shift relates to the social classes. The old middle classes represented by university men, lawyers and other professional groups have begun to yield leadership in the states to classes which had so long been denied power. The Chief Minister of one of the provinces in the period before the general election of 1962 belonged to a scheduled caste (formerly untouchable), while the leadership in another has been in the hands of communities which though not untouchable have been considered as belonging to the lower classes. The rise of groups like the Jharkhand Party—representing aboriginal tribes—tells the same tale.

The processes of democracy have thus continued effectively the work of Mahatma Gandhi and the non-co-operation movement in awakening the masses and shifting the power from the middle classes to the common people. This is the great social integration now taking place in India, bringing to the forefront through education, use of political power and better distribution of wealth, the masses who at all times in the past have been like dumb driven cattle. The calling forth of the untapped human wealth of India, in its economic, social and intellectual urges—this indeed is the great revolution that is now taking place. The new classes emerging from below represent new India more than even the middle classes of the past whose role in intellectual leadership, in science and technology will no doubt continue to be important, while they will be forced to yield political power to those who wield the vote.

CHAPTER VIII

The Awakening of Women

The most spectacular and in many ways the most fundamental social change that the Gandhian movement effected in India is in respect of the position of women.

It would be wrong historically to consider that the great part that the women of India played in the non-co-operation movement and the position they have achieved for themselves in modern Indian life was the result of a sudden transformation. For over a century the process had been at work. In 1822 Ram Mohan Roy in his book entitled *Brief Remarks Regarding Modern Encroachment on the Ancient Rights of Females* had drawn attention to this problem, and had tried to prove that the condition of Hindu women in his day, when in many parts of India they were subjected to many cruel social customs, was not in keeping with the liberal teachings of early Hinduism.

Undoubtedly women in ancient India enjoyed a much higher status than their descendants in the eighteenth and nineteenth centuries. From the earliest days there had been many notable women in India—poets, scholars, capable administrators and leaders of religious movements. Even the eighteenth century produced women of the type of Ahalyabai Holkar whose administration of Indore State was considered a model for all India. But there is no doubt that, speaking generally, the condition of Indian womanhood had sunk low. Kept rigorously secluded behind the *purdah* in many parts of India, denied facilities of education and compelled under a system of child marriage, at least among some of the higher classes, to maternity when their sisters in other countries were in schools, and kept under subjection during marriage and forced, among the Brahmins and upper castes, to live a life of misery during widowhood, Indian women in the beginning of the nineteenth century were probably among the most backward of their sex all over the world.

The Brahmo Samaj led the movement for emancipation. The ancient rules of purdah were broken: and Brahmo women moved freely in society: but this was but a false dawn as it was far in advance of popular opinion. As even the educated classes generally showed a disinclination towards the emancipation of their women-folk, the movement for the uplift was slow in taking shape. By the beginning of the twentieth century the position had begun to show some change. The education of women had gradually become popular, and some of those who had tasted the fruits of modern education had taken seriously to the work of women's uplift. Pandita Ramabai Ranade, in the Maharashtrian country, Mrs P. K. Ray in Bengal and Maharani Chimnabai of Baroda, were among the pioneers of this awakening. It was however only with Gandhiji's non-co-operation movement that women were encouraged to come forward and participate in the life of the nation.

From the first days of his movement Gandhiji realized that there was a source of immense untapped power in the womanhood of India which could most advantageously be turned to the work he had nearest to his heart—the rehabilitation of the villages. His appeal was addressed directly to women. Originally he seems to have been uncertain of the response, or at least of the kind of work that women could do in the national movement, for though he was a passionate believer in the equality of women, he seems to have been doubtful whether the women of India who had for so long a time been shut up in seclusion could shoulder the active leadership of a movement which called for so much physical suffering.

But when the movement was actually started, women were everywhere at the forefront. In picketing liquor shops, in enforcing the boycott of foreign cloth, and in undertaking civil disobedience they shamed men in such a way that Gandhiji continually spoke of them as the main support of his movement. There were many prominent women associated with the movement everywhere, in villages and in towns. Women all over India came forward, defying all social taboos, sacrificing physical comforts, and denying the validity of all restrictions which had been enforced against them, to take up every kind of work connected with the national movement.

They were from all classes—from Sarojini Naidu, poet, social reformer, President of the Congress, to humble women of the untouchables, Princesses like Rajkumari Amrit Kaur and wives of millionaires to the commonest village folk. And strange was the fact that the wives of many loyal officials working in all earnestness and sincerity on the side of the British Government were brave enough openly to take up the constructive side of the movement. In a very famous pronouncement dated December 22, 1921, Gandhiji declared: 'I had hoped that in the initial stages at any rate women would be spared the honour of going to gaol. They were not to become aggressive civil resisters. But the Bengal Government, in their impartial zeal to make no distinction even of sex have conferred the honour upon three women of Calcutta. I hope the whole country will welcome this innovation. The women of India should have as much honour in winning Swaraj as men. Probably in this peaceful struggle women can outdistance man by many a mile . . . now that the Government of Bengal have dragged women into the line of fire, I hope that women all over India will take up the challenge and organize themselves. In any case they were bound, when a sufficient number had been removed, for the honour of the sex to step into their places. But now let it be side by side with men in sharing the hardships of gaol life.'[1]

Equal participation of women in the struggle thus became the motto of satyagraha and this spirit of active interest in public life grew with the prolongation of the movement for over twenty-five years. If the first movement of 1921 had succeeded and Swaraj had then been won, the awakening of Indian women would have only been superficial. It is the hardening effect of the continuing revolution and generation after generation of women growing up in an atmosphere not only of tension but calling for every sacrifice that gave women their present place in Indian life. There was no suffragette movement in India, no feminism, for the share of women in the battle of freedom gave them their position of equality without their having to fight for it separately. It was a matter of surprise to the outside world that independent India should have appointed women to the highest posts so freely, as

[1] *Young India* (weekly) of December 21, 1921.

members of the Cabinet, as Governors of Provinces, as Ambassadors and as leaders of delegations to international conferences, for *ex hypothesi* in an oriental country such as India, women are presumed to be held in subjection and therefore all this seemed to be unnatural. What caused even greater surprise was that these women, hardened by many terms in gaol, should have been not merely ornamental figures but able in every sense to hold their own with the ablest of any country.

It is not the distinction achieved by a few women of genius that is the true test of the changed position of women in India. What really is epochal and marks a revolutionary change is their free and equal participation in all spheres of national activity, and at every level, from work in villages to the government of the country. It was never a part of the Indian tradition that women were by nature inferior: on the contrary the ancient tradition emphasized their equality, though later social disabilities rendered it impossible for women to exercise that equality or to participate in many fields of activity. What the Gandhian movement did was to release women from the social bondages that custom had imposed and conservatism had upheld.

The legislative reform establishing the equality of women has been one of the most significant political achievements in the period of partial self-government. Their right to independent property, to freedom of marriage, to education and employment has been recognized by law. Many important pieces of legislation, especially the raising of the age of consent of marriage and the prevention of the dedication of women to temple services, have helped to change their status. These were but the reflection of a general awakening among the women themselves. During the last twenty-five years the Women's Conference, organized under the leadership of such personalities as Sarojini Naidu, Marahani Chimnabai of Baroda, and Rajkumari Amrit Kaur who had already achieved national distinction by their work in many fields, attained the proportions of an all-India movement. It viewed Indian life as a whole, attacked the special problems of women in the spirit of practical needs and put social reform as an important plank in the programme of the Indian Revolution.

The contribution of women to modern India may therefore be said to have been a challenge to some of the basic principles of Hindu society. More than that, it was a reintegration of social relationships on different ideas. It has forced the creation of a new code of laws, a new morality and a new principle of family organization, for the one thing which could not survive the growth of women's influence was the joint-family of the Hindus.

PART III

THE INTELLECTUAL SETTING

CHAPTER IX

The New Learning

India was at all times in her known history a country devoted to intellectual pursuits, where learning and scholarship were held in high esteem and where men seeking knowledge for its own sake were held in greater veneration than men of wealth or power. This is perhaps the most valuable part of the Brahminical tradition. It has also been a characteristic of India that knowledge as such was never denied to anyone, for, from the puranic times at least, we have records of men of all castes who had achieved distinction in different fields of knowledge. The period of anarchy which preceded the establishment of British power in Bengal was no exception. Over vast portions of India, for example in the Maharastra country, in the South, in Rajputana and even in Delhi and Lucknow there was a vigorous intellectual and artistic life in the eighteenth century of which the supreme examples in architecture were perhaps the beautiful city of Jaipur in Rajputana and the Padmanabhapuram Palace in the former Travancore State. In Bengal, the scene of much political and economic anarchy, intellectual life had no doubt sunk low, but the literature of the period, though it reflects misery and gloom, was not lacking in vigour or beauty. Somehow through popular effort, even when all government had broken down, the classes devoted to learning continued to receive their education.

What the reforms of the nineteenth century did was to give a new direction to this undying interest in education and in the search for knowledge. Men like Ram Mohan Roy in Bengal and Kesava Das in Travancore had even at the beginning of the century opted for Western knowledge, and both of them and many others of their time were masters not only of English but of other European languages as well. But what was in store was something different from this voluntary pursuit of knowledge. In 1813, the Charter of the East India Company ordered that a modest sum of Rs.1,00,000, or about £10,000 according to its then value, be set apart 'for the revival and improvement of literature and the encouragement of the learned natives of India and for the introduction and promotion of a knowledge of the sciences among the inhabitants of the British territories in India'.

No definite policy in the matter was laid down till Thomas Babington Macaulay was appointed President of the Board of Education. A child of liberalism of which he was the most distinguished advocate in his time, Macaulay had an invincible faith in the greatness of European civilization, and in the value of the English language as the supreme expression of its spirit. More unjustifiable was his contempt for all oriental learning, for, as he declared, he was prepared to sacrifice for a shelf of English books the entire literature of the East.

Macaulay's propositions were simple. He held 'that we ought to employ them (our funds) in teaching what is best worth knowing; that English is better worth knowing than Sanskrit or Arabic; that it is possible to make natives of this country thoroughly good English scholars, and to this end our efforts ought to be directed'. The Government of India accepted this view and laid it down (1835) as a fundamental article of policy that 'the great object of the British Government ought to be the promotion of European literature and science among the natives of India and the funds appropriated to education would best be employed in English education'.

Twelve years before Macaulay wrote his famous minute and the Government of Lord William Bentinck accepted it as the basis of its policy, Ram Mohan Roy had in a petition to Lord Amherst, protesting against the opening of a Government College for the study of Sanskrit, declared: 'The Sanskrit system of education would be the best calculated to keep this country in darkness if such had been the policy of the British legislature. But as the improvement of the native population is the object of the Government, it will consequently promote a more liberal and enlightened system of instruction, embracing mathematics, natural philosophy, chemistry and anatomy with other useful sciences by employing a few gentlemen of talent and learning, educated in Europe and providing a college furnished with the necessary books and apparatus'. In fact the demand for Western education had come most insistently from Indians themselves, and with Macaulay and Bentinck it became the official policy.

Thus were laid the foundations of a scheme, perhaps unique in this world, under which the effort of a powerful government, for a century and half, was directed towards the education in a foreign language of a country with more than 300 million people.

Macaulay's minute provided the basis, and colleges and schools teaching English came into existence in the provincial capitals both as a result of public effort and government initiative. It was however only in 1854 that a co-ordinated educational system on a national scale became the objective of British policy in India through the Wood Despatch, a memorable document which may be said to constitute the charter of Indian educational development. 'It is neither our aim nor our desire,' the Despatch declared, 'to substitute the English language for the vernacular dialects of the country. . . . It is indispensable therefore that in any general system of education the study of them should be assiduously attended to, and any acquaintance with improved European knowledge which is to be communicated to the great mass of people can only be conveyed to them through one or other of these languages'. Education was to be promoted on a general, India-wide basis, with primary schools in the vernaculars in every district, with higher education exclusively through the medium of English, though Indian languages were also made subjects of study.

Universities were started in Calcutta, Bombay and Madras in 1857, reflecting the educational fashions of the time in England. A vast field was opened for missionary effort, and non-official Indian activity also entered the field in competition with missionary institutions. The main features of the system for which Macaulay laid the foundation still survive. The Universities and Colleges which continued to be founded year after year had as their 'great object the promotion of European literature and science among the natives of India', though changed circumstances have altered the emphasis and added other objects such as a knowledge of their own country, a study of their own civilization and a cultivation of their own languages among the lesser objectives of intellectual enquiry.

Many of these universities, notably those of Bombay, Madras and Calcutta, have achieved world-wide reputation as seats of learning; others have attained distinction in scientific research and even the lesser and newer universities maintain a standard of education which is recognized to be the best outside Europe and North America.

The scientific institutions of India also came to be opened in due course. The Indian Institute of Science of Bangalore, the Forest Research Institute of Dehra Dun, the School of Tropical Medicines of Calcutta had achieved a respected position in the world of science. As evidence of a hundred years of conscious effort to promote 'European literature and science among the natives of India' these are indeed remarkable.

The evils of the new system were however many. Gandhiji who was among its most uncompromising critics put the position lucidly when he stated: 'The medium of foreign language through which higher education has been imported in India has caused incalculable intellectual and moral injury to the nation. We are too near our own times to judge the enormity of the damage done. And we who have received such education have to be both victims and judges—an almost impossible feat.'[1] After discussing from his personal experience, which is indeed the experience of all, of the immense wastage involved in studying all subjects through the medium of English Gandhiji went on to say, 'I knew what I took four years to learn of arithmetic, geometry, algebra, chemistry and astronomy, I should have learnt easily in one year, if I had to learn them not through English but Gujerati. My grasp of the subjects would have been easier and clearer. . . . I would have made use of such knowledge in my own home. The English medium created an impassable barrier between me and the members of my family who had not gone through English schools. My father knew nothing of what I was doing. I could not, even if I had wished it, interest my father in what I was learning . . . I was fast becoming a stranger in my own home. I certainly became a superior person.'[2]

Besides creating this impassable chasm between the English educated classes and others, including those educated in the

[1] For Gandhiji's views on education see notably *Young India*, September 1, 1921. The quotation is from his reply to Srinivasa Sastri in *Harijan*, dated July 9, 1938.

[2] Ibid.

traditional way, and apart altogether from the immense wastage of effort involved not only in the mastery of a foreign language, but in studying all other subjects through it, this system because of the importance attached to the English language placed a wholly disproportionate emphasis on literary studies to the neglect of vitally important subjects. In the first stage at least the result of the system was a large-scale production of young men with a competent knowledge of English and therefore useful in the subordinate ranks of administration, but uncertain of their surroundings. They had lost touch with the rich human soil and were mentally divided in their allegience. It did not train men and women to become useful members of society, but merely produced a literate class. It had a tendency to de-Indianize them intellectually, but because of the iron grip of the joint-family and the social system they had to live lives of mental dishonesty, accepting meekly in society what their minds rejected. The system in fact made its products unhappy in every way.

Also it has to be conceded that this attempted transplantation of a European culture on Indian soil took a long time to get acclimatized. For a considerable period the Indian mind seemed to be lacking in originality, purely imitative and reproducing without a full realization of their meaning the phrases learnt from books. The barrenness of Indian thought during the first half-century of English education is remarkable and there is hardly a single notable contribution that India made to the literature, thought or science of the world during this period.

When all this has been said and the truth of the criticism accepted, the credit balance of this unique experiment still remains substantial and impressive.

In the first place the system of higher education in English provided India with a class imbued with social purposes foreign to Hindu thought. The continuity and persistence of those purposes achieved the socio-religious revolution on which the life of modern India is based. While British administration did little, if anything, to emancipate the spirit, to extinguish the prejudices, to eradicate the ravages of ignorant custom and pernicious superstition, to encourage and stimulate thought, the New Learning which came to India through its introduction to the English language on a nation-wide scale undoubtedly did all this. Indeed it may be argued that the essential contradiction of the British rule in India lay in this: the constituted government upholding the validity of customs, maintaining and administering laws which denied the principles of social justice, refusing to legislate for changes urgently called for by society, watching with suspicion the movement of liberal ideas, while the officially sponsored and subsidized educational system was undermining everything that the Government sought to uphold. The schools and colleges taught young men the idea of liberty while the Government did everything to suppress it. In the education system the Government created and maintained an opposition to itself on a plane where its own methods were ineffective.

The mining of the ancient fortress of Hindu custom was a major achievement for the reason that it operated all over India. If, as modern critics suggest, the new education had been through the Indian languages, the emphasis of the movement would have been different from province to province, according to the development, flexibility and character of the language used. No doubt the reformation of Hinduism would still have come about, but it would not have been on an all-India basis. So to say, there would have been no 'master plan' of change, and instead of the Hindu community being unified, it would have split into as many different units as there were languages in India, and would have repeated the pattern of Europe with its conglomeration of mutually hostile units within the same Christian community. From this development India was saved by the common medium of education which Macaulay introduced into India.

In the second place, it is a point of major significance in the evolution of India as a single nation that this uniform system of education throughout India through a single language, produced a like-mindedness on which it has been possible to build. That it gave to India a common language for political thinking and action is of less importance than the creation of this like-mindedness, this community of thought, feeling and ideas which created the Indian nationality. The mind of India is united spiritually by Hindu religious thought, by the binding force of the great tradition which Sanskrit embodies and which, through the Indian languages that still reflect and convey that tradition, continues to be a living factor, and by the new community of ideas and approach which English education has spread among the dominant classes. Of these three factors the one which unites India politically and makes it possible for Indians to act as a single nation and build up a new society is the last. The first two are the permanent bases of Hindu civilization. They need not and cannot have by themselves created a unified nation without the cementing force of like-mindedness in politics. The unity of Hindu life and the common tradition of a Sanskrit culture are analogous to the Christian religion and Latin tradition in Western Europe, and yet by its emphasis on regional languages and the absence of a cementing factor in secular life Europe's development was through fragmentation. But for a hundred years of uniform education through the English language the result would have been the same in India.

Further, this education through the English language enabled India to share, not derivatively or at second-hand, but directly the results of the great movement of Enlightenment in Europe. The historic and truly magnificent work of the eighteenth century thinkers of Europe had, after a period of revolution and unsettlement, become the living thought of the nineteenth century. Through a hundred channels it was fertilizing the life of Europe, at the very time that English education was spreading in India. From explosive revolutionary slogans, liberty, equality and fraternity had become transformed into the respectable creed of liberalism. Even in traditional England, law was undergoing a reform which was soon to affect India also. The greatest good of the greatest number had become an acceptable formula in a country to which an exclusive Whig Oligarchy had given prosperity, security and an empire spread over the four corners of the world. To this thought India became an adopted heir, and though English administrators spoke contemptuously of 'natives talking the language of their masters and aping the manners and mannerisms of their betters' and not understanding the inner significance of the words by which they were swearing, it is undeniable that as time went on and one generation after another grew up on these principles, the apparent contradiction became reconciled. The Hindu middle classes had got acclimatized to European thought in a way that few people had anticipated.

There were as usual in such cases two parallel tendencies, one of breaking with the past and accepting the West wholesale with all its trappings; the other of continuity and adaptation of the old to the new, of widening, reforming and modernizing. The Brahmo

Samaj in its earlier phase may be said to represent the first. The attitude of Indian converts to Christianity continued that tradition for quite a long time. But it is an evidence of the strength of Indian culture and the adaptability of the Indian mind that the process by which the revolutionary principles of Europe were assimilated into Indian thought was one of quiet, almost imperceptible modification. The incompatibility of the system of caste with democracy, of secular thought with a mode of life dominated by religious ritual; of equality of sexes with women in *purdah* and subjected to social and legal restrictions, all these which at one time seemed to stand permanently in the way of Westernization, gave way to the pressure of ideas without a revolutionary upheaval.

India emerged by a peaceful revolution as a modern society mainly because the gradual penetration of ideas was through education spread over a fairly large and representative class.

CHAPTER X

The Emergence of the Indian Languages

It is often alleged against the Indian system of education that it failed to filter through to the masses. On a careful examination, this criticism will be found to be unjustified. It is true that the authors of the scheme had hoped that as a result of infiltration, Hindu society, which was then considered to be in a process of dissolution, would disappear and the population of India would be saved for Christ. This was the Grand Design which made the missionaries ardent advocates of the scheme. That hope did not materialize. In fact, far from India turning Christian, the progress of English education only led as we have seen to a large-scale reformation of Hinduism and a more rational interpretation of its dogmas. It led to a remarkable strengthening of the hold of Hinduism on the masses and its emergence as an important world religion. In that sense the theory of filtering down had the very opposite effect from what Macaulay and his friends in their complacency had imagined. It is therefore no matter for surprise that the missionary educators should consider that the object for which they had spent so much money and energy had failed.

The extent to which the theory of infiltration succeeded can best be seen by the extraordinary growth of the regional languages of India during the last half-century. Few European scholars have tried to understand the literary activity which transformed these languages into great and live vehicles of thought and artistic creation entitling them to recognition among the literatures of the modern world. Languages like Hindi, spoken by over 150 millions, Bengali, the mother tongue of 70 millions, Gujerati, Marathi, Telugu, Tamil, Canarese and Malayalam—the least of them spoken by a population of more than 15 millions—have all of them during the last half-century witnessed an immense amount of literary activity the echoes of which have only very occasionally reached the West. It will hardly be denied that this activity, which is the genuine reflection of the new humanism which India has developed, is the result of the infiltration of Western ideas and thought. Indian intellectual effort has so far been judged by the work of Indian writers in English. Insignificant in number and not too original, and with but little distinctive quality, the poets, essayists and literateurs of Indo-Anglian literature, as it is called, cannot claim to represent either the modern Indian mind or be considered the examples of India's creative capacity. The genuine results of English education in India, the reaction of the Indian mind to the vital movements of European cultures introduced to them through English, are to be seen in the work of Tagore, Iqbal, Sarat Chandra Chatterji, Prem Chand, Vallathol, Bharati and a host of other great writers who have enriched the literatures of modern Indian languages. Some idea of the quality of their work reached the West through the popularity that the translations of Tagore's works achieved in Europe; but generally speaking it has been a closed book to European scholars.

Three stages may be noticed in the development of these languages. At the beginning of the nineteenth century each one of these languages could boast of a literature which contained some of the masterpieces of poetic inspiration. There were in Hindi the great works of Tulsidas, Surdas and Kesavadas: in Bengali of Vidyapati, Chandidas, and Kirtibas. In Tamil there was a classical literature which claimed to rival the glories of Sanskrit. In Marathi, Gujerati and the rest the position was similar. There was a poetic literature of undoubted excellence, which was greatly cherished by the people; but all the same they were vernaculars, for education was through the classics, Sanskrit or Persian. Learning and scholarship had relation only to the classical languages. It was therefore true of all these languages that they had no books which could be used as textbooks in the new educational scheme.

This period also witnessed the secularization of the vernacular literature. As mentioned before, the development of literature in these languages was almost exclusively in the realm of poetry and the themes of such poetry were dominantly religious. All the great names in the different vernacular literatures before the nineteenth century—Tulsidas, Surdas, Kabir, Mira, Vidyapati, Chandidas, Tukaram—were of those associated with devotional religion. In fact, historically, the revival of religion in the Middle Ages and the growth of vernacular literatures were two aspects of the same development. The popularization of the Rama and Krishna cults, which constituted so important a feature in the life of medieval India, was achieved through the work of these poets, and as a result the literatures of what became modern Indian languages started, in the nineteenth century, with a heavy religious tradition. The secular tradition in these literatures was confined mainly to erotic poetry.

The secularization of literature was the work of the first part of the nineteenth century, mainly as a result of the infiltration of English ideas. For this development the essential preparatory work such as the production of authoritative dictionaries and grammars was done in most cases by missionaries and other foreigners who had the necessary scientific training in other languages. For example, it was the German missionary Gundert who in the middle of the nineteenth century wrote an authoritative dictionary for the Malayalam language. It is Bishop Caldwell's *Comparative Grammar of the Dravidian Languages* that formed the groundwork of linguistic studies in the South. The work of the Serampore missionaries in laying the foundation of the modern developments in Bengali is generally recognized.

With the foundation thus firmly laid it became possible to utilize the vernaculars in the schools. The first stage was the production of textbooks, often written under orders of the Department of Education, for no old-fashioned scholar was likely to come forward voluntarily to undertake this work. The period of what may be called the production of textbooks created for the first time the models for prose writing to which no serious attention had been paid in the past. Not much work which would pass as literature was produced in this period, but a standard prose style was evolved, which was greatly helped forward by the growth of vernacular journalism. As everywhere else in the world, the language of journalism was artificial, but it helped the growth of new ideas, made expression flexible and related it to the political, social and economic problems of the day.

The second stage was a period of imitation when the literary talent of the Western-educated classes came into evidence first by the translations of English classics and later by original works under the inspiration of Western masters. This was the period when Bankim Chandra Chatterji wrote novels in the manner of Scott, Madhusudan Dutt wrote in the style of Milton, and Dwijendralal Roy wrote historical plays following the European technique. Similar tendencies were reflected in other languages a little later, for the leadership of Bengal in this matter was widely accepted at this time.

It is, however, necessary to emphasize that at this period the languages themselves continued to be dominated by Sanskrit. The poverty of vocabulary in some of the vernacular was easily remedied by turning to the immense wealth of Sanskrit, and both the prose writers and poets of the age heavily weighted their language and gave it richness and colour by an unashamed Sanskritization of their style. Bankim Chandra's novels, no less than Madhusudan Dutt's epic, teem with pure Sanskrit words. The extent of the domination of Sanskrit over the literary vernacular of the time may be judged by the fact that in the famous song *Vande Mataram* in Bankim's novel *Anand Mutt* more than ninety per cent of the words are of pure Sanskrit formation. The same obtains, it may be added, in Tagore's equally famous *Jana Gana Mana* which is now used as the national anthem of India. In the other Indian languages also, with the exceptions of Tamil and Urdu, this dominance of Sanskrit in poetry, no less than in prose, was equally visible.

The period also witnessed a systematic attempt to render into the vernaculars the treasures of Sanskrit literature. The translations in the earlier period were mainly of religious books like the Ramayana and the Mahabharata but the immense secular literature of Sanskrit was the preserve of classical scholars. The translations of the dramas and epics of Kalidasa, of the works of Bhavabuti and other classics from Sanskrit, meant to bring the riches of Sanskrit within the reach of the common man, was undertaken both for educative purposes and for enriching the vernacular languages.

Though these tendencies were mainly imitative and lacked originality, other trends were also becoming evident. Historical writing, criticism, biography, essays, and polemics began to make their appearance. Research in literary origins made considerable progress, and even before the century had closed many notable works had appeared in the vernaculars which evidenced a widespread intellectual ferment. Critical editions of texts, a general questioning of intellectual standards, and other evidences of wide interests were also not lacking. But generally it will not be untrue to say that till the beginning of the twentieth century pseudo-classicism preserved its authority, both in form and in language. In Malayalam, for example, the literary masterpiece of the period was *Mayura Sandesa*, a work of merit cast in the mould of Kalidasa's 'Meghaduta'. Other works which attained authority and popularity, though they appeared in the first decade of the twentieth century, were Mahakavyas written in the style of Magha, Harsha and Bharavi, following not only the canons of Sanskrit poetics but using the rigid metres of classical *chhandas* or metres. Though the north Indian poets used popular metres, the forms of Sanskrit Alankaras (rhetoric) and *rasas* dominated them equally.

The new generation was not satisfied with this and it found a master in Rabindranath Tagore. With the appearance of Tagore as a major influence in Indian literature, the transformation of the vernaculars into great modern languages may be said to have been completed. The generation of which Tagore was the representative genius and supreme prophet struggled to give expression to the trends of India's new life. Simultaneously, the movement spread in all languages. It is significant that the period also marked the growth of an integral nationalism, following the partition of Bengal, the *Swadeshi* agitation and the appearance of the school of activists led by Tilak and Aurobindo. A great patriotic fervour becomes visible in the poetry of the period between 1903–1914, the period of *Jana Gana Mana*, of the exaltation of India and of patriotic motives in drama, novels and poetry.

Tagore's genius stamped this movement not only in Bengal but everywhere in India with the characteristics of modernism. He infused into the language itself vitality and flexibility, provided and popularized styles and forms which broke away from the old tradition, introduced an international outlook into Bengali literature and established its independent position in the world. But Tagore, though exceptional in his genius, was not a singular phenomenon. There were many notable poets and writers in other languages who were also moved by the same patriotic fervour and the same desire to burst through the shackles of the earlier imitative period. Two are especially worthy of mention,

Subramania Bharati, the Tamil poet and Mohammed Iqbal, whose earlier work voiced the spirit of patriotism and revolt.

The inter-war period witnessed 'the protest of the children against the fathers'. Everywhere the search for new literary forms, experimentation with new modes of expression, the desire to get away from the stereotyped emotions became apparent. Social unrest began to be reflected in the literature which saw in 'realism' the ideal it was seeking. Ibsen, Dostoevsky, Chekov and others replaced the earlier enthusiasms. The Gandhian movement, which held the political stage, sent young men to the villages and re-established the primary relationship with the soil. Munshi Prem Chand and Sarat Chandra Chatterji are perhaps the most representative novelists of this period. The novels of Bankim Chandra and of similar romantic writers became the reminiscences of school days.

The controversy about poetical forms and themes extended far beyond the realms of literature. The realist and 'progressivist' slogans with which the atmosphere was overcharged stood for something more than literary creation. They were the voices of social revolution. The earlier poets and writers had come from the higher strata of society, the educated nobility or the middle classes. In many ways the literature itself was aristocratic. With the change of emphasis in national life the common man began to assert his rights in the republic of letters.

By the twenties, literature had ceased to be either a polite occupation, or one dependent on the favour of official textbook committees for a steady royalty. The reading public in all the Indian languages had grown tremendously, and literary work became for the first time a full-time occupation capable of earning a livelihood. Proust, Lawrence and Joyce were the European masters who influenced the technique of the period, while in poetry the later years witnessed an extraordinary growth in the influence of Eliot and Hopkins.

'Progressive' influence made some headway. It helped to change the emphasis from the time-honoured love themes to the conflicts on the economic level, but the ideal of a 'class literature', in which creative literary work becomes the handmaid of proletarian propaganda, failed, in spite of the allegiance of some writers of notable talent, to achieve any marked success in the sphere of poetry. Proletarian literature in the form of 'People's Theatre', of short stories in which class-struggle is the main motive, and novels laying bare the poverty of the peasants and workers and their exploitation by feudalists and capitalists, is, however, no longer insignificant and has come to stay. The short story especially has been developed by the 'progressives' as a literary *genre* suitable for their purpose. The ancient system of story-telling in the East and its appeal even to the illiterate helped the 'progressives' in this direction, and the perfection they have achieved in this form is indeed remarkable.

Change is the single uniting factor in the literary climate of the quarter-century that preceded independence. Unlike Europe, India did not have the disillusionment of the twenties and the conflicts of the thirties which had so profound an effect on English and continental literature. But she was agitated by a general feeling of social restlessness, by a revolutionary upheaval of the masses, by the intoxicating wine of Marxian thought which began to penetrate influential classes during this period. The ideal behind the modernist movement of the period can best be understood in terms of Chekov's assertion that there is more humanity in electricity and steam than in chastity.

Though realism and progressivism may be said to have represented the vital and younger movements, the older 'polite letters', romantic, pseudo-classical, caring for perfection of form and language did not lose their popularity. Especially in poetry they more than held their own while even in the more unsettled sphere of novels, drama, etc., their influence continued to be considerable.

CHAPTER XI

The Discovery of the Past and the Revival of Arts and Science

Another development of significance during this period which can also be traced directly to the new learning is the spirit of research and criticism of ancient texts. Sir Rama Krishna Gopal Bhandarkar may be described as the first Indian scholar to apply the modern methods of criticism to Sanskrit studies. His work on Vaishnavism and Saivism set the model of research into Indian religions and sects, while his *Peep into the Ancient History of the Deccan* may well be considered the beginning of the present attempt to reconstruct the earlier history of India. Men like Rajendralal Mitra had contributed to earlier researches, but the inspiration of their work had come from European scholars. The Government of India had begun a systematic attempt to collect, decipher and edit inscriptions and also to preserve ancient manuscripts. The search for manuscripts was taken up all over India and produced some remarkable results including the discovery of the historic work on politics and administration by Kautalaya (fourth century BC) and the plays of Bhasa (second century BC). A vast unsuspected literature of the medieval period, which included notable works on law, astronomy and mathematics, was discovered and edited. The literature of Sanskrit Buddhism, for long lost to the tradition of Hindu culture, was rediscovered and reinstated in its place in classical studies. In fact the revival of Buddhist studies, especially the Mahayana, of which the sacred texts are in Sanskrit, and the recognition of Buddhist achievements in India as an integral part of national tradition, so significantly emphasized by the acceptance of the capital of the Asokan pillar as the symbol of new India, are different aspects of the same movement.

The most notable achievement in this field of research and

scholarship is undoubtedly the great Bhandarkar Institute Edition of India's national epic—the Mahabharata. This colossal task which has successfully reconstituted the authorized text of the great epic has been a model of scientific accuracy, of unprejudiced application of the technique of modern criticism and a demonstration of what can be achieved by the co-operation of the scholars of Europe and India.

The recovery of Indian history and its reinterpretation are also the results of the intellectual ferment created by the new education. The foundation for this great task was laid by European scholars who deciphered inscriptions, collected and collated references in foreign languages, especially in Greek, Latin and Chinese, excavated ancient sites, interpreted the legends on coins, and created a school of archaeology and epigraphy in India. But they produced no history. The chaotic accumulation of facts they made available, however, constituted the documentary foundations for writing a proper history.

So far the textbooks of Indian history read more like telephone directories, a vast jumble of names unrelated to each other, with emphasis on the period of British rule in India. What gave to Indian history a perspective was Nehru's *Discovery of India*—a layman's attempt to understand the main currents of India's past. Nehru had inherited from Europe a sense of world civilization and it is interesting to note that his first adventure in the unfamiliar field of history writing was a synthesis of world historical tendencies entitled *Glimpses of World History*. Nehru would have accepted without question the memorable words with which Jacques Pirenne opens his *Great Currents of Universal History*, 'History is essentially a continuity and a solidarity.' The world perspective is always there in the *Discovery of India* and Nehru's vision of Indian history is not obscured by national prejudices or an undue sense of national glory.

The growth of 'national' history is also a development of this period. It started mainly as a reaction against the prejudiced and anti-Indian point of view officially propagated in Government schools and colleges. Mahadev Govind Ranade, scholar, statesman, and jurist, was the father of this movement. His *Rise of the Mahratta Power* helped greatly to restore the sense of national pride which the loss of freedom had brought in its train, and the works of Parasnis, Sardesai, Jadunath Sirkar, Krishnaswamy Aiyangar,

Nilakanta Sastry, R. C. Mazumdar and others created a historical tradition based on patient research, deep learning, accurate analysis and critical appreciation. Except in limited fields like Maharashtra and Vijayanagar histories and specific periods like the reign of Aurangzeb which saw the downfall of the Mogul Empire, the national school of historians did not attempt systematic histories or integrate known facts on a broad general basis but limited themselves to monographs and specialized works. All the same the growth of a historical sense, giving to Indian life an increased sense of its continuity, a growing appreciation of its political and social roots, a pride in its past achievement, has been an important factor in the development of modern India.

A factor closely related to this sense of recovered history is the awakening of the Indian mind to the expansion of Hindu culture in the past across the Himalayas to 'Serindia', Tibet and China and across the seas to the Indonesian Archipelago, to Malaya, Siam and Camboja. This was mainly the work of European scholars of all nationalities mostly the French and the Dutch, Sylvian Levi, Chavannes, Coedes and others among French scholars, Kern, Stutterheim and others among the Dutch. Indian expansion to these areas was an epic achievement spread over 1,200 years, of great and powerful Empires established in distant lands, or art and architecture carried across the seas, of continued naval power, of flourishing trade and commerce. Every part of India shared the glory that was disclosed by the work of these scholars. India had a share, not perhaps a dominant one, in the architectural achievements of Borobudur and Ankor Vat and in the mural paintings of the Tunghuan caves. She could legitimately claim a share in the artistic heritage of Java, as may be seen from the fact that Coomaraswamy's great work on Indian Art is entitled *Indian and Indonesian Art*. All this contributed greatly to a new sense of nationalism.

Indian art also witnessed a renaissance in the twentieth century. India's ancient and continuous artistic tradition was all but submerged in the flood of Westernization in the second half of the nineteenth century. The new generation educated in English had been taught that nothing of beauty had originated outside Greece. The architecture, painting and sculpture of India were represented as the crude and primitive attempts of a people who had not seen the vision of Attic beauty. Strange and unfamiliar to

India's early European teachers were the architectural conceptions of the Hindu temples, the ideals that shaped Hindu sculpture and the form and colours of Indian paintings. They were prepared to admit that Indo-Saracenic architecture was beautiful, as they were familiar with the traditions of Islam in Europe. This point of view found classical expression in the statement of Sir George Grierson that 'outside handicrafts Indian Art was a monstrosity'. Even a 'historian of Indian Art', Vincent Smith, went on record to say that India produced no sculpture after the Gupta period.

The result of this teaching was that the new educated classes were for a time ashamed of the artistic tradition of India, and looked passionately towards Europe for inspiration. Raja Ravi Varma who caricatured Hindu gods and goddesses and made them look as far as possible as Indian versions of Apollos and Venuses was the representative of that imitative age. But the genuine tradition though eclipsed was still alive. The so-called Patna school is a remarkable example of the vitality of India's artistic tradition. This school, whose last representative died in 1933,[1] was in the direct line of descent from the painters who adorned the Court of Akbar and his successors. Forced out of Delhi as a result of the breakdown of the Moghuls, they settled down at Patna, where Sewak Ram who may be called the founder of the school established his studio in 1750. From then down to 1933, when its last distinguished master passed away, the Patna school kept up in difficult circumstances the purity of the Indian tradition, no doubt modified to suit changed conditions, but definitely Indian in all its essential characteristics.

Elsewhere also the Indian tradition maintained itself precariously against the onslaught from the West. In the States of Rajputana hereditary painters submitted as 'Nazar' at Dusserah Durbars specimens of their work, and in Jaipur, Bikaner, Udaipur and Alwar, the tradition of such painting continued to be very vigorous, though the rulers to whose patronage they looked showed but little appreciation. In the principalities of the Himalayan valleys the old Kangra school continued and the work of recent representatives of this style has found appreciation by leading critics.

The tendency to abandon the ancient artistic tradition which the popularity of Ravi Varma showed, was not, it is clear, the

[1] See Millicent Archer, *Patna Painting*, Royal India Society, London.

failure of technical competence. Painters and master craftsmen could as before produce masterpieces, but Indian art had lost its appeal to those who were its natural patrons. The Princes of India preferred to buy art from second-hand dealers in Europe hoping thereby to impress their masters with their cultured and modern taste. The Western-educated middle classes had been taught that all beauty was represented by the Greek tradition. The artistic masterpieces of the past conveyed nothing to them.

The beginnings of a national renaissance in this sphere were not long delayed. Under Abanindranath Tagore the Calcutta School of Art became the centre of a revival of Indian artistic traditions. Abanindranath himself was an artist of genius, and at least one of his disciples, Nandalal Bose, has a place among the masters. The so-called Bengal school is not however to be judged by the achievement of its individual members, though even from that point of view its work both in quality and quantity is not negligible. Its great national contribution is the undoubted fact that it awakened India to its own traditions in art and cried a halt to the sterile imitation of the West which had become the fashion in the nineteenth century. It not only gave rise to vigorous regional schools, but also awakened India to its own artistic heritage.

The restoration of values in art to educated India is primarily the achievement of the first quarter of the twentieth century. Coomaraswamy's studies in Rajput painting laid the foundations of modern art criticism in India. Ganguli's *South Indian Bronzes*, and the Royal India Society's and Hyderabad Government's publications on Ajanta, provided the impetus which helped India to recover her lost soul. In E. B. Havell it found a zealous champion and his vigorous publications helped to open the eyes not only of India, but of Europe to the significance of Indian art. The Royal India Society of London, the 'Kala Bhavan' of Benares and other institutions took up the work, so that today it may well be claimed that Indian art has gained world-wide recognition as one of the cultural heritages of humanity.

In architecture the blighting hand of an unimaginative bureaucracy did all it possibly could to cover the face of India with buildings which, however useful, had no claims to beauty. It is only in the South of India and in Kathiawar that religious architecture followed the traditional forms and produced some works of undoubted excellence during this period of barrenness. Even the courts of Indian princes reflected the tendencies of British India of imitating European styles in buildings, the most curious example of which is the strange Italian villa in the State of Cutch, and the parody of Versailles with which the Maharaja of Kapurthala adorned his capital. The majority of palaces and gardens that the Princely Houses of India built during this period had neither character nor beauty, but again it is significant of the strength of the Indian tradition that in many places like Bikaner, Jaipur and some of the Kathiawar States Indian architecture has had a revival, which has produced some remarkably beautiful buildings both religious and secular.

There is one field of intellectual activity in which the Indian mind has been particularly barren during the last 100 years and that is in philosophical thinking. Until quite recently philosophical teaching in the Indian universities was confined to the systems of Western thinkers and when Indian systems came again to be taught the categories had become confused. The translations of Indian philosophical systems into English added to the confusion, for these tried to express Indian thinking in terms of Western philosophy. Thus Western education in this field has been altogether sterile and may be said to have helped to dry up the roots of philosophical thinking in India—except among classes among whom this education had not penetrated. The great monasteries like the Sringeri Mutt, and seats of ancient learning like Nawadwip, keep up a faint light, but it is significant that not one of the universities has produced a philosopher of any distinction who has made a contribution of value either to the traditional systems of thought or to the modern schools.

It is a pleasure to turn from the record of this failure to the achievements of modern India in the fields of positive science. For the first time after a thousand years India again claimed a seat at the High Table of science with the emergence of Ramanujan as a mathematician of world-wide eminence. Since then, during the last quarter of a century in Physics, Chemistry, Astrophysics and fundamental research Indian contributions have been significant and they have earned general recognition. Outside the nations of Europe and North America and Japan, India is the only country which can claim to have made positive contributions of far-reaching importance. The pioneer of this movement was

Acharya P. C. Ray who trained a school of researchers in Chemistry at Calcutta University. Dr Ray's *Ancient Hindu Chemistry* also provided inspiration to the younger generation by drawing attention to the achievements of their forefathers in this branch of science. The discoveries of Sir J. C. Bose in the field of plant life, and more important, the studies of Sir C. V. Raman leading to the discovery of what is known as the 'Raman Effect' gave to Indian science its international status, while others like Meghanad Saha, Bhabha, Krishnan, Ghosh, Chandrasekharan and Bhatnagar have added lustre to the name of India in the scientific world.

There are of course many wide and important gaps in Indian scientific work. The older generation of scientists had to carry on their work without adequate facilities or much national encouragement. Laboratories and scientific institutions—with the one exception of the Indian Institute of Science, established through the munificence of Jamshedji Tata—were not provided either by the Government or by the public. The British Government depended for defence purposes on English scientific research. Indian industries followed at a distance the technology and scientific achievements of other countries, as the basic industries which depended on continuous research had not yet gained a foothold in India.

With the universities, the defence authorities and industries neglecting scientific work, the remarkable thing is not that there are gaps in Indian scientific achievements but that modern India should have been able to produce a corps of pure scientists at all.

From the above brief analysis, it will be seen that the policy of education through English had a much greater success than even Macaulay anticipated, though it was along lines which his Christian spirit could not foresee. That a Western system of education would set in motion forces which would lead to a strengthening of Hinduism and to a wide acceptance of the principles behind Western social thinking while rejecting Christian teaching was inconceivable to the men of Macaulay's generation, who were convinced that Hindu institutions, like the Walls of Jericho, were only awaiting the trumpet call of an archangel to crumble and fall to pieces. But the process of infiltration, as it worked, gave rise to what may appropriately be called modern Indian humanism, which spread the basic ideas of Western civilization, interpreted in terms of Hindu thought, through modern Indian languages.

It is not merely the creative activity which the literatures of these languages reflect that is important. It is the continuous, unceasing popularization of ideas, discussion of fundamental problems, controversies between the ancients and moderns, that go on day by day in the magazines, journals and periodicals that are even more significant. The growth of Indian-language newspapers and periodicals during the twentieth century has been something phenomenal, and while a few exist for the defence of the orthodox view, the preponderant majority preach the message of the new humanism.

What are the basic ideas of this new humanism? They can be briefly stated as a modern and Indian interpretation of liberty, equality and fraternity. They are modern because the economic movements of the nineteenth century have given a new content to these ideas. They have taken an Indian form because liberty, for example, means in India not merely the acquisition of political independence, but the emancipation of women, freedom for the suppressed classes, liquidation of feudal elements within the country and many other things which have ceased to have significance in Europe. In the same way, equality is a dynamic and revolutionary conception in India, as society has always been organized on the basis of inequality, of caste and untouchability. Fraternity also has a different significance in India, for while the universalism of Hindu thought emphasizes the motive of action as *Loka samgraha* or welfare of the world, the practical experience of the subordination of the non-White races and the prevalence of discrimination by European peoples have given to Indian thought on this subject its colour and temper. It is the fraternity of the oppressed which has moved the mind of modern India. The Marxian doctrine of fraternity 'Workers of the world unite', found in India a corollary 'the oppressed of the world unite' and this feeling has been deeply ingrained in the Indian mind.

The fact that the Macaulayan system of education through the English language is now being extensively modified is in itself an evidence of its success. It fulfilled its function when it trained a sufficiently large class of people in India in the basic concepts of modern civilization, when it succeeded in transforming the vernaculars of India into modern languages capable of carrying on the work it inaugurated, when it integrated the permanent values of the West in the thought of India. The nationalization of education has thus been rendered possible, and the present programme giving instruction even in universities through the medium of Indian languages is but the logical fulfilment of the scheme that was introduced in 1835.

How will it affect the study of English? What will be the place of English in independent India? These are questions of vital importance to the future of India and of Asia. It is obvious that the pre-eminence that English has enjoyed in India as the medium of instruction in colleges and universities will not in future be accorded to it. Increasingly the emphasis will be on Indian languages. As Gandhiji has put it: 'The nobility of its (English) literature cannot avail the Indian nation any more than the temperate climate or the scenery of England can avail her. India has to flourish in her own climate and scenery and her own literature, even though all three may be inferior to the English climate, scenery and literature. We and our children must build on our own heritage. If we borrow another we impoverish our own.'

Such a change, however, is unlikely to affect the influence of the English language, for apart from its being a compulsory second language in schools and universities, it will have to continue at least for a very considerable time to be a second official language of the country. The English language, by ceasing to be the language of the conqueror, is likely to be naturalized more easily as one of the languages of India as Persian was for over 400 years. Indo-Persian, during its 400 years of existence in India, developed an independent literature, and the language itself is still a part of Indian tradition. A similar development of English is not only possible but probable, more especially because, as the most widely used international language, its cultivation will continue to be of the highest importance to India itself.

Besides, Indian law and the Constitution are built on the foundation of English, so that any breach with their sources, until they take firm root, may have unforeseeable consequences. The English text is the original of the Indian Constitution. It is expressed in terms which have, by association, judicial interpretation and common acceptance, come to have specific significance, which no translation can convey. To take two instances, both of which are fundamental to the Constitution. The President of the Republic is to be '*advised*' by a Council of Ministers and on this wording is based the whole structure of parliamentary responsible government. The word 'advise' bears in this context a meaning which can be understood only in reference to English constitutional practice and its extensive literature. No translation can convey its significance, and constitutional evolution in India will take unexpected twists and turns if the Hindi version is recognized by law as being the authoritative official text. A second illustration is the phrase '*due process of law*'. Autocratic rulers of Indian princely states used to claim that arrest without warrant on their verbal orders came within this phrase, as the law of the State vested all power in the ruler and therefore his order was constitutional. Again without reference to the interpretations in England and America this phrase would bear a different significance altogether.

Nor can it be forgotten that the whole corpus of Indian law—perhaps the most comprehensive and extensive legal and judicial system in the world—is in English. It would take decades of human effort even to translate the whole body into Indian languages. But the bare facts convey but little. The judicial interpretations of the various high courts lie buried in law reports which are all in English. It is obvious that for political work and for the administration of law English must continue to be the official language of India for years to come. It is significant that the Government, while deciding on Hindi as the national language of India, has provided for the continuance of English as an additional language till parliament otherwise decides.

It will be seen from what has been briefly stated above that the intellectual ferment which provided the background of the movement for political independence was essentially the result of the assimilation of European thought and ideas by the educated classes and its infiltration through the Indian languages. Its results have not been insignificant. It has created in India a new humanism, which attempts to create a synthesis between the East and the West, accepting many of the ideals of European civilization and modifying them in terms of India's own tradition. It has begun to contribute effectively to the scientific work of the modern world, has added to the world's heritage in the realm of art and beauty. More, it has produced an influential class of men who, while they are intensely nationalist and have their roots firmly in Indian soil, are also the inheritors of European culture and do not look upon it as something alien, different or undesirable. The intellectual temper of modern India is international and cosmopolitan, no doubt partly as a result of her European inheritance, but mainly from her own tradition of leadership which stamped the peoples of South Asia with her civilization and culture.

PART IV

THE CONSTITUTION

CHAPTER XII

Territorial Integration

It used to be a common criticism in the days before independence that India was only a geographical expression. So are England, France, China and the names of other [illegible] geographical areas. It is true [illegible] has not always been the same [illegible]. There have been many changes [illegible] of the United States during the last 150 [illegible] France has extended and contracted during [illegible] years and Germany today is not what [illegible] to speak of the pre-Bismarckian [illegible] India no doubt [illegible] [illegible] their constituent into a [illegible] government [illegible] India has been [illegible] and day.

As [illegible] In [illegible] [illegible] Pakistan [illegible] [illegible] that the [illegible] large [illegible]. The [illegible] of [illegible] South [illegible]. The [illegible] and North [illegible] the [illegible] kingdoms, [illegible]

CHAPTER XII

Territorial Integration

It used to be a common criticism in the days before independence that India was only a geographical expression. So are England, France, China and the names of other countries, for they all indicate a geographical area. It is true, however, that the territory of India has not always been the same. Nor is this a peculiarity of India. There have been many changes in the political boundaries of the United States during the last 150 years of its existence. France has extended and contracted during the last seventy-five years and Germany today is not what it was twenty years ago, not to speak of the pre-Bismarckian period. In the heyday of British power, India no doubt included territories to which she has never had any historic claim, for example, Baluchistan, Burma, Aden and the trans-Indus tribal areas. Today, by the secession of the Provinces which have a majority of Muslims and their constitution into a separate sovereign State, the territory of India has been definitively laid down.

As a result of the partition, the territory of India has contracted to a certain extent, but the historical identity of India has remained unaffected. From the Himalayas to Rameswaram, from between the Ravi and the Beas to the Brahmaputra, the country which includes the Gangetic valley and the peninsula, India has been united into a single state under a common authority, professing undivided allegiance. Compared to the historical empires of the past, the Indian Republic has not merely a greater unity but a larger territory. The Empire of the Mauryas did not extend to the South beyond Mysore. The Empire of the Guptas effectively ruled only North India and though Samudragupta conquered some of the southern kingdoms, his imperial sway did not extend over them. The Empire at the time of Akbar the Great extended only up to the Deccan, and the Moghul Empire under Aurangzeb reached only the Tungabhadra and was unable to bring under its control the historic lands of the South. Under the British, no less than two-fifths of the area of India remained under the Princes, who no doubt accepted the paramountcy of the British Crown but over whose territories neither the Indian Government nor the British Parliament claimed or exercised any sovereign authority. Today the territory of India is one, for what has emerged is a single nation-state, claiming sovereignty over the entire territory, and exercising undisputed authority from one end to the other.

The rise of a nation-state in India is a matter of supreme importance, as it is a basic departure from the traditional policy of India. From the time of the Vedas, to the withdrawal of the British, the political ideal of India has *at all times* been that of a *Samrajya*, a paramount State with subordinate territorial organizations under it. The conception of the *Samrat* or the emperor emerged distinctly in the later Vedic literature, and in the Mahabharata all the kings of India were said to have been brought under the suzerainty of the *Kurus*, from whom the *Pandavas* wrested the sceptre of Empire. But the imperial conception meant no more than the acceptance of the paramountcy of a powerful ruler or dynasty by the other states. At no time did a conqueror or a great Empire think of annexing the territories of the *Samantas* or subordinate rulers in the outlying areas, though the dynasties were often replaced either directly by the paramount power or by local revolutions. The Allahabad inscription of the great conqueror Samudragupta (fourth century AD) gives a description of the areas which were directly governed through Viceroys and other imperial officers, those which were under subordinate rulers and those over which the empire exercised only a protectorate. Even under the more centralized administration of the Moghul Empire, in North India itself, vast territories were under the effective authority of local kings who willingly accepted the Emperor as the traditional *Samrat* but continued to reign over their hereditary dominions as before. The entire area of Rajputana, the vast territories of Bundelkand, Bagelkand and Chatisgarh remained in the very heart of Hindustan almost untouched by Moghul administration. Nor was the case essentially different under the British. As mentioned before, over two-fifths of the entire territories continued to be ruled by subordinate kings.[1] A look at the map of the British Empire in India would demonstrate the fact that direct British rule was confined to the Punjab, to the Gangetic Valley and to the coastal areas. The vast tract in the interior extending from the present boundary of Pakistan, south of the Punjab, practically to the Bay of Bengal, was shaded yellow, indicating that it was under the rule of Indian princes. The Nizam of Hyderabad and the Maharaja of Mysore between them ruled over 100,000 square miles of the tableland of the south, while the rich coastal area, famed in history for its unbroken contact with the West, was under the Rulers of Travancore and Cochin. It used to be pointed out as evidence of the divided character of India that the railway line from Delhi to Bombay, known as the BB and CI, in its direct route of 1,000 miles covered only 150 miles of British territory.

Such indeed was the position on August 14, 1947, the day before the British Government handed over authority to the Indian Union. On the 15th, however, all except three States, Hyderabad, Junagadh and Kashmir, had voluntarily acceded to the new Dominion, surrendering to it all essential powers for the exercise of effective direct sovereignty. Within the course of a year and a half the Princes had voluntarily withdrawn from the Government of the States and nowhere, except in Hyderabad, had even a show of force to be used. One after another the great sovereign Princes of India, who had represented the tradition of Indian monarchy for over 2,000 years, and some of whom claimed to have ruled over the same State for over 1,500 years, voluntarily handed over their territories, accepting a financial settlement for themselves and retiring into private life.

How did this remarkable revolution, so historic yet so bloodless, come about in a country known to be strongly wedded to ancient traditions and forms? How did the descendants of Rulers and potentates who had fought valiantly against the Moghuls to maintain their independence, like the Maharanas of Udaipur and the representatives of the great Maratha Empire who had contested with the British the sovereignty of Hindustan, and how did the successors to the dynasties like that of Cochin which were

[1] On the position of the Princes see Panikkar, *Indian States and the Government of India*, Martin Hopkinson, London, Second edition, 1932.

already ancient when Vasco da Gama negotiated with them, so meekly surrender their authority?

Those who claimed to know India well, British administrators who had lived in India for a lifetime, were convinced till the last moment that the Princes would not submit themselves to the authority of democratic leaders and, as they had their own armies, would resist any encroachments on their power, threatening certain civil war in which even the structure of the new India might perish. This was a widely held and frequently expressed view and seemed to have reason on its side, for what guarantee was there that the Indian army would obey the orders of its political masters, especially against Rulers to whom many in the army owed personal allegiance? The Rulers were, generally speaking, the leaders of the martial classes from which the army was recruited, Sikhs, Jats, Rajputs and Marathas. It was argued by these 'experts' that the communal loyalty and pride of these troops would have to be taken into consideration before the new Government decided to take any step against the States such as Kolhapur, whose dynasty was descended from Shivaji, the founder of the Maratha Empire, Udaipur, the recognized head of the Rajputs, Bharatpur, the leader of the martial Jats. Even Indian observers had not foreseen the disappearance of the Princely States which had from the beginning of history been a permanent characteristic of the Indian polity.

And yet to those who had tried to look beneath the surface, the inevitability of the new development should have been clear. In a work entitled *Indian States and the Government of India*, the present writer had drawn pointed attention to this fact as early as 1932. He emphasized that the States had ceased to be separate entities after the sense of Indian nationhood had come into being, that the system of education, the integration of economic life, the consolidation of communities and the growth of all-India political parties had rendered the conception of independent state units within India obsolete: that 'a barren dynasticism' was all that was standing in the way of unification, which the people of the States had already realized. The processes by which this unification of the mind had come into existence even before the departure of the British may be briefly examined here.

The strength of this 'integral nationalism', which made the people of the States and of British India feel and think alike as

Indians, had all along been underestimated. The Princes were maintained in their power by the British Government, whose authority, though questioned by Indians, was accepted by the Princes without reservation as they had become increasingly dependent on it. The basis of their authority over the people during 100 years of dependence had shifted to the power which the British Government put at their disposal. This was visibly demonstrated in almost every major principality during the half-century that followed the rebellion of 1857 when the paramount power had to intervene to prop up the authority of the Rulers, first against rebellious nobles and later against popular movements. The basis of hereditary authority had vanished in many States and weakened in many others.

The most remarkable instances of this change came from two of the most progressive and best-governed States in India, Mysore and Travancore. The prestige which the reigning dynasties of these two States enjoyed was immense. Their administrations were considerably in advance of those that most areas in British India possessed. They were in fact substantive States with a long and respectable tradition of good government. Feeling secure in the loyalty and affection of their people the Rulers hesitated to accede to the Indian Union. The State of Travancore especially, with a coastline of its own and rich natural resources, openly proclaimed its desire to remain independent. The Indian Union had not even come into existence: its prospects were uncertain and the Rulers hoped that they would be able to rally their loyal subjects on a cry of independence for themselves. But the results were the opposite of what the Rulers had anticipated. With no help from outside, for the Crown still claimed to protect the Rulers, the people of the two States rose as a man and forced their unwilling governments to surrender and join up with India. It was the strength of the national sentiment and the awakening of the masses by the Gandhian struggle which united India and forced the Princes to surrender their authority.

The fact was that the monarchical system in the States had lost its inherent strength: the authority of the Princes had become derivative, their administrations but reflections of the British Government and their sovereignty, though clothed in the decayed and tattered mantles of Indian kingship, was in the final analysis supported and propped up by British bayonets. No doubt, even the worst of them enjoyed the loyalty of his people, but only in comparison with the British Government. As against Indian nationalism, the hold of the Rulers had become weak long before the crisis arrived, as the fight for the tricolor (the national flag) in the different States had so clearly proved.

Many things had widened the cleavage between the Princes and the people. The contradiction of the Ruler's position had made him a supporter of British rule, and its agent in fighting the forces of nationalism. This became very marked during the period of Gandhiji's non-co-operation movement. That the popular awakening and the movement of non-co-operation should provoke the hostility of the Princes was understandable, but their open attempt, in alliance with reactionary forces in England, to break away from India by a dubious interpretation of their treaties, and their repeated offers in times of conflict between the National Congress and the Government 'to place their entire resources at the disposal of the Crown' to put down the popular movement placed them openly in the enemy's camp. Gandhiji's satyagraha at Rajkot—the capital of the Princely State of that name and the headquarters of the British Representative to the Kathiawar group of Rulers—made this contradiction a national issue. No compromise with the Princely system of government was possible after that incident. Even the meanest intelligence in India understood that the alliance between the Princes and the foreign Government was anti-national.

The people of the Indian States were the first to awake to this fact. The Gandhian movement had ignored the arbitrary political boundaries and had spread to the States. In the Princely States the British Government, unhampered by the limitations of its own law and interpreting its obligations in terms of the loyalty of the Rulers to the Crown and its corollary, the duty of the Crown to uphold the authority of the Rulers, intervened openly against the popular movement and assisted the Rulers in their repressive policy. The position of the States at the end of British rule in India may be described appropriately by quoting Professor Barraclough's description of the German Princely system before the Napoleonic invasions. 'Their boundaries still broken by enclaves and determined by the whims of dynastic accident corresponded to no reality. They were artificial creations unable to stand on their own feet and only existed as clients of France or opponents of France. The Princes who ruled them had no object except to continue to rule, unless it were to make their rule more profitable by adding more acres and more bodies to contribute to taxation. With rare exceptions they still acted largely as landed proprietors, who farmed their patrimony to raise an income to support their households, courts and palaces. Thus the resources of the land, dissipated in small fractions, were wasted on the upkeep of a senseless multiplicity of court establishments which served no useful purpose. When we view places like Zwinger in Dresden, or Bruchel, the residence after 1772 of the Prince-Bishop of Speyer, with their colonnades and wings and orangeries and pavilions, our admiration should be tempered by the knowledge that they were bought by the sweat of an oppressed peasantry, by the acceptance of subsidies from France. . . . It should be tempered also by the knowledge that the object of these establishments was to create an impression of solidity, permanence and magnificence, which was the very opposite of the truth, with the object of magnifying the distance between prince and subjects and holding the latter in political subjection. . . .'[1]

The claim to complete independence which some of the Rulers, especially the Nizam of Hyderabad, the Maharaja of Travancore and the Nawab of Bhopal, put forward and, in the case of the first at least, pressed to a desperate conclusion also proved to the people of India the danger of allowing dynastic loyalties to continue. The intrigue was not new. From 1927 an attempt had been made by some of the more ambitious Princes in alliance with powerful groups in England to break the administrative unity of India by keeping the Princes and States under the special protection of the Crown in England. But it was found that the economic and other ties which had been forged by a century of paramountcy could not be broken without ruining the entire fabric. The Federation Act of 1935 attempted to find a compromise, giving to the Princes and States a dominant voice in a united India. But mainly through the intransigence of the Nizam and the Nawab of Bhopal and other ambitious Princes the scheme could not be put into operation. When in 1946 the British Government affirmed their intention to withdraw from India, they added to it a condition that their authority over the States would automatically lapse and the Princes would regain their

[1] Barraclough, *Origins of Modern Germany*, Blackwell. pp. 389–90.

original status. Some of the major Princes, unaware of the strength of the forces of nationalism, were misled into thinking that the time was opportune for them to declare their independence. Hyderabad and Travancore took steps to implement this decision. In Travancore a popular upheaval drove out the dewan, while in Hyderabad it led to such a state of civil war and breakdown of administration that the Government of India had to intervene. The attitude of Hyderabad, Travancore and Bhopal brought home to the Government and people of India the realization of the grave danger represented by dynastic ambitions divorced altogether from national sentiment. It should however be added that the vast majority of Princes accepted the change as inevitable and patriotically surrendered their authority. More, many of them adjusted themselves to the conditions and sought honourably to serve the new government in different capacities as Governors and heads of new State units and as Ambassadors of India.

Thus it will be seen that the independence that India achieved was not only a liberation from British rule, but also a liberation from an age-long doctrine of fragmentation which had kept India divided even when the form of unity had been achieved. This was the work of the people themselves, because it was the people of the States that achieved this liberation and forced their own union with the rest of India. This represented a qualitative break with the past, giving to the period of history which began with the Act of Independence a significance which no mere transfer of power could have given.

The integration of the Princely States has been compared with Napoleonic policy in Germany and with Bismarck's establishment of the Second Reich. But the comparisons ignore a basic difference. The Napoleonic settlement of Germany was essentially an incorporation of the smaller States into the bigger ones, imposed in the interests of French policy by an external power. The Bismarckian settlement remained fundamentally feudal which, while it united the German people, also exalted the Prussian monarchy. It was in no sense a decision which reflected the will of the German people but only an agreement forced on weaker princes. The disappearance of the Indian Princes was fundamentally more important not only because it swept away a tradition which was as old as Indian history itself, but because it reflected the revolutionary democratic urge of the people, and the economic, social and spiritual unification that had been achieved by a slow process during a period of 100 years.

There are, no doubt, incurable historical romantics both inside and outside India who regret the passing of a system which added colour, pageantry and variety to Indian life, who echo Burke's eloquent description of the liquidation of the French nobility by the Revolution and lament the inevitable decay of the 'court culture' that the Princes had promoted in their different States. But, weighed in the scale of history, their assimilation was inevitable, as the Princes of India had long ago ceased to fulfil any political or social function, and had become an anachronism, picturesque no doubt, but dangerous to the course of Indian development and perhaps even to its new-found freedom.

The unity that has been achieved is not merely a political one, though the recolouring of the map and the elimination of local sovereignties are the most spectacular of its results. One hundred years of administration had united the areas into a single political structure known as British India and the territorial principalities, which lay interspersed with British India, had by copying the British administrative system followed closely behind. A customs union had transformed the whole of India, with the exception of Cutch, into a single unit for the purpose of external trade. After the first Great War, India had been recognized internationally as a single unit, and the treaties made with foreign powers on behalf of India had become binding on the States. But these political developments would hardly have counted, as the secession of Pakistan was clearly to demonstrate, towards the creation of a single united state in the rest of India, unless the people had believed in its necessity. Essentially, therefore, it was the people's conception of an integrated national State which suppressed the historic particularisms created by the language, past history and provincial rivalries and brought about the unification of India.

Also, it should not be forgotten that there were many material factors, which did not exist in any earlier period of India's history, making integration possible. A centrally-controlled railway system operated the length and breadth of India. Hard-surfaced roads intersected the provinces, making communications easy and isolation of provincial units difficult. Posts, telegraphs and telephones bound the country together. Air communications and a nationally-controlled broadcasting system brought even the most distant areas under the authority of the Centre. A uniform system of education created a like-mindedness against which the artificial boundaries of provinces and States provided no barrier. The social and religious movements which changed the face of India were nation-wide in their effects.

A common legal system and a uniform judicial administration helped to create not only a sense of community but provided a common background to political rights. The Rule of Law, by no means an alien conception to Hindus, gained a new content as regards relationships between man and man without reference to caste and between man and the State, undermining the doctrine of monarchical rule in Princely India. The national movement also ignored political divisions. The Princes themselves realized this and attempted to organize themselves through a Chamber of Princes, the very creation of which reduced them from their pretended status as monarchs of independent States to that of a privileged 'Order' in the national life of India.

A no less important factor in this process of unification was the creation of a single economy for the whole country. Economic life was not organized on a provincial basis. The markets for the products of the States lay in 'British' India. Indian industry was concentrated in certain centres and provincial or State considerations did not enter seriously into calculation. Industry developed where opportunity existed and its financial structure knew no territorial bounds. The unity of India is therefore not an artificial political creation but the genuine emergence of a single nation, welded together by social, economic and political forces. At first there remained outside the union two separate remnants of old Colonialism, Pondicherry, Karikal, Chandernagore, and Mahé under France and Goa, Daman and Diu under the Portuguese. The French authorities realized early that in the changed conditions of India it was impossible to maintain these isolated possessions and negotiated a peaceful transfer of territory to the Indian union. The Portuguese not only refused all negotiations but went to the extent of declaring Goa and the other Portuguese possessions in India as provinces of Portugal. In the face of Portugal's refusal to discuss any kind of voluntary liquidation the Indian Government felt compelled to eject the Colonial authorities and integrate the enclaves with the rest of India (December 20, 1961).

CHAPTER XIII

The Constitution

The Constitution of India embodies the changed sense of Indian unity brought about by its hundred years of evolution under British rule. The political concepts behind this document, which is the charter of India's freedom and national life, require careful analysis. It is a formidable document of 396 articles and numerous schedules, and reflects three main tendencies.

The first may be described as the circumstances of its own origin. The structure of the Constitution Act is taken from the Government of India Act 1935, a statutory enactment of the British Parliament. Though it is thus a written constitution, it is also based on the unwritten conventions of British parliamentary government. Nowhere in the document is it provided that the President of the Republic is a constitutional head of the State, that the Cabinet functions under a principle of collective responsibility, that the Prime Minister has the right of asking for the resignation of his colleagues, that he can advise the President to dissolve the House of the People and all the other accepted conventions of the British parliamentary system. In fact a perusal of the Constitution may even lead the student to the contrary conclusion. The Council of Ministers only 'advises' the President, who is expressly stated to be the head of all the armed forces of the Republic. The President appoints all the Governors of Provinces, summons and dissolves legislatures and is even given the authority to promulgate laws. Where then is it provided that the President is to act only on the advice of his Cabinet? The answer is in Bagehot, Dicey and Anson. The written Indian Constitution has to be read, interpreted and understood not in terms of its own express text but in terms of the unwritten conventions as expounded in English constitutional law.

In form the Constitution is federal: but it would be more accurate to describe it as statutory decentralization. The Federal doctrine has a curious history in India. When it was originally accepted by the Indian National Congress as its official policy, the object that Gandhiji and the national leaders had in mind was to give the Muslim majority provinces (now the Republic of Pakistan) the widest possible freedom from central control consistent with the unity of the old Indian Empire. The preponderance of Hindu authority in a Central Government, in whatever form it was constituted and whatever checks and balances were provided, was the unavoidable fact which made the Muslims feel that their position would be endangered in a united India, even though they were in a majority in some provinces. The Congress went to the extent of agreeing to a central authority limited to the most essential subjects and to all residuary power being vested in the provinces. The danger of such a constitution with an attenuated centre in a country like India was recognized by the Congress, but in the face of the implacable opposition of the Muslims it was felt to be the lesser of the two evils. With the separation of Pakistan the *raison d'être* of this weak federation vanished. Gradually the position veered round to a federal form with a unitary spirit, a strong centralized structure, with wide powers to the provinces.

In a country of the size of India where some of the provinces are larger in area and population than the largest European powers outside the Soviet Union, no form other than a federal one would have been feasible. Provincial problems, especially those associated with land tenure, irrigation, forestry, show marked differences arising from the continental character of India, and these can best be administered by provincial authorities. The maintenance of law and order over so vast a territory cannot also be effectively achieved except by provincial machinery. Distances alone make the centralization of judicial administration impossible, and to this should be added the wide differences in custom, in personal laws and in property rights in land. Federation alone provided a solution of these difficulties.

But it was equally clear that the fissiparous tendencies inherent in the Indian situation, which had led to the disruption of previous empires, would have to be carefully kept under check if the unity of India, achieved after so much struggle, was to be preserved;

consequently those forces which had contributed to that unity, such as a common legal system, the growth of a single economy, the maintenance of all-India civil services, the subordination of provincial administrations, the development of communal solidarity through the legislative reform of social customs, would have to remain within the sphere of the central government. Above all, if the backwardness of India in industry, technological skill, agricultural production and the numerous other economic factors which render her ineffective in the world, are to be remedied and the crucial problem of transforming her from an under-developed area into a great modern nation solved, by raising the standard of living, of health, of education and of general welfare, then the planning for all this has to be under a central direction unhampered by the statutory rights of state governments. The prolonged legal battles in the United States and Australia on these issues had convinced the fathers of the Indian Constitution that wisdom lay in altering the balance in favour of the Central Government and entrusting the provinces only with such powers as would not hamper the policy of the Centre in matters of general interest to the whole of India.

The Constitution thus gives all residuary powers to the Central Government. While following the general federal formula of a clear division of powers between the Centre and the units, the Indian Constitution also demarcates a very large area of concurrent powers, where the units are entitled to legislate subject to the overriding authority of the Centre. The concurrent sphere is the reserve area of the Centre, where it can intervene at will and oust provincial authority. Provincial Governors are to be nominated by the Central Government and are expressly given the authority of watching over all-India interests. Overall audit and powers of financial supervision remain with a centrally-controlled department. And finally the extraordinary power of superseding a Provincial Government is placed in the hands of the Centre. The Constitution also provides in express terms that the executive authority of the units should be so used as not to impinge on or interfere with the authority of the Central Government.

This brief summary will show how far the federal doctrine has been attenuated and the central authority strengthened in the new Indian Constitution. The theory of the co-ordinate powers of the Centre and the units, for a long time the favourite theme of constitutional lawyers, would hardly apply to the Indian Federation where the Centre is invested with such extraordinary powers and the provinces reduced frankly to a position of subordination. In fact, it may be said, India is starting her federation from the point which the United States has been trying to reach through a laborious process during the last 150 years. India has garnered the experience of federal constitutions in the past and tried to avoid their pitfalls. The essential difference has been that while the Fathers of the American Constitution were determined to give the Centre only the minimum, so that the maximum of sovereignty might be reserved for the States, the process was reversed in India, where the call for unity was stronger and dangers of disruption through lack of power at the Centre more real. Further, the history of India from the Regulating Act (1773) was one of the gradual growth of central power, and the country had thus become accustomed during a period of 175 years to an effective and complicated machinery of administration controlled from the Centre. The cry of the provinces in the past was not for sovereignty but for administrative decentralization, and with that background to have disrupted the structure of Indian unity to approximate more to the theory of federation would have been unwise as well as dangerous.

The second major tendency reflected in the Constitution is its desire to guarantee freedom of justice, liberty, equality and fraternity to the people of India. The preamble of the Constitution makes an unequivocal declaration to this effect. It reads: 'We the people of India having solemnly resolved to constitute India into a Sovereign Democratic Republic and to secure to all its citizens, JUSTICE, social economic and political, LIBERTY of thought, expression, belief, faith and worship, EQUALITY of status and opportunity and FRATERNITY assuring the dignity of the individual and *unity* of the nation . . . do hereby adopt, enact and give to ourselves this constitution.' (Italics added.) The entire Constitution can be interpreted in these terms and its every provision is designed to uphold and safeguard the unity of India achieved after so much struggle and to assure to all alike Justice, Liberty, Equality and Fraternity, each of which also finds a definition in the preamble. The primacy given to Justice—which finds no place in the revolutionary slogans of France—is especially significant. It has its origin both in the historic past of India, where the maintenance of Dharma was considered the supreme duty of the State. This ancient conception was extended and greatly transformed by the Rule of Law and a new approach to social and political justice which the composite character of the Indian population necessitated. The doctrine of economic justice is the outcome of socialist thought which has during the last 100 years transformed political conceptions in Europe and given to the problem of poverty and economic maladjustment in India an immediacy amounting to a revolutionary urge. When we consider the composition of India's population, its millions of depressed classes and backward tribes, its impoverished peasantry living on the margin of existence, its inherited social inequalities and its religious minorities, nervous and agitated about their future under a democratic government where power is related to numbers, the importance of this emphasis on social, economic and political justice will be fully appreciated.

Liberty, expressly defined to include thought, expression, belief, faith and worship, goes much beyond the narrow conception of political freedom. It is again a guarantee to the religious minorities for the undisturbed profession of their faiths. The emphasis on religious freedom has to be understood especially in terms of the fear and apprehensions of the Muslims and the Christians. For 400 years before British rule Islam had enjoyed a pre-eminence in India as the official religion of the Delhi Empires. After the establishment of British rule, this privileged position no doubt vanished, but, as mentioned before, a sense of political rivalry between Muslims and Hindus had grown up during the last half-century which poisoned the feeling of mutual toleration. The Muslims felt that in an independent India, which was predominantly Hindu, their religious freedom might not be respected. The widespread upheaval which followed the declaration of Independence, when over vast areas Hindus and Muslims shed each other's blood, made the minority community even more apprehensive of its future. It was therefore essential that adequate guarantees for the free profession of religion should exist in the Constitution.

So far as the Christian community was concerned, they felt that the activities of earlier missionaries, whose animosity towards Hinduism had caused widespread resentment and whose attempt to disrupt Hinduism had met with such determined resistance, might now react against themselves. They also were therefore apprehensive, especially as the privileged positions, which the Anglican establishment and the prestige which the missionaries generally as belonging to the ruling race enjoyed, had given them an artificial importance which they could no longer claim. This provision is also a declaration of faith in the tolerance of differences which is the basis of civilized life, of political action through moral persuasion and not coercion.

Equality is defined as both of status and of opportunity and has to be understood in the context of India's caste society, a reversion to which is a danger which had to be foreseen and prevented by every means. The main conception behind the doctrine of fraternity is the unity of the nation, the idea of an Indian nation in which all castes and communities are children of the same motherland. This is an idea which could not be said to have existed in India before the growth of Indian nationalism. Its slow development during the last 100 years, reaching its stage of fruition during the last twenty-five years of struggle, is what constitutes the central fact of the Indian Revolution.

The Constitution also embodies the gains of the social revolution of the past century. Following continental models, it has incorporated in the Act a declaration of Fundamental Rights in two parts, the first forming part of the Law of the Constitution, enforceable through the Courts, and the second described as Directive Principles of State Policy which, 'though not enforceable by any Court, are fundamental in the governance of the country' which it shall be the duty of the Government to promote—a charter of human rights which, by its comprehensive character, its tolerance, wide humanitarian feeling and general appreciation of the dangers, inherent in all States, of emphasizing power as against Liberty, may well be said to represent the ideals of Freedom which modern India cherishes.

The first part includes the right relating to equality, the basic provision of which is that the State shall not discriminate against any citizen on the grounds of religion, race, caste or sex. This is expressly extended to cover access to shops, hotels, restaurants, etc., and to the use of wells, tanks, roads, etc., maintained out of public funds. The purpose is clear. Jim Crowism of every kind, disabilities which previously existed as a result of caste and untouchability, are expressly banned in order to give to the doctrine of equality substance and authority so far as the untouchables and other depressed communities are concerned. Equality of opportunity in matters of public employment is guaranteed to women also. Untouchability is formally abolished and its practice made an offence punishable in accordance with law. Apart from providing for freedom of speech and expression, of assembly, of association, of circulation and other normal rights of the individual, this part also lays down that no child below the age of fourteen years shall be employed to work in any factory or mine or engaged in any hazardous employment.

The rights relating to religion which entitle the citizen to freedom of conscience and the right freely to profess, practise and propagate religion include a notable exception. Power is reserved expressly to legislate for social welfare or reform, for if the Constitution provided for neutrality in these matters on the ground that social institutions in India were tied up with religion, then the imperfectly achieved social revolution would have been interrupted and Hindu society especially would have gone back to its age-long customs and habits. Adequate guarantees for the protection of the cultural interests of ethnical groups and religious minorities are also included as fundamental rights.

Without proper and adequate sanctions, provision of human rights, however specific, will have but little meaning. In this matter the Indian Constitution leans heavily on British and American practice, the British system of writs by judicial courts, of *habeas corpus*, *mandamus*, prohibition, *quo warranto* and *certiorari certiorin* and the American practice of moving the Federal Court for the maintenance of the rights provided in the Constitution. In the absence of a written constitution the structure of freedom in England is founded on the right of the Courts, by the issue of writs, to enforce the rights under Common Law against the State no less than against other parties. In America, the rights being defined under the Constitution, it is made subject to litigation in Courts. The English system of writs has long been in operation in India and has been in the past an effective safeguard against which the administration had fretted and chafed. The application of the American system is new to India and, in a country given to the exercise of extreme subtleties in law and with a strong bent towards litigation, the opportunities for appealing to Courts for the maintenance of such a comprehensive scheme of fundamental rights may, while ensuring every freedom to the individual, tend to obstruct government at every turn.

The main Directive Principle of State policy lays down emphatically: 'The State shall strive to promote the welfare of the people by securing and protecting as effectively as it may a social order in which justice, social, economic and political, shall inform all the institutions of national life.' What is laid down specifically in order that this general principle may more effectively inspire the policies of Government constitutes a social programme of the highest importance. The general tendency of these directives is to introduce a wide measure of socialism in the economic sphere, to provide social security and better standards of sanitation and care for all, to emphasize the duty towards women and children and the obligations towards backward and tribal classes. The clauses dealing with the future economy of India lay down specifically that the State should ensure that the ownership and control of material resources of the community are so distributed as best to serve the common good; that the operation of the economic system does not result in the concentration of wealth and the means of production to the common detriment. The clauses relating to social welfare direct that the State shall, within the limits of its economic capacity and development, make effective provision for securing the right to work, to education and to public assistance in case of unemployment, old age, sickness, disablement and other causes of undeserved want.

It is obvious that the overwhelming anxiety of the Constituent Assembly and the Fathers of the Constitution has been to guarantee in every manner possible a sense of justice, equality, freedom and security to all minorities in India and to uphold the principle of a composite secular State. Every section of the Constitution provides evidence of this burning desire to satisfy the racial, religious and ethnical groups outside Hinduism that India is not going to be a Hindustan—a country exclusively of Hindus in which other communities exist only by sufferance: that the religion, culture and interests of all alike are safeguarded in the Constitution, and the sense of distrust and fear, which had for so long made India a cockpit of communal strife, may now be laid at rest.

The establishment of a Supreme Court, independent of the executive government, and of public services free from the taint of political affiliations are two other features of the Constitution meant alike to uphold the unity of India and to ensure impartial administration of rights. The Supreme Court is the coping stone of the constitutional structure. As in England the Judges cannot be removed except by a resolution of the two Houses. The powers entrusted to the court in the matter of constitutional interpretation are plenary and beyond the question of executive authority. More specifically, the Court has been vested with the authority to enforce the fundamental rights of the individual both by writs as well as by decisions on issues raised before it.

The provisions with regard to the civil services are perhaps unique, as no parallel exists either in British constitutional practice or in the federal constitution of America. The Indian Constitution provides for central and provincial public service commissions outside the day-to-day control of parliamentary government. The motives behind these provisions are two. They are meant in the first place to create an administrative steel frame for the unity of India. An all-India machinery, free as far as possible from provincial allegiances, and dealing with the problem from a united central point of view, was imperatively necessary if the regional tendencies were not again to assert themselves. The superior administrative services of India include not merely the ICS or its present counterpart the IAS, but the Indian Police, Audit and Account, Customs, Post, Telegraphs and Railways. The superior administration in these spheres in the states are in the hands of these centrally recruited and centrally trained All-India services.

The second object of this system is to ensure that every community has an equal chance in the services. All recruitment is on the basis of competitive examinations conducted by the Public Service Commission. The rights, privileges and emoluments of officials are made independent of the whims and caprices of politicians. The Public Service Commission is a guarantee to all the minorities that the bureaucracy of the future will not be recruited from any favoured castes or communities, but on the basis of merit. In this matter India had the advantage of a long civil service tradition built up by the All-India services under the British Government. Although in the last twenty-five years of British authority a strenuous attempt was made to introduce into the services also a communal virus, by determining proportions of appointments, the idea of an independent administrative machine, upholding the rights of all and secure in its tenure, is an inheritance from British rule.

These features of the Indian Constitution, which secure and uphold the right of the minorities, have already demonstrated their importance in building up a national life. The minorities, especially the Muslims who for a period of forty years had enjoyed the right of separate and exclusive representation in every sphere of popular government through the device of separate Muslim electoral rolls, voluntarily gave up the privileges which had isolated them from the rest of the community and created the theory of two nations. The Anglo-Indian community which felt orphaned by the withdrawal of the British, as it had for over a century identified itself with the interests of the Europeans in India, and whose economic existence had been dependent on special spheres of secure employment, such as railways and telegraphs, where their loyalty to the rulers was considered an important asset; the Christians who felt that the latent animosity to the missionaries, whose anti-Hindu propaganda in the past had earned them a wide measure of unpopularity among all classes, might be reflected against their community; the Untouchables who feared that free India would be dominated by caste Hindus who, even if they did not enforce against them the restrictions of the past, might at least neglect their further progress and endeavour to stabilize the present position of superiority of caste Hindus, were all equally assured by the comprehensive safeguards introduced by the Constitution. The Indian people after mature deliberation rejected 'Hindustan' as against Pakistan, and opted for a secular India, where every community had equal rights, privileges and duties.

CHAPTER XIV

The Composite Secular State

'The co-existence of several nations under the same State is a test as well as the best security of its freedom. It is also one of the chief instruments of its civilization', declared Lord Acton. He elaborated the same conception when he added: 'If we take the establishment of liberty for the realization of duties to be the end of civil society, we must conclude that those States are substantially the most perfect which include various distinct nationalities without oppressing them'.

The circumstances of India's historical evolution gave the Indian people a choice of ways, the creation of a composite secular State, or of a Hindu State. The separation of the areas having a majority of Muslims and their organization as an Islamic State, as officially proclaimed by Pakistan, gave rise to a parallel movement among the Hindus that India should be established as a Hindustan based on the conceptions of Hindu Dharma. The movement secured considerable support among certain sections of aggressive Hindus who had long opposed what it called the policy of Muslim appeasement. It also appealed to the embittered millions who had lost their all in the uprooting of communities that followed partition. Why, it was asked, should India not follow a liberal policy towards the minorities while declaring itself to be a Hindu State and basing its constitution on Hindu ideals? Western history provided ample illustrations to support such a course. Was not England itself a Protestant State, which supported an official church and where the monarch was not free to profess any other religion and where the Catholics still suffered some though minor legal disabilities? Is not Catholicism the official religion of Eire and did not other European countries recognize the pre-eminence of the faith of the majority? Why should the Hindus who number no less than 310 millions out of a population of 360 million (1951) deny themselves a pre-eminent position in India merely for the sake of placating a Muslim minority, which, by its unquestioned acceptance of the two-nation theory in the past, had shown itself to be disloyal to any idea of a composite State? Such was the theory of which the Rashtriya Swayam Sevak Sangh (RSS) was the champion. Primarily it was Gandhiji and the Congress as shaped by him that stood against this doctrine.

And it was for this that the Mahatma had to lay down his life.

Out of India's total population of 360 million (in 1951 when the Constitution was framed), no less than 30 to 35 millions were Muslims. The Christian population numbered 7 millions, the Sikhs 6 millions, Buddhists over a million, Parsis a hundred thousand. There are also spread all over India small communities of Jews, Armenians and Arabs who have settled down in the country and consider India as their home. While no doubt the population is predominantly Hindu, the tradition of India during the last 150 years has been pre-eminently secular, probably for the reason that the Government being in the hands of foreigners it had perforce to follow a policy of neutrality.

But the composite character of India's political structure is not derived from European traditions. Even in the days when the kings professed orthodox Hinduism, they welcomed and gave not only protection but special rights to religious minorities. The Parsis in Gujerat, the Christian communities on the Malabar coast and the Jews at Cochin, all enjoyed special rights and privileges. In fact the doctrine of the religious State, which excluded other forms of worship, or when it tolerated other faiths gave them an inferior position, was never a part of Indian tradition. The expulsion of the Moors, the Test Acts and Exclusion of Dissenters, the Revocation of the Edict of Nantes and other such manifestations of the doctrine of a single community enjoying political power in the State is a Christian conception developed in Europe.

What is the Secular State which India claims to be? It postulates that political institutions must be based on the economic and social interests of the entire community, without reference to religion, race or sect: that all must enjoy equal rights but no privileges, prescriptive rights or special claims should be allowed for any group on the basis of religion. Secondly it eliminates from the body politic all ideas of division between individuals and groups on the basis of their faith or racial origin. In a country which has had forty years of history based on separate electorates, communal proportion in all appointments from the meanest to the highest, where a man's preferment depended mainly on his separateness from, if not animosity towards, members of other religions or communities, this is a definite breach with the immediate past. In the third place it is obvious that a composite secular state must accept as the basis of its policy what Aristotle termed 'distributive justice', that all communities must share the power as they must share the duties and responsibilities of being a citizen.

How far India has upheld these principles in practice and not merely enunciated them theoretically may now be examined. As we have seen, the Constitution provides the most specific and precise guarantees with easy processes of effectuation for the protection of the faith and worship of all religions, for the maintenance of culture of different communities, for non-discrimination in avenues of public employment, etc. In practice effect has been given to this ideal in every sphere of employment. In the Central Government of India, every major religious group is represented: so also among other major appointments like Judgeships of the Supreme Court, Governorships, etc. In diplomatic appointments abroad the percentage of the members of the minority communities is much larger than their numerical strength warrants. It is only where the recruitment of service is through open competitive examination that some of the communities may claim that their representation is not adequate. Broadly speaking however it can be claimed that the composite secular state is a working fact in India, in Acton's words 'the test as well as the best security of its freedom'.

The opposition to the secular state came mainly from a section of the Hindus who felt that a great opportunity was lost for identifying Hinduism with the new State. It also came from a section of the small but aggressive Sikh community, which demanded the right to be treated as an entity enjoying special political rights. The Sikhs are a religious group, a militant sect born out of Hinduism. They are concentrated mainly in the Punjab. In the time of the British they were a specially favoured community as they were counted among the more important martial classes from which the British Indian Army was recruited. The Sikh regiments in the Indian Army were famous for their fighting spirit and their loyalty and consequently during British rule they were given weightage in political representation, election on the basis of separate rolls and a higher percentage in appointments than their number warranted. In the partition of the Punjab the community suffered heavily, as a little more than half of its population was in West Punjab, where they owned vast tracts of irrigated land. They were uprooted to a man from that area and became displaced persons in India. Some among them felt that they had special claims, that the Constitution should provide special political and other rights for them. A secular state which, while guaranteeing all minorities their freedom of religion and culture, refused to treat them as a political community entitled on the basis of their religion to political rights, seemed to them a denial of what the British had for so long a time given them, and considerable opposition to the scheme of the Constitution was voiced by the more communal-minded among them. But the principle of the secular state was not one on which new India could compromise, and the effective action that the Government took in suppressing that agitation and the support which it received not only from the other communities but from the more progressive sections of the Sikhs themselves is the best demonstration of the strength of the new idea.

It is however necessary to clear up one misunderstanding. Secularism in Europe, especially in the Third Republic and the revolutionary regime in Mexico, Spain and other countries, is associated with movements against religious education, against the influence of religious bodies in public life, against the recognition of any special position for religious organizations. The secular state in the West has therefore become identified with an active movement for the elimination of religious influences in the State and especially in education. This is not the meaning given to the secular state in India.

The Constitution recognizes the right of every community to maintain its own educational institutions to teach religion to those belonging to the faith. What it does prohibit is the compulsory teaching of the doctrines of one's religion to others, for the State has the obligation to see that if it permits private organizations to undertake the work of education, which is its own function, the the right so given is not abused in the interests of particular religious faiths. The secular Indian State gives large subsidies to the Benares University which is a Hindu endowment, to the Aligarh University with its emphasis on Muslim studies, and to many other institutions maintained by religious bodies. It arranges special facilities for Muslims to make their annual pilgrimages to Mecca, maintains under semi-official control Buddhist, Hindu and Muslim places of pilgrimage and assists in the renovation of temples, mosques and shrines. The Indian State by becoming secular has not become irreligious. Its secularism is negative in the sense of not permitting religious considerations to enter into the principles of state action, and this arises basically from a desire to be just to the members of all religious communities inhabiting India.

The fact that Pakistan had opted definitely for an 'Islamic' State and had declared her intention to establish a democracy based on the teachings of religion made it necessary for India to define clearly her own attitude. The very doctrine which led to the establishment of Pakistan as a separate State—the theory of India being composed of two nations, Islamic and Hindu—contained within itself the germs of two theocratic States, Pakistan and Hindustan. The Indian National Congress has from the very beginning denied the two-nation theory as historically incorrect, ethnically baseless and politically dangerous. Even after the secession of the Muslim majority provinces was accepted as inevitable, the Congress had courage enough to hold to its convictions and declare that India held to the theory of the composite secular state and, whatever position Pakistan might give to other religious groups, India would not depart from her principle of equal rights for all, irrespective of religion, within the Indian State.

CHAPTER XV

Democracy

Gandhiji's political ideals, as we have seen, centred round the village. His idea of an Indian Democracy was as a union of self-governing, self-supporting and self-educated villages, with the minimum of intermediate and central governments necessary to keep them together. A scheme of village councils electing representatives to district bodies who in turn elect a provincial assembly, culminating in a supreme central legislature strengthened by men dedicated to the service of villages, seems to have been his conception of the constitution of India. This arcadian scheme bears a curious and strange similarity to the Soviet constitution in which, beginning with village and factory Soviets of peasants and workers, the elaborate structure culminates in the Supreme Soviet of the USSR. The differences were mainly two but basic. Firstly, while in the USSR the emphasis is on the factory workers, in Gandhiji's scheme it is almost exclusively on the peasants. Secondly the Soviet Centralism invested the Supreme Soviet with the plenitude of power while Gandhiji wanted only a minimum of government from the top. But Indian opinion decisively rejected the Gandhian idea in this matter. It was not a rural democracy—an idealized system of village republics—that the Constituent Assembly after two years of earnest consideration decided to adopt. It was a parliamentary system, a democratic structure in which power was concentrated not at the bottom but at the centre, that India chose to erect on the foundations left behind by Britain.

In fact, India had but little choice. A central legislature had been in existence in India from 1848. A hundred years of history could not easily have been wiped out. Gradually the legislature had been enlarged (1861, 1895, 1909, 1921) to include, first, nominated Indian representatives and later, members elected indirectly from provincial legislatures, and finally in 1921 it was transformed by the acceptance of direct elections on a broad franchise into a national parliament. In the provinces also a similar evo ution had taken place. Local self-government in districts and municipal areas had been made popular in 1882. Thus the structure of parliamentary democracy had been reared on a solid foundation over a period of 100 years. India did not start on her democratic career on the date of her independence. She had travelled along the road for a considerable distance and it was impossible for her to retrace her steps.

The structure of her democracy was also decided by other factors, political, economic and social. The security of her frontiers became an urgent and overwhelming problem with the achievement of independence. Partition created an undefended land frontier on the east and the west. The sense of fear, distrust and suspicion, which the uprooting populations on both sides of the frontier left as a heritage both to India and Pakistan, forced on the nation a policy of building up a strong central government which would be able to safeguard its liberty. The requirements of national security, and the crises that followed one after another, made it imperative that the Government should be so constituted as to have control over the entire national resources. The resettlement of over 8 million refugees, a problem which both by its suddenness, magnitude and the unimaginable tragedy behind it awakened the newborn State to the responsibilities of freedom, would in itself have been a factor of outstanding importance in the shaping of the Indian Constitution. But the troubles that followed the riots, the killings and the unsettlement, though fortunately limited to certain areas, showed that liberty had to be defended from internal, no less than from external foes. The troubles in Kashmir and Hyderabad only strengthened this feeling. The evolution of a leviathan State, in which considerations of its own security took first place, was thus rendered unavoidable.

The context of international affairs also led to the same result. India found herself thrust forward into a world divided into two opposite camps. A major revolution was changing the face of her neighbour, China. Burma, which had been so closely associated with India for many decades and with whom her ties were intimate, was then torn by civil war. In Vietnam and in Indonesia colonial powers were carrying on a life and death struggle with the forces of nationalism. Nothing seemed more obvious than that India would be incapacitated from playing her part in the affairs of the world unless her political structure was firm and unbreakable, her forces organized effectively to meet every danger and her authority firmly established over the whole of her territory.

Economic forces pulled the same way. Her major areas of food supply had gone to Pakistan. Stark famine faced many parts of the country during the first three years. The world itself was passing through a period of economic controls as a result of which the flow of food into the country was possible only through governmental efforts. Naturally this led to an enormous increase in the authority of the Centre and a general recognition that, in view of the chronic nature of the problem, all preconceived notions of limiting central authority to a few subjects should be discarded.

The problem that India had to face as a result of these complex factors was how to reconcile free institutions with the growth of a leviathan state, clothed with the plenitude of authority, of which even the British Government, in its days of bureaucratic centralization, would never have dreamed. A parliamentary system in which all authority was concentrated in a Cabinet responsible and strictly accountable to a legislature elected on adult franchise seemed to be the most acceptable method. It is not that India did not give the fullest consideration to the American system of presidential government. The checks and balances of the American Constitution, its sharing of power between different elected authorities, its parliamentary procedure, and its still powerful tradition of State rights all came up for consideration in the Committees of the Constituent Assembly. What finally decided the fathers of the Constitution to follow in the main the British model was the necessity to entrust the Cabinet with the totality of government power in order to enable it, under the supervision and mandate of Parliament, to deal effectively with every issue of national importance.

The main features of the Indian parliamentary system are adult franchise and direct elections to the House of the People, indirect elections through State legislatures to the House of the States, financial authority and budgetary control confined to the Lower House, the resolving of differences between the two Houses by joint sessions, the vesting of executive authority in a Cabinet enjoying the confidence of the Lower House, the President acting only on the advice of his Cabinet, and the constitutionality or otherwise of legislative actions being determined by the Supreme Court. On two fundamental points it differs from the British system. The British Parliament is absolute in its sovereignty and no act of Parliament can be challenged in a Court of Law. The Indian Constitution, following the model of the United States has, as we have seen, established a Supreme Court which is entrusted with the right and duty of upholding the Constitution. Legislation which impinges on fundamental rights or encroaches on the authority of the units can be challenged in the Supreme Court, and thus an absolute safeguard is provided against the encroachments of Parliament on the basic freedoms of the people. Secondly, unlike the United Kingdom, India is a federation with State legislatures functioning with sovereign authority within their own sphere. The Provincial or State legislatures within the range of their own powers exercise absolute and final authority and are not subject to the control of the Central Parliament. It is true that this sphere has been limited by the wide range of concurrent legislature authority, but nonetheless the states retain final powers in regard to a number of important aspects of Government. Federation, though attenuated by the desire of the Indian people to strengthen its Central Government, remains the basis of India's democracy.

There is no doubt that the democratic structure of India is a victory for the forces of liberalism. The creation of a leviathan State based on the principles of parliamentary democracy as the outcome of a prolonged revolutionary agitation may look strange. The reasons, apart from the requirements of a dangerous situation arising from the partition analysed above, lie in the traditional conservatism of the middle classes who were unwilling to try new experiments or to jeopardize their newly-won liberty by following blindly either those who beckoned from afar to a dubious new-fangled paradise based on the theories of class struggle, or others who pleaded for reaction by pointing to the mystic greatness of glorious eras in the past. The erstwhile advocates of civil disobedience, whose motto was *Inquilab Zindabad*, victory to the revolution, became the champions of ordered society, and equally those who had seen virtues and glories in the past and talked about constitutions suited to India's tradition and genius became the advocates of the secular state.

The liberalism of the Indian intelligentsia found a middle way.

The principles that the Constitution embodies and the political structure it has endeavoured to erect are undoubtedly Western. India no doubt had her own republican forms of Government and methods of democratic organization in ancient times. Great republican states existed for over a 1,000 years in the Gangetic Valley. There is also ample evidence that the methods of election, vote and rule by the decision of the majority were known and practised at certain periods. But no one would deny that the present Constitution of republican India derives its inspiration from Western models and is devised to uphold principles which have also been assimilated from the West.

While this is indubitably true, so far as the Constitution itself is concerned, the administrative structure which supplements the Constitution is wholly Indian, though in its organizational aspects it may bear the British stamp.

The Mauryan Empire, the first governmental organization in India of which we have any detailed knowledge, was essentially a bureaucratic state, undertaking a comprehensive control of economic functions. In fact all the empires in India including that of the Moghuls were bureaucratic in their organization, with the district as the basis of administration. It is on this system inherited from the Moghuls that the British had built, introducing with it, however, one major innovation, that of selection by open competitive examination, borrowed it would seem, from the Chinese.[1]

It is this imperial bureaucracy which republican India has today inherited and which functions as the effectuating machinery of the State. As has been stated elsewhere, 'The system that Chanakya perfected or inherited, or in any case described, endured without much change through the ages. The Hindu Kings to the last followed the organization of the Mauryan Empire, in its three essential aspects: the revenue system, the bureaucracy and the police. The organization as it existed was taken over by the Muslim rulers and from them by the British. If the Indian

[1] See Panikkar, *The Origin and History of Civil Services*, Srinivasa Sastri Lectures, Madras University, Madras, 1956.

administration of today is analysed to its bases the doctrines and practices of Chanakya will be found to be still in force.'

It is important to realize that the great European States developed nothing like the centralized bureaucracies of the Asian Empires. Feudalism, which was essentially a fragmentation of State authority, prevented the growth of the non-hereditary official who specialized in administrative work. The great civil services of India, both administrative and technical, are therefore in the genuine tradition of the country and not borrowed from Europe. Even their functions, revenue administration, water control and direction of economic activities, have not basically changed. It is on this ancient foundation that the political superstructure has been raised and the unity of the State established.

In the reorganization of the state structure of the federation which was undertaken in 1956 the governing principle, as stated by the Commission appointed to enquire and report on this question, was the primacy of the Union as against the units of the Federation. While conceding the principle of linguistic homogeneity as a major factor in the reconstitution of the States, the Commission emphasized the necessity to uphold all-India interests in the economic and political sphere, and made recommendations to strengthen the Central Administration and to prevent the growth of separatist tendencies. Parliamentary legislation has given full effect to these by giving greater content to the conception of a common citizenship, by taking over final authority in the matter of inter-state water rights, by investing itself with the right to give directions to State governments about the treatment to be accorded to minority groups, etc. As a result of these changes, the reorganization of the States on a generally linguistic basis, which many people feared might loosen the bonds of unity by encouraging local loyalties, has enabled the Central Government to forge additional links of union.

Equally significant is the pattern of integration which is reflected in the all-India institutions. The central institution for military training is to be located near Poona. The chief base for the Indian Navy is at Cochin, in the extreme south. The aeroplane factory is located in Bangalore while her shipyards are in Vizagapatam and Bombay. The research institutions that the new State has started are to be dispersed all over India. The economic planning of the country looks at India as a single community, and provincial and local considerations are not being allowed to stand in the way of all-India decisions. Most irrigation and power plans cover more than one province: the Bhakra Dam scheme, for example, includes within its scope the Punjab and the northern area of Rajasthan. The desire to bind together the regions not only by constitutional provisions but by economic ties is written large in the history of the last fifteen years.

These are but indications of the single purpose which lies behind the Indian political structure, the welding together of India into a single community united in democratic freedom, guaranteeing to each man and each group the right to the fullest existence possible in civilized society.

The picture of India fifteen years after her independence is of a country anxious to preserve its liberal traditions of freedom, but egged on to move quickly by a sense of fear and an ambition for rapid achievement—a fear that she may be left behind again in the race for economic prosperity and progress in the conditions of the New World: a fear that with her population increasing at the rate of eight millions a year she may not, without super-human effort, be able to eradicate the poverty and malnutrition which holds her people down; and an ambition to justify before the world her claim to be a progressive community and a State wedded to a policy of social and economic amelioration. The terrors that haunted it were not few: famine, social reaction, pressure from outside, failure of capital, crisis in confidence, millions of displaced persons uprooted from their homes—liabilities which would have strained the statesmanship and the finances of any Government in the world. Some of these were inherited from the past: especially the problem of food which had been raising its ugly head for many decades.

There was also the terror caused by the Kuomintang example: the failure of a revolution that started so well and collapsed because it could not safeguard freedom, or deal with essential economic problems. The fate of the Kuomintang was a dire warning, which helped India to realize that she must, even in the extreme crisis that faced her, hold aloft the banner of liberty and place social amelioration and economic advancement as the primary objects of her government. All these are reflected in the democracy that India has built up. Her constitution maintains and upholds the essential democratic freedoms. It has written prominently into its fundamental laws the conception of a State whose main duty is to achieve economic and social justice and to ensure that the wealth of the nation is used for the benefit of the nation.

Revolutions are inevitably followed by disillusionment. The New Jerusalem does not descend immediately and the more eager spirits feel thwarted and frustrated at the slowness of practical achievement. In India, if the widespread disillusionment of the first eighteen months did not lead either to the growth of reaction, to the development of a Communist challenge, or to a dictatorship, it was due to achievements, both idealistic and practical, which struck the people's imagination; the evolution of a constitution embodying the principles of freedom, no less than the liquidation of the feudal Princes; the determination at all costs to hold on to the ideal of a sovereign republic, no less than the vast schemes of irrigation and industrialization and resettlement of refugees to which the Government devoted all their attention.

PART V

THE MAHATMA AND MARX

CHAPTER XVI

The Mahatma

Though the foundations of new India are buried deep in her own past, the present structure of her society, her political organization and economic life are the outcome of many factors—not the least important of which has been her prolonged association with the liberal movements in Western Europe. The Indian mind in the nineteenth and the early twentieth century was, as we have seen, greatly influenced by the liberal thought of the West. But in the quarter of a century that preceded her independence two other major factors began to shape both her thinking and her action. Mahatma Gandhi took over the leadership of the national movement and for over twenty-five years shaped not only the course of India's history but left an indelible imprint on the thinking of India. The political and social heritage of India bears his imprint and it is necessary to examine how far the Mahatma's influence is a continuing one in independent India.

The second factor which undoubtedly is of growing importance is that of Marx. Socialism became a major influence with the younger generation of India in the thirties but, during the struggle for independence, its influence was limited to a group of intellectuals. With independence, however, it became a growing factor, especially in relation to India's economic thinking. It is, therefore, important to assess the contribution of Marxian ideas to India's new life and the prospects of their permanent impact on Indian thought.

Mahatma Gandhi's contribution to the achievement of India's independence is universally recognized. It is he who converted Indian nationalism, a movement confined to intellectual middle classes, into a revolutionary mass struggle. It is he who developed its organization and disciplines and provided it with a method of effective action. Beyond all this, it is to his credit that he endowed it with an urge for social justice, with a passion for equality and aroused the conscience of India to the conditions of the depressed classes and other underprivileged sections of the community. The emphasis on rural India and the moral fervour which he imparted to the national movement in respect of the uplift of the untouchables were also important aspects of the Gandhian movement. The Mahatma's wide sense of tolerance and his consistently friendly attitude to the British people, while denouncing the British Government as satanic, also left their mark on the Indian national struggle. The question, however, is not the influence that Gandhiji exercised in his lifetime, but how far it is a continuing process in Independent India.

Mahatma Gandhi is generally styled the Father of the Nation. All parties in the country, including the Communists, pay homage to him. In fact, the leaders of most Indian parties—the Congress, the Praja Socialists, the Socialists and the Communists—were, at one time or other, associated with him or worked under his leadership. His ideas and teachings are not the exclusive possessions of any party, and even those who are today opposed to what may be called Gandhism have been greatly influenced by him. While all this will be accepted by most students of Indian life, the question remains and is often asked whether in the political life of India today, after fifteen years of independence, the Mahatma exercises any considerable influence; whether such influence as he still exercises is not a diminishing one, and whether, when those who were immediately associated with him, an ageing group who in the course of the next few years are bound gradually to disappear, cease to guide Indian politics, anything will be left of Gandhism.

To a casual observer, the achievements of India after Independence would appear to be based on other than Gandhian principles. It is not on the basis of handicraft industry, as Gandhiji hoped and Gandhian economics taught, that India has during the last fifteen years built up her economy. Her giant steel mills and other enterprises in the public sector represent the very opposite of Gandhian teaching. In fact, the so-called Gandhian economists in India denounce them as a betrayal. Rapid large-scale industrialization is the ideal that India has set for herself. That it is different from Gandhiji's vision of India requires no proof for his whole life was a protest against industrialized society.

To him *khaddar* or *khadi* represented an ideal of civilization, a symbol of human necessities being satisfied by men and women individually working in villages. True, most Congress leaders even now wear *khadi*; on formal occasions such as Gandhiji's birthday they even spin. The Central and local governments also give considerable financial and other support for the production and sale of *khadi*. But for all this demonstrative allegiance to the Mahatma's doctrines, very few will today claim for his teachings any influence on India's policy. We no longer hear of *ahimsa* or non-violence—a principle to which Gandhi attached fundamental importance. On the other hand, India is straining every nerve to arm herself to the teeth. That every nation requires armed forces for its defence—however much Mr Krushchev may talk of total disarmament—is obvious. Not even during Gandhiji's lifetime did the Congress leaders in India accept the doctrine of non-violence in regard to defence. But India's policy has gone much beyond the doctrine of essential self-defence. No doubt this is due to the growth of conditions on her borders which compelled India to interpret the requirements of her defence rather elastically. The growth of Pakistan's military power as a result of her alliance with America and the supply of up-to-date arms and equipment and her threatening attitude in regard to Kashmir rendered it necessary that India should also develop her defence forces adequately. The change in Tibet's status and the gradual build-up of Chinese military forces on India's northern border--not to speak of the Chinese occupation of a stretch of Indian territory in Ladakh—created for her problems which the British Empire in India did not have to face. Consequently, during the last few years India has been increasingly devoting her attention to military problems, strengthening her forces in every way. It is not the urgency of this problem nor its justification which is under question. That India should develop her defence resources to full capacity if she is to uphold her independence and maintain her influence in international affairs will not be denied by anybody. That she should provide herself with the most up-to-date arms and that for these she should not be dependent on others are indeed obvious facts. That this policy could not be reconciled with *ahimsa* and the doctrine of non-violent resistance to evil is also obvious. In fact, no one concerned with politics in India today talks of *ahimsa*.

The same oblivion has not fallen on the Mahatma's doctrine of satyagraha as an effective weapon in politics only because minor political leaders here and there show a tendency to degrade it by invoking its name to cover every kind of ridiculous agitation. But the failure of these so-called satyagrahas has only helped to discredit what was in the hands of the Mahatma an irresistible instrument of mass action. With free political institutions functioning at all levels, from the central government to village panchayats, with freedom of speech, and full civil liberties, it becomes difficult to wield satyagraha as a political weapon on a national scale. To use it for limited local purposes has been found to be ineffective when other and more effective courses of action are open to the public.

If satyagraha, as Gandhiji viewed it, has disappeared from the political scene, fasting as a political weapon, which also was one of the Gandhian techniques, today stands totally discredited. The Mahatma resorted to this weapon only when he considered moral issues were at stake. But fasting by political leaders in the post-independence period has been mainly to secure some political point which had no moral issues behind it. Poti Ramulu's fast was meant as a protest against the Government of India's delay in constituting the Andhra State. The latest instances of political fasting, Master Tara Singh's fast unto death to get the Government of India to accept the principle of a Punjabi Suba and the Muniraj's counter-fast to ensure that Master Tara Singh did not succeed in his object, reduced the whole method to an absurdity and had the result of discrediting fasts and hunger-strikes as political weapons.

Another aspect of Gandhian thought was the Mahatma's distrust of state action. It was one of his sayings that he liked that government which governed the least. His idea of a state was that of an individualist who considered state action, outside a limited sphere, to be interference with the individual's liberties. He was in fact a determined opponent of the leviathan state. In this sphere also he could not be said to have influenced Indian thinking. The major characteristic of India's development after independence is the growth of state functions in all directions. Economic planning, social legislation, community development, educational policies—in fact in every sphere of human interest—the new Indian State has extended its activities. It has even tried to organize the *sadhus*, sanyasis who have renounced the world. Nowhere has the departure from the Gandhian ideal been so great as in the development of state activities. Indian politics are libertarian but the Indian State is totalitarian only as a welfare state can be.

In what may be called minor issues also, Gandhian ideals have come under eclipse. Prohibition was an idea very dear to the Mahatma. In his lifetime the elimination of alcoholic drinks was an important plank in all Congress programmes. So deeply was the Congress committed to this policy that its impetus continued for a time even after India became independent. But what is the position now? Though Congressmen as a body claim to be teetotalers, prohibition as a national policy is not even being talked about. With some difficulty the States in which prohibition was introduced in the first enthusiasm are carrying on with it even now. There is however no talk now of enforcing it on an all-India scale.

If *ahimsa* and satyagraha are not doctrines which exercise any great influence in Indian polities, if *khadi* economics and handicraft civilization have been discarded in favour of large-scale industrialization based on continuous planning and state control, if India is developing into a welfare state with planned activities extending to every sphere, what then is left of the Mahatma's inheritance? It is obvious that India is now developing along lines which the Mahatma had opposed during his entire lifetime. This cannot be denied. In fact the true blue Gandhians in India from Vinoba Bhave and Mira Ben[1] down to the least important occupants of ashrams in different parts of India openly complain that Gandhiji has been betrayed and that the India that is developing before their eyes is something which would have appeared monstrous to Gandhiji's eyes. Would it then be right to say that the Mahatma is now no more than a legend to which people pay homage and that his teachings have no more influence with the people of India? That would indeed be an exaggeration. Though his economic ideas have been discarded—and in fact would never seem to have been seriously accepted or believed in—and his political methods are no longer considered useful or effective, there are important spheres of national life where the Mahatma's

[1] See in this connection the moving autobiobraphy of Mira Ben (Miss Salde), entitled *The Spirit's Pilgrimage*.

teachings continue to shape national policy. The most important of these is the burning sense of social justice which he brought into national life, and which showed itself most prominently in his identification with the Harijans in India. Nothing moved him so much as the inhumanity with which Hinduism had throughout history treated the Depressed Classes. To him untouchability was the great sin for which India was paying the penalty. His approach to this question was not of a social reformer but of a humble penitent who identified himself with the oppressed. He lived by preference in Harijan colonies. He was prepared to sacrifice everything, even his life, to safeguard their interests. This passionate revolt against a crying injustice was perhaps the most important aspect of his political life and some of it he has been able to transmit not only to his followers but to the people of India as a whole.

The sense of social injustice which is one of the characteristics of new India is undoubtedly a part of what India has inherited from Gandhiji. If untouchability has been abolished and its practice in any form made a penal offence, if the so-called untouchables of yesterday share effective political power both in the Centre and in the States, if special provision is made for their educational, economic and social advancement, it is undoubtedly due to the great impetus that the Mahatma gave to the sense of social justice as a basis for national life.

Again, India's emphasis on the village and on what has been called *panchayati raj* is a part of the inheritance of Gandhiji. All his life Gandhiji had insisted that real swaraj can only be swaraj for the villages. Cities were anathema to him. He considered urban life as representing something evil. In an interview with foreign correspondents at Mussoorie in 1946 Gandhiji declared: 'I consider the growth of cities to be an evil thing, unfortunate for mankind and the world . . . and certainly unfortunate for India. The British have exploited India through its cities. The latter have exploited the villages. The blood of the villages is the cement with which the edifice of the cities is built. I want the blood that is today inflating the arteries of the cities to run once again in the blood vessels of the villages.' That so strong an advocate of village life should picture the independence of India in terms of the village is not strange. Writing in the *Harijan* on July 26, 1942, Gandhiji expressed his idea of village swaraj:

'My idea of village swaraj is that of a complete republic, independent of its neighbours for its own vital wants and yet interdependent for many others in which dependence is a necessity. Thus every village's first concern will be to grow its own food crops and cotton for its cloth. It should have a reserve for its cattle, recreation and playgrounds for adults and children. . . . The village will maintain a village theatre, school and public hall. It will have its own water-works ensuring its own water supply. This can be done through controlled wells or tanks. Education will be compulsory up to the final basic course. As far as possible every activity will be conducted on the co-operative basis. . . . There will be a compulsory service of village guards who will be selected by rotation from the village. The government of the village will be conducted by the Panchayat of five persons annually elected by the adult villagers, male and female, possessing minimum prescribed qualifications. . . . The panchayats will be the legislative judiciary and executive combined to operate for its year of office.'

While it is undeniably true that India's great and fundamental reform of *panchayati raj* can be directly traced to this teaching of the Mahatma and is perhaps the most abiding of all the lessons that she has learnt from him, the very significant differences between what India has adopted and what he taught are illustrative of the character of Gandhiji's influence. India has rejected totally and utterly Gandhiji's objection to the growth of cities. In fact the period of India's independence has witnessed the planning and development of many cities especially around industrial complexes. Chittaranjan, Durgapur, Bhilai, Rourkela are but a few of the more outstanding examples. Great ports like Kandla have been built up from marshes. Townships like Nilokheri and Faridabad have been created to accommodate refugees from Pakistan. New capital cities, Chandigarh and Bhubaneswar, have come into being. Within twelve years the population of Delhi has jumped from a mere 700,000 to 2,500,000. Many satellite towns have grown up around the older cities. In fact all over India this development of cities and townships is going on and the Government far from discouraging it, as it should do according to Gandhian principles, is actively encouraging the movement. The Government believes that in India the percentage of rural population is higher than it should be and a deliberate effort is therefore being made to absorb them in urban industries. While emphasizing the value of small industrial units based on villages, the Government also holds that the economic development of India will never be satisfactory unless it is based on modern large-scale industries which have to be grouped around towns or which would inevitably develop townships around them. Consequently the basic assumption of the Mahatma that cities are the handiwork of the devil and are 'evil' is decisively rejected by new India.

Even in respect of village organization, Indian leadership does not follow Gandhiji the whole way. Nehru has accepted from the Mahatma the doctrine of the village as the base on which to build the political democracy of India. But his *panchayati raj*, while giving to the village an effective voice in many important aspects of village life, integrates it with higher organizations. With Gandhiji the village is an independent unit. In the *Panchayati raj* which Nehru has introduced the village is a constituent unit, enjoying no doubt effective power but subordinate to higher organizations. Gandhiji wants theatres, schools, co-operative organizations independently in each village. The community project which is the attempted practical realization of the Mahatma's ideas wants to group villages together in order that such facilities may be more easily available and that there may be better organization and more effective leadership. In fact, Gandhiji's idea of each village 'being a complete republic' finds no support in the policies of new India but they have accepted and given shape to his essential doctrine that real India lives in the villages and that India's freedom, if it is to mean anything substantial, must not only mean a better life for the people of the villages, but a life which they will be allowed to shape themselves. This indeed is the living part of Gandhiji's teaching that the predominantly urban leadership which took over from him has not forgotten. It is no mere lip service they pay to this doctrine, as in the case of *khadi* and handicrafts, but a genuine effort to translate it into practice so that India will not be merely a formal democracy, but essentially one in which the millions in the villages will be effective participants.

India's approach to private wealth may also be said in a measure to be an inheritance from Gandhiji. No doubt it has much earlier roots. At no time did India consider wealth to be the measure of value; nor did a man receive honour or exercise power in terms of his wealth. It was perhaps one of the few good results of the caste conception that the money maker or Vaisya came only after the Brahmin and the Kshatriya. No doubt the worship of wealth and the political importance of money are results of an industrial society, for even in feudal Europe wealth as such counted for little as against status. In India the persistence of caste gradation added to this tendency. But with the transition to an industrial society the danger was no doubt there of the new capitalist classes getting control of the machinery of government and utilizing it for their benefit. It was generally insinuated in anti-Indian circles—indeed at one time it became a part of British propaganda—that since a few millionaires were included in the Mahatma's circle and he at times used to stay with them, that the Congress under his leadership had become the instrument of the capitalist classes. There was never any danger of this. From the beginning the Mahatma identified himself with the *daridra narayan* (God as a poor man) —was the champion of the poor and the dispossessed. He was never impressed by wealth, nor was he willing at any time to accept the idea that wealth conferred any privilege. Speaking at the London Round Table Conference in 1931 he defined his attitude to special interests as follows:

'Above all the Congress represents in its essence the dumb semi-starved millions scattered over the length and breadth of the land. Every interest which in the opinion of the Congress is worthy of protection has to subserve the interests of these dumb millions: and so you will find again and again apparantly a clash between several interests, and if there is a genuine clash, I have no hesitation in saying, on behalf of the Congress, that the Congress will sacrifice every interest for the sake of the interest of these dumb millions.'

This was an unequivocal dedication on a formal occasion before the representatives of all sections of opinion both in India and in Britain. And it was a clear warning that vested interests whether British or Indian would not receive any consideration at his hands when they came into conflict with the interests of the poor. This emphasis on the overriding interests of the masses and the determination to make all other interests subserve the masses is one of the most valuable things inherited by modern India from Gandhiji's teaching.

Independent India has made no secret of the fact that its policy as far as possible is to eliminate glaring inequalities in wealth, and to use for this purpose the entire power of state machinery—through heavier and often differentiating taxation on the rich, through exclusion of private interests from many important spheres of economic activity, by abolishing zamindaries and other forms of landlordism, by placing a ceiling on landholding, etc. This policy no doubt has a two-fold origin, from the Mahatma as well as from Marx. While undoubtedly the influence of socialist thinking is a major factor in the shaping of India's economic policy, as we shall try to show later, this idea of levelling economic differences and of considering the wealthy as a sinister interest whose claims to importance and influence should be watched and controlled is undoubtedly a part of Gandhian teaching which has taken deep root in India. Whether it would have been as effective as it has proved to be without the economic and social urges provided by socialism is something which requires examination.

Briefly, it may be said that some of the teachings of Gandhiji have passed into the general traditions of India, but strangely enough not those to which he attached the greatest importance, *ahimsa*, satyagraha, voluntary poverty, etc. Indeed, in the case of the importance he attached to villages as the basis of national life, India has rejected certain essential aspects of his approach to the problem, as for example his view that villages should be republics, that cities in themselves are evil. His successors have taken over only as much of his teaching as can be accommodated in an industrial society, in which rural life would itself be urbanized to a large extent and *panchayats*, while entrusted with wide powers, would be integrated with national life. What India has inherited from Gandhiji is thus important and is undoubtedly a continuing factor. In many cases, like social reform, betterment of women, Gandhi's influence has given only an additional impetus to an already growing movement 100 years old. In others, like the abolition of untouchability, the widening of Hinduism to include in it all the classes which had been considered *avarnas*—or outside the caste system—his teaching, practice and influence was the predominant factor. All in all, the Mahatma is justly acclaimed the Father of the Nation, though with the growth of an industrialized society, it is difficult to be certain whether his influence will continue.

CHAPTER XVII

Marx: The Two Faces—Socialist and Communist

MARX—THE SOCIALIST

None can doubt the influence of Marx on new societies. After the first Great War, Marx came to have a hold on the younger intellectuals of India. In the 1930's that influence began to show itself in India's economic and political thinking. After independence, Marx's has been one of the major influences that has shaped Indian policy. But it must be stated at the very beginning that what has been influencing India are not the ideas of Marx as interpreted by Lenin, but as popularized by the Fabian Society and the London School of Economics. It would not be true to say that Marxist-Leninist thinking in India has had no influence. Indeed it is represented by the Communist Party which has grown into a force of some significance during the last few years. Its position in the life of the Indian people will be discussed in a later section. Here it is sufficient to say that the socialist pattern that India has declared to be her goal, while undoubtedly indebted to Marx for much of its economic thinking, is in many essential points in conflict with Communist doctrines. The essential difference so far as India is concerned is that Socialism bases itself on the liberal freedoms, i.e. freedom of speech, of worship, of organization, etc., while emphasizing the necessity for economic equality and the control by the State of the basic industries on which the life of the nation depends. In its social policy it follows the line of gradually changing the structure of society so as to bring it into a socialist pattern. The Communist view rejects this gradualism in respect of social policy and ridicules the idea of land reform without the 'liquidation' of the feudal classes, and of the State sharing with private capitalism the control of private enterprise. Communism, even while granting in theory the possibility in present-day conditions of a peaceful transformation to socialism, holds that without a violent revolution the capitalists, feudal landholders and even the peasants will not accept economic equality or a socialist organization of society.

So far as India is concerned, the influence of Marx and socialist thinking has been essentially on her economic policy. We have already seen that the reorganization of India's social structure was guided by other principles, broadly by the idea of modernization based on the liberal experience of the nineteenth century. Politically and from the point of view of civil rights also India has followed more American and British ideas than the doctrines of Marx. But in the economic field it is socialist thinking that has held the field. Ten years before Independence, in 1937, when the Congress first assumed power in the provinces under the Government of India Act of 1935, Jawaharlal Nehru was able to secure the co-operation of the Central and provincial governments and the leading public organizations for the establishment of a Planning Committee, with the object of studying the economic, industrial and financial conditions of India as a whole and of working out comprehensive plans for development. This was only a preview of what Congress under his leadership would do when it came to power.

Planning today is an activity of governments of all types, military dictators, fascists and even liberal democracies. France has a powerful planning commission and it was under the guidance of the Monnet plan that she achieved her astonishing recovery. Western Germany also reconstructed her war-devastated economy according to certain priorities and plans. In practically every newly independent country there has been established a planning commission for the purpose of economic development. It is however seldom remembered that economic planning is an essentially socialist conception deriving directly from the founding fathers of socialist thought. In his *Anti-Dühring* Engels, the co-founder of Socialism with Marx, declared: 'The conditions of existence forming man's environment which up to now have dominated man, at this point (at the time of change into socialist society) pass under the dominion and control of man who now for the first time becomes the real conscious master of nature because and in so far as he has become the master of his social organisation.' It is on this principle that Lenin was led to formulate his first five-year plan, and to lay down a policy of bringing the immense natural resources of the Soviet Union under a planned system of development for the benefit of society as a whole.

Originally, planning was for production and economic development. But it soon became clear that the State's interest cannot stop there, and the distribution and utilization of the wealth so produced for the benefit of the community as a whole must also be a function of planning. So planning had to extend its activities to the development of health services, education, housing, public utilities, scientific research—in fact to all aspects of the community's life. There was nothing in common between this conception and the general idea of the liberal state. It seemed to deny all the assumptions of *laissez faire* economics, and the old liberal tradition of the least interference possible with the individual and his rights.

The first planning committee which was established under Congress auspices had a chequered career. Its president, Mr Nehru, along with many of his leading colleagues, was arrested and incarcerated within three years of its establishment. The Congress governments in the provinces whose co-operation had been secured resigned office soon after war was declared and the British administrators who replaced them were indifferent to the work of a body which was originated by the Congress. In spite of the difficulties, the commission did much useful work but its main achievement was the popularization even among progressive industrialists of the idea of a planned society. The Bombay plan associated with the names of J. R. D. Tata and G. D. Birla, the leading representatives of capitalist interests in India, was an indication of the general acceptance, even among conservative circles, of the necessity of co-ordinating economic developments on a national basis, and of its conscious direction towards defined social objectives.

With Independence the importance of planning both in its economic and social aspects came to be emphasized much more. In 1949, planning was made the national policy and the commission was reconstituted on a wider and more effective basis under the direct authority of the Government, with the Prime Minister as Chairman and some of his colleagues as members but with a number of full-time members, each in charge of specified departments. The two successful five-year plans which India has completed, transforming effectively her economy and social structure under a democratic and parliamentary system more rapidly than most people had expected, demonstrated the success of her planning. It also brought out more and more clearly the socialist character in India's thinking. An economy in which the basic industries were owned and managed by the public sector, a limited private capitalist section subserving the general economic policies of Government, control of trade and banking, public ownership of power, utilities and other essential things, these were undoubtedly some of the socialist aspects of India's planning. A tax structure meant to ensure a better distribution of wealth and to bring in to the public treasury profits of industry beyond a certain limit, a ceiling for land holding, encouragement of co-operative cultivation, these again are economic policies with a social objective influenced considerably by Marxian thinking. The welfare state which India seeks to establish is indeed socialism within a liberal framework.

This is clear from the Directive Principles of State Policy incorporated in the Constitution which lay down that—

> 'The state shall in particular direct its policy towards securing
> (*a*) that the citizens, men and women equally, have the right to have an adequate means of livelihood;
> (*b*) that the ownership and control of material resources of the community are so distributed as best to subserve the common good; and
> (*c*) that the operation of the economic system does not result in the concentration of wealth and means of production to common detriment.'

It was never intended to disguise the socialist character of this policy though it was only in 1954 that Parliament openly adopted the socialist pattern of society as the objective of India's social and economic policy. As the report of the Planning Commission says, 'This concept which embodies the values of socialism and democracy and the approach of planned development involved no sudden change as it had its roots deep in India's struggle for independence'.

It is not our purpose here to estimate the success of the objective which the Government of India set for itself as a socialist pattern, nor the continuing influence of socialist ideology. It will no doubt be conceded that the economic policy followed by the Government of India was mainly influenced by the desire to create a socialist pattern. The powers of taxation were frankly used to secure this object. The mixed economy on which India embarked from the beginning was tilted in favour of the public sector, the basic industries being generally reserved for it. Co-operative cultivation has been declared to be the objective in agriculture. Even in commercial policy direct state trading has become a factor of importance. Briefly it may be said that socialism is a gradually increasing tendency in India's economic life, and while preserving her liberal and democratic traditions in politics, India is making a serious effort to introduce socialist ideas in her economic life.

But even in the economic sphere, the influence of a liberalized democratic socialism has had to compromise with the survival of Gandhian tradition in favour of handicrafts and village industries. One of the features of India's planning is the large financial aid provided for *khadi* and other systems of handicraft production. Proposals in this regard are clothed in high-sounding phrases about the development of the rural population, the spreading of production to as large a base as possible, etc. But there is no denying the fact that *khadi* as a national scheme of producing cloth and all efforts in making its use popular are only the outcome of a sense of loyalty to the Mahatma. So far as handicrafts are concerned an economic justification for it could be found on the basis of its providing luxury products of high quality. But it is often forgotten that handicrafts are *broadly caste occupations*, and financial assistance and artificial support given to them only help to uphold and prolong the life of the caste system. The fact would seem to be that against the combined strength of Gandhism and traditional caste organization Socialism had to effect a compromise.

If in the economic field itself Socialism, though a growing influence, has to compromise with caste prejudices and old-fashioned economics, it would be nothing surprising if traditional Hinduism and its social structure have been able to offer continued resistance to its inroads. No doubt against the combined forces of democracy, socialism and economic growth, these institutions are fighting a losing battle. In India today there are no convinced advocates of caste; no one upholds untouchability or the denial of equal social rights to the backward classes, or compulsory widowhood for women. Parliament has effectively enacted laws which, as we have seen, will in time transform Hindu society. Yet for all the efforts of social reformers and the achievement of legislatures, the unseen resistance of age-long custom to these reforms is something which cannot be overlooked. Socialism has made but little gains outside the sphere of economic activity.

It would no doubt be an exaggeration to claim to the credit of Socialism the growth of the trade union movement, regulations for the safety of workers, the limitation of working hours and the entire gamut of progressive legislation in the interests of labour. Though they might have socialist origins, they came to India mainly through the liberal traditions which she inherited. There is no doubt a socialist strand in Indian trade unionism. But basically its origin was as a part of the nationalist movement, and even today a major section of the trade unions, the Indian National Trade Union Congress (INTUC), works in close association with the National Congress. The other political parties, the Praja Socialists and the Communists, have also unions associated with them.

Broadly, it may be said that liberal socialism is a growing influence in the economic reorganization and provides also the urge for some of India's egalitarian legislation. But its influence on the life and thinking of India in the sphere of social structure is negligible and unlikely to increase. The social transformation which is taking place in India is, as we have seen, the result of the penetration of liberal and radical ideas in the nineteenth century which have become a part of the Indian middle-class tradition and is hardly related to Socialism.

MARX—THE COMMUNIST

It is not only in his social democratic garb that Marx began to influence India in the twenties of the century. Marxist-Leninism or Communism also made its entry at the same time. A major difference between the two has to be noticed at the very beginning. Socialism entered India as a body of ideas providing an economic leaven to the Congress movement. It was originally an influence among the intellectuals, an outlook rather than a political ideology. Even in the thirties when it became more defined, it did not organize itself into a separate party but formed only a socialist group in the Congress. Communist penetration was on a different basis. It was as the projection of a great international party, controlled at that time by the Comintern, that the Communists entered India. From the first, for quite a long time, it was controlled from outside and its policies determined by directives from the Comintern. Later the Comintern, finding it difficult to control the party effectively from Moscow, asked the Communist parties in imperialist countries, in this case England, to maintain close contact and give guidance to the parties in colonial countries, a policy which M. N. Roy denounced as smacking of imperialism. In fact organizers like Spratt and Hutchinson were sent out from England to put the party on a sound basis.

The history of the Communist party in India falls into five well-defined periods, each a record of political failure and ideological chaos. The first was the period till the Meerut conspiracy case when the party was broken up and its leaders jailed (1922–34). The second was the period of underground activities and penetration into the national movement through the socialist group (1934–40). The third was the period of collaboration with the British authorities on the plea of helping to fight the anti-fascist war. The fourth was the period between 1946–52, when the party, feeling that conditions were likely to be unstable in India following Independence, embarked on a programme of sabotage and the creation of confusion in the hope of capitalizing on it. After 1952, faced with the problem of a functioning democracy based on adult franchise, the party decided, after a period of hesitation, to work the Constitution, no doubt keeping its machinery of conspiratorial and revolutionary activity also ready and well oiled, as otherwise its claim to be a revolutionary party would altogether have disappeared.

The first period was marked by a basic contradiction. The Comintern had laid it down as general policy that Communist parties should support bourgeois nationalist parties in colonial countries and work through them. While it was undoubtedly a right line of action in countries where the nationalist movements were weak and where a determined body of Communists could take over the leadership, in India with the mass movement under the leadership of Mahatma Gandhi, assisted by men of outstanding ability, possessing influence with the people both at all-India and state levels, there was never any possibility of a small group of

Communists, however able and determined, taking over control of politics or the machinery of the Congress. In fact, whatever the Comintern might decide as a matter of policy, the Indian Communists realized that Gandhi's influence should be weakened if not destroyed if they desired to gain authority in the national movement. This was their great handicap. Gandhiji could not be taken in. Nor were the masses in India prepared to accept from the Communists that the Mahatma was a reactionary. Besides, the British Indian police were very vigilant and the Cawnpore conspiracy case and the prosecution of individual Communists made it very difficult for the party to organize itself effectively, so much so that a representative of the British Communist Party, Glading, who was sent out to report on the situation in India declared (1925) that no Communist party existed at all in India. It was after this that the British Communist Party was entrusted with the duty of advice and guidance and Spratt, Hutchinson, Bradley and others were sent out from London. M. N. Roy also arrived on the scene at almost the same time. Again the party came up against the two main forces that blocked its way: the influence of the Mahatma and the administrative efficiency of the British. The Mahatma's influence prevented them from gaining any great influence with the people, while the British administration unearthed the conspiracy and brought the organizers to trial (the Meerut conspiracy case). The leaders were sentenced to varying terms of imprisonment and the Communist party was declared illegal (1934). For these twelve years of activity there was but little to show in the way of revolutionary gains. The attempt to blow up India, as Spratt called it, had failed. All that could be claimed was that, though as a party the Communists had not functioned effectively, dispersed groups had come into existence at different centres who were beginning to exercise some influence on national opinion.

The party was proscribed and declared illegal in 1934. Only two courses were open to the organizers and active members. The first was to create front organizations and work through them. The second was to penetrate and capture existing organizations. During nationalist agitations, extremism of any kind has an aura and is generally welcomed as an evidence of dynamism which established parties lack. The intellectuals especially were frustrated by the inactivity following the great salt satyagraha (1930–31).

This provided an excellent opportunity for the Communists to penetrate subsidiary nationalist organizations like the student movement and also to establish 'progressive' movements under their control. It is interesting to note that the first 'progressive writers' conference was inaugurated in Allahabad by Jawaharlal Nehru. Peasant movements, professional organizations, etc., became the centres of their activity and began to gain importance in national life.

But the most important gain, though it was as usual only temporary, was the arrangement by which individual Communist members were allowed to join the Socialist party (1936). Thus the Communist party, deprived of its own organization, found a handy, ready-made machinery with the prestige of an important Congress group. Jaya Prakash Narayan was its Secretary and Minoo Masani, later to become the most determined opponent of Communism, was the Joint Secretary of the group. The alliance lasted only for a year, when from a document which fell into their hands the Socialists came to know that the Communist allies were working according to a definite programme with the object of capturing their machinery. The Communists were again in the wilderness.

This was also a period when they made a determined attempt to gain control of the trade unions. The fifth Comintern Congress (1924) had laid down the policy that the Indian Communist party should bring the trade unions under its control, that it must eliminate outside interests, the leadership at that time being provided by liberals and Congressmen unconnected with industrial labour, and further that it should be organized on the basis of class struggle. Its early attempts met with little success, but in the period between 1934–42, the Communists began slowly to gain ground with some sections of industrial labour.

When the war broke out in 1939, the Communists were able to shout the loudest in the agitation against India taking part in the 'imperialist war'. As this was also the Congress view, the Communist could then pretend only to be giving active effect to the Congress policy. But with the entry of the Soviets into the war, the Communist attitude had perforce to change. The imperialist's war became overnight transformed into the anti-fascist struggle, and the Communists became active supporters of India participating whole-heartedly in the war on the side of the Allies. Here they had to part company with the Congress. The Congress was determined on a last great struggle against British authority and prepared for the Quit India movement under the leadership of Mahatma Gandhi. At this time when the issues were clearly defined, the Communist Party, obedient to the directives from Moscow, became the allies of the British Government in India, which it had so long denounced as imperialist, and became their agents in anti-Congress propaganda. M. N. Roy, who had no doubt broken with Communism but had remained a Marxian, emerged from his retreat in Dehra Dun to accept money from the British Indian Government for propaganda among the workers.

The alliance was not without immediate benefit to the Communists. They got a privileged entry into the trade union movement and were able to build up their organization among certain sections of the working classes. The Communist challenge in the labour movement as a result of this remained serious, till the Congress after Independence, with the blessings of the National Government, started the Indian National Trade Union Congress (INTUC) from which Communists were excluded.

The Communist attempt to weaken the Congress movement and to wrest the leadership of the younger generation did not end with the war. But the Congress also hit back. It excluded from the Congress all Communists and denounced the party for its anti-national activities during the war. Though as a result of co-operation with the British organizationally the party was stronger after the war, the public attitude to it was not one of sympathy. Nor were the Communists clear as to what they wanted in the political sphere. When the Cabinet Mission came to India to negotiate the withdrawal of British authority from India, the point of view which the Communists urged was that there *should be no united India but that the country should be split into a number of states on the model of the Balkans*. What persuaded them to put forward this strange proposal is not clear, but again they showed themselves to be in opposition to the national point of view.

Even after India's independence, the party's policies continued to be tortuous and in many cases unnational. It persuaded itself that India continued to be a colonial country even after Independence. Mr Nehru was denounced as a lackey of British Imperialism. The Constitution which the Constituent Assembly adopted was roundly denounced as a 'slave constitution', 'a constitution of a fascist type'. Actually the party for nearly three years thought that success was round the corner and if the revolutionary machinery was kept well oiled and tensions and troubles created in the country, it could take over by decisive action. In Telingana it had established a base, 'a liberated area', a 'Yenan', and the party expected to establish other such centres all over India from which they could take over the central administration when the expected revolutionary situation developed. The Government of India, after its police action in Hyderabad, was able to liquidate this pocket and to eliminate altogether the danger of armed revolt led by the Communist party.

With the approach of the general election based on adult franchise under the new constitution in 1951, the party was faced with a difficult problem. To boycott the election would have been to confess a lack of popular support. To contest would be put to test the party's alleged mass following. After an agonizing re-appraisal, the Communists decided to contest the general elections, and though their popular strength was demonstrated in certain pockets, the overwhelming victory of the Congress, in the general election which was universally recognized as having been conducted with strict fairness and without the use of undue influence or pressures, showed two things. First, that on an all-India basis the party could not expect to challenge the Congress or to claim to have any great national support. Secondly, it showed that Communism had become a strand, though a minor one, in the pattern of Indian life.

The elections also demonstrated that the party had made but little influence over wide areas like Uttar Pradesh, Bihar, Madhya Pradesh, Karnatak, Rajasthan, Gujerat, and that where it had a considerable following, as in Kerala or Andhra, there were special circumstances of a local character which helped its growth. After three general elections now it can be safely affirmed that the danger of the Communists achieving power in India through parliamentary action is practically non-existent. Nor could it be claimed that the party has much chance of subverting by revolutionary action the established government of India. The reasons for this conclusion we shall analyse later in this section.

The fact is that after forty years of existence, hard work, organization, agitation and suffering, Communism in India has been politically an undoubted failure. Its impact has been local as in Kerala and Bengal and marginal as in the trade unions. Why has this been so, when the party leadership consists of men of proved ability, strong conviction, intelligence and perseverance, prepared to suffer and sacrifice for a cause, and when that cause itself has been proved to possess a great appeal to large sections of people even in Western liberal democracies like France and Italy? We have to look elsewhere for reasons.

The causes of the failure of Communism to gain over the masses of India or even to establish a party with an appeal lie both within the party and outside it. Within the party it is significant to note that Communist analyses and forecasts in the past have either been wrong or against clear national interests as understood by the people. To mention only a few outstanding instances. From 1922 the Communist leadership held the view and proceeded on the assumption not only that Mahatma Gandhi was a reactionary force but, having 'decapitated' the movement (after Chauri Chawra when he had called it off), his influence was on the wane. Many a time they proclaimed that 'the Mahatma was a spent force'. Again in 1947 Nehru was a tool of British Imperialism helping to hold down the progressive forces in India. In 1947, revolution was round the corner and the proletarian leadership had only to issue 'the call' for the people to rise. Instances of their wrong analysis leading them to conclusions against clear national interests as understood by the vast majority of the people in India are also flagrant. Their decision to co-operate with the British Government in India after the Soviets had joined the war, when the Congress and the national movement were engaged in a bitter struggle for securing independence, is of course one example. The demand for the Balkanization of India and the doctrine of different nationalities to which the Communist party gave its approval from 1942 to 1947 is another instance of the party's analysis running directly counter to national interests. The adventurist attempt in the period immediately following India's Independence to create chaos in the country, to promote sabotage, armed insurrection, etc., may have been in conformity with the Communist theory of revolution but, as events proved, was based on a totally wrong analysis.

Many reasons could be advanced for this consistent misreading of the Indian situation. In the earlier days, in fact till India's Independence, the party was under tutelage. Until its direction was handed over to the British Communist Party of Great Britain, it was in a way an orphan child about whose guardianship nobody seemed certain, though M. N. Roy was the most persistent claimant. This leadership from afar, without an adequate appreciation of local circumstances and a realistic valuation of mass psychology in India, led the Communist leaders astray in their evaluation of Mahatma Gandhi and his movement. That it was a profound mistake is now accepted, and may be seen from the change in the Communist evaluation of the Mahatma's contribution to the national struggle. The Soviet leaders have themselves accepted their mistake on this point. The recent penetrating and sympathetic study of Mahatma Gandhi by Prof. Hiren Mukherji is evidence that the Communists today recognize that their original judgment of Gandhi was wrong. So far as Jawaharlal Nehru is concerned, Communists who in 1947 denounced him as the agent of imperialism had reluctantly to accept that their judgment was based on wrong premises and that today he represents and leads a force independent alike of Imperialist and Communist states. It is, however, interesting to note that the Soviet leaders gave expression to this view even before the Indian Communists accepted it.

Generally speaking, it may be said that the Communist failure to understand the situation in India and to evaluate it objectively comes from their argument by analogies. The Indian Communist Party, for example, considered it necessary to put forward a doctrine of nationalities in India on the analogy of Stalin's famous document. They did not realize that the analogy was an entirely false one. The Empire of the Tsars was one in which Russia conquered and held in subjection other historic nationalities like the Ukranians, the Georgians and the Armenians. They had been at all times rebellious groups demanding freedom from Russian control, and if the Russian Communist revolution was to gain the support of these nationalities their aspirations had to be satisfied at least for the time. In India the position was otherwise. Whatever may be the claims of regions, languages and states, the demand of the Indian people was for unity. Argument by analogy led the Communists in 1942 to a tragic error, from which they were unable to recover even in 1946 when they demanded separate constituent assemblies for fifteen different states in India.

Perhaps the Communists also had a vague idea that if India were divided into eighteen or twenty sovereign states, the chances of success in individual states were greater. It must have been obvious to them that with vast areas in the Gangetic valley, Central India, Rajasthan, outside their influence, a federal government for the whole would be able to nullify whatever success they achieved in any province. Imagine for instance that their success in Kerala was achieved not under a federal system with the Centre laying down the conditions of government but in an independent state; this would have provided a base for extended action. From the party point of view, a Balkanized India had, therefore, its advantages, for with the apparatus of a government at their disposal, if they could capture even one, they could proclaim a policy of liberation for the rest.

Another instance of their programme based on analogy was the border area doctrine which Mao Tse Tung had elaborated at Yenan. The idea was that if Communist action was spread over two neighbouring states, the jurisdictional conflicts would enable them successfully to defy both. The Telingana movement attempted to repeat this strategy. For a time it was successful when the administrations of Madras, which included the Andraha area at the time, and Hyderabad followed different policies. But when the Central Government intervened in Hyderabad and brought its administration in line with the rest of India and full co-operation was established between Madras and Hyderabad, the base so carefully built up was easily liquidated and the 'liberated area of Telingana' became only a memory.

Perhaps the greatest mistake based on argument by analogy was the parallel between the Kuomintang and the Congress which became a dogma with the Communists from 1947 to 1952. The Congress, they said, because of its very size, the conflict of interests within it, and the vested interests ('the big bourgeoisie') who were said to control it, would soon become corrupt and inefficient, thereby losing the hold it had on the people. Nehru was equated with Chiang Kai Shek who had also been a national hero once. It was argued with conviction that with the 'Tatas and Birlas' exacting their price, and the Congress incapable of finding a radical solution for the tremendous problems which India was facing, the national movement would break up, with the progressive section slowly coming round to the view of a new democracy on the basis of a coalition with the Communists. The analogy seemed perfect. Every element of the analysis could be fitted in beautifully. But this argument by analogy overlooked certain essential facts. The Kuomintang after the death of Sun Yat Sen in 1924 was essentially an organization controlled by the military. Its leadership outside Chiang Kai's relations lay mainly with the generals who surrounded him. The Congress had no tradition of militarism behind it. Secondly, the Kuomintang had no democratic basis for its political activity. The only major election it held was in 1947–8 under American pressure, and even that was openly rigged up. The Congress, on the other hand, was democratic not only in its party organization, but from the beginning, its governmental apparatus at all levels, from the Central government to the District boards, was based on elections on an adult franchise. Besides, if the Kuomintang had in its early days under Sun Yat Sen a social purpose and an economic policy, it quickly forgot them. Socially, it spearheaded reaction with a slogan of neo-Confucianism: economically it developed a system of bureaucratic capitalism which concentrated economic power in the hands of a few families, who monopolized political power also. In India, on the other hand, the social urge was converted into a political programme resulting not only in a large-scale reorganization of Hindu life but in an attempted nation-wide transformation of rural society, through community development, national extension programmes and similar activities. Economically, as we have seen, the Congress followed a progressive policy of planned industrialization with the basic industries under state control. In fact, in every major respect the Congress in India was the very opposite of the Kuomintang and yet the Communists, arguing on analogy, based their programme for a time on the idea that the Congress would go the way of the Kuomintang.

Instances of this kind of argument by analogy and interpretation of political events on the basis of experience in other countries can be multiplied. The point that is sought to be emphasized is that till recently the Communist party made no serious attempt independently to analyse or interpret social and political developments in India even from the 'Marxian' point of view. Their politics, therefore, remain unreal, though of late there have been attempts to rectify the situation. But the size of India, the differing conditions of social and economic life, not to speak of the varying degrees in which caste, even though weakening in its hold, functions, make a uniform analysis of social phenomena difficult, if not impossible. The problems in Kerala are different from those of Bengal or Andhra. Consequently the Communist party which can only function on the basis of theses, studies and analogies—and cannot deal pragmatically with problems—finds itself continually at sea, making mistakes and going off in wrong directions, withdrawing only when it is too late. Marx in his Leninist version has proved an unsafe guide so far as India is concerned, though it is no fault of the prophet himself.

CHAPTER XVIII

The Prospects of Communism

We have seen that the political developments of the last forty years have given to Communism a position of some influence in Indian life though at the present time it is mainly peripheral in most provinces and confined to certain pockets elsewhere. But what are its prospects for the future? In the complex pattern of Indian life, every opinion which moves men will necessarily find a place as in all open societies. But does Communism present a serious danger to democratic life in India and its political growth? This is an issue which worries many people not only in India but in many parts of the democratic world.

The success of the Communists in China, from small beginnings and under circumstances which appeared most discouraging, has created an apprehension that the danger is real. There are many factors which at least superficially favour the Communists. India has a growing industrial proletariat concentrated in such centres as Bombay, Calcutta, Kanpur, Ahmedabad, and in the new industrial towns like Rourkela and Bhilai. Besides, the workers in the public utility undertakings under the Government like the railways and post offices are politically organized and could be made effective instruments of direct action. Also, spread all over India there are millions of people—the former untouchables—who are now awakened to their rights and realize their strength. There is, too, a growing body of discontented intellectuals who at all times provide the leadership for revolutionary action.

With all these advantages, most of which have existed during the forty years that the Communists have been active in India, it cannot be said that their prospects have improved with time. On the other hand today, after fifteen years of Independence, Indian democracy stands more firmly established than the most ardent optimists could have hoped at the time of Independence. The prospects which the Communists might have foreseen in the early days of freedom seem to have receded further than ever.

There were two 'dangerous decades' when the possibilities of Communism gaining ground and developing into a challenge to Indian democracy appeared serious. The first was the period following the Meerut conspiracy case, when the party was declared illegal by the Government. It was a period of general national frustration, and the Communists who had gone underground were working through front organizations and, after the so-called Lucknow agreement with the socialist group in the Congress, were permitted and even encouraged to penetrate the national movement. At that time the Communists were looked upon by the people in general as an organized and dynamic forward movement. Few people saw any danger from them, and the obvious earnestness, energy and ability for organized action of the Communists impressed the general public, who were more concerned with the achievement of freedom than with the form of government to follow. The Communists succeeded to some extent and gained an effective voice not in the socialist wing of the Congress, but in trade unions and peasant organizations. But the clear vision of Gandhi and the firmness of his hold on the Congress prevented them from attaining any power in the Congress or in shaping its policy. Their prestige as a spearhead of nationalism, as a group which was balancing the Conservative elements in the National Congress, and as workers among peasants and factory labourers continued to grow till they threw the whole of these assets away by their alliance with the British Government after the Soviets entered the war.

The second period when chances appeared at first sight bright for the Communists was the one immediately following Partition. The disastrous incidents on both sides of the frontier seemed to indicate a weakening of administration and the possibility of law and order breaking down in large areas. The food position continued to be menacing. In the Deccan, the Nizam was challenging the authority of the Government of India. The Communists felt that a revolutionary situation was developing. But, as in the earlier period the party had to meet the determination of Mahatma Gandhi, in the crisis after Independence they had to face not only the personality of Nehru, but his Socialism. Nehru met the Communist challenge not merely by putting down ruthlessly their attempted resort to force and sabotage, but by a policy which cut at the root of Communist lines of action. The Congress Government under his leadership annexed the principalities where feudalism had flourished; abolished the zamindaries, jagirdaries and other forms of parasitic landlordism, initiated vigorous measures of social reform, established a democratic state with freely conducted elections, started on a comprehensive scheme of rural transformation in order to enable the population in the villages to share effectively in the new life, and, side by side with this, embarked on a programme of planned industrialization, meant to correct the imbalances of the Indian economy and generally to raise her standards of living. In fact, he carried out courageously a policy of democratic Socialism which even received the active support of the Soviet Union so far at least as his industrial plans were concerned.

Lenin is said to have remarked when he read of Stolypin's policy of land reform in Russia, that if the Czarist government were able to carry it out, the Revolution for which he was working would be postponed for fifty years. An Indian Lenin objectively studying the achievements of Nehru's Government may well say that the prospects of a Communist Revolution in India have receded far into the background as a result of fifteen years of progressive government which learnt the lessons of modern life from everywhere, from Moscow, Washington and London, and transformed them to suit Indian conditions. It was the good fortune of India that in these two periods of crisis, when if leadership had been weak, Communism could have made great headway, she had the inestimable advantage of being led by two men, Mahatma Gandhi and Mr Nehru, who not only enjoyed the full confidence of the people, but each in his way was a champion of the poor and the depressed, the real proletariat. The Mahatma's economics were no doubt unrelated to modern life; but his identification with *daridra narayan* (the poor and the lowly) was sufficiently strong to withstand the attacks of Communists. The correspondence between Gandhi and the Communist leaders bears witness both to his firmness in the rejection of Communist doctrines and their chagrin at not being able to weaken his influence or to bypass him. Mr Nehru's case was different. He frankly admired the achievements of Communism in many fields. He accepted from Communism many ideas—especially the idea of a planned economy. He worked in friendly co-operation with the Soviet Union on many issues. But he was essentially a democrat who thought that a socialist pattern of society could be achieved through democratic processes and without the forcible liquidation of classes. The result of the last fifteen years of his administration has been, therefore, to endow India with the framework of a society based on democratic socialism. If India follows broadly the policy which Nehru has chalked out, the prospects of the Communist party achieving power in India would cease to be a matter of practical concern.

What happens if India after Nehru goes conservative and follows a policy of social reaction and economic development of capitalists? No doubt the Communist party will gain by such a development as then it may well succeed in creating a broad front of progressive groups in the country and working through it penetrate more effectively into labour and peasant organizations, as it tried in effect to do during the period of repression following the Meerut conspiracy case. In a country like India where there will always be causes for public agitation, a reactionary and conservative leadership in the country would enable the Communists or front organizations working under its leadership to claim to be the champions of popular causes. In short, in a developing country like India reaction and conservatism help the growth of Communism. This, as is well known, was the position in China. With the growth of militarism, reaction and neo-Confucianism in the Kuomintang, the radicals, the liberals and other reform parties rallied to the side of the Communist party which promulgated attractive doctrines under the slogans of a 'coalition government' and a 'new democracy'.

A reactionary government may lead to a strengthening of Communism, especially by the penetration of legitimate political institutions, but in India it is most unlikely to lead to the capture of power. Nowhere in the world—in political experience so far—has Communism been able to gain a victory on the ground of the reactionary nature of the government, the repressive nature of its laws or the conservative character of its policy. Only through two processes has a Communist revolution succeeded or can succeed in the future. One, by a coup at the top as in the case of the

Soviet Union, with the Communist system establishing itself through political propaganda and large-scale liquidation of opponents and a rigorous control of all activity through a pervasive administrative machinery. Secondly, as in China, by a civil war. In all other cases, in Poland, Rumania, Hungary, East Germany, it was through the action of the victorious Soviet Army and in Czechoslovakia through the strength of its presence in the background that Communism gained control of the state machinery. In North Vietnam and North Korea, also, it was as a result of conditions following the war that Communism came to be established.

The poverty of the people, the reactionary or dictatorial character of the regime, social and economic backwardness—these and other reasons often advanced do not lead to Communist revolutions. They may help to strengthen a Communist regime *once* established. It is where the Communists can conceal their aims in a slogan with an all-embracing appeal without reference to classes or parties, and which have a strength to override other prejudices, like national liberation from a foreign foe or the acquisition of independence, and when the administrative machinery of the government opposed to it fails, that the Communists have in the past succeeded in taking over a state.

China is an interesting case study.

When the Communist Revolution burst upon the world in 1917, China was practically in an anarchical state with its vast territory partitioned under local dictators, known to history as war lords. Effective administration had broken down as the recruitment to the mandarinate had been given up as a result of the short-sighted demand of the Western powers in 1904 that the classical examination system should be given up, and the great civil service tradition which had upheld the greatness of China even during the period of Western supremacy had in fact vanished. The nationalist movement which Sun Yat Sen had organized was itself in the doldrums. Sun himself, though at all times a liberal, was uncertain in his attitude towards Russia and Communism. In this he differed fundamentally from the Mahatma whose penetrating eye had seen through the nature of Communist ideology. But this much may be said in favour of Sun Yat Sen, that he was compelled by the circumstances of China to organize a military force with which he could bring about the downfall of the war lords. Only the Soviets were prepared to help him to organize an army, and the Communists were therefore able to get in on the ground floor of the Kuomintang party when it was reorganized in Canton. The penetration of the national movement which the Communists in India also attempted was accepted as normal and legitimate in China when the Whampoa Academy began to function. It was only after reaching Shanghai that Chiang Kai Shek got rid of the Communists in his movement.

The nationalist government that Chiang had organized at Nanking found soon that it had the Communist problem on its hands. Mao Tse Tung, who in 1927 had taken refuge in Chinkan Shan, had only a few followers with him and it was only by his association with local bandits that he was able to terrorize the area around him. This is what he himself said to Edgar Snow:

'Two former bandit leaders named Wang Tsu and Yuan Went Sai joined the "Red Army" (Mao's own followers) in winter 1927. This increased the strength to about three regiments. Wang and Yuan were both made regimental commanders. . . . While I remained in Chinkan Shan, they were faithful Communists. Later on . . . they returned to bandit habits.'

It is the manner in which this small ill-organized force was dealt with that was characteristic of China. Chiang Kai Shek led his 'annihilating campaigns' with no serious results till his German Chief of Staff took the matter in hand. Then Mao Tse Tung realized that Chinkan Shan was no longer a safe area for him and that he had to take his forces behind his enemy's area if he was to survive. Thus came about the Great March, at the end of which a small force of 20,000 bedraggled soldiers found refuge in Yenan. Today in the myths of Communism, Yenan stands as a great symbol of patient preparation, persistence and determined action, and yet there was nothing in Yenan or in the organization of the small party which Mao Tse Tung led there that in itself held the promise of the brilliant future which awaited the refugees.

The Communists would have remained merely a faction, a thorn in the side of Kuomintang but for a major development at this time—the intervention of Japan in China. This enabled the Communists to ride the wave of Nationalist sentiment and stand forth as the party of resistance to external aggression. The policy of appeasement which Chiang and the Kuomintang followed in the early stages of the Japanese annexation of Manchuria and subsequent intervention in North China helped the Communists to mobilize popular opinion all over the country in their favour. Chiang was forced in the end to ally himself with the Communists, to agree to reorganize the Eighth Route Army and equip it and to accept the help of both the Communist Party and the Red Army in the fight against Japan. This arrangement afforded the Communists the opportunity they had long desired. The red steel was tempered in extensive guerilla warfare against the Japanese. Under Nationalist colours and under the slogan of national liberation, they were able to overrun large areas behind the Japanese lines, recruit troops, indoctrinate the peasants and generally build up their strength. From a faction which had been unable firmly to establish itself in any area, they had, at the end of the war with Japan, grown into a mighty force of veterans under generals whose names had struck terror even in the minds of Japanese soldiers.

The agreement of 1936 under which the Kuomintang undertook to train and arm the Communist army was undoubtedly the turning point. Chiang Kai Shek always recognized it as his greatest mistake and never ceased to regret it. Once the army was trained and provided with modern weapons, from a faction it became a rival party, which during the war claimed to be the spearhead of nationalism and after the war claimed to be fighting for the liberation of China from the American yoke.

Thus it will be seen that the spectacular success of the Communists in China was due largely to factors other than the appeal of Marxian ideology to peasants and workers, factors which do not exist in India. Primarily the victory of Communism in China was achieved in the military field, but, after the Kuomintang had betrayed the revolution, the allegiance of the intellectuals had also shifted.

The real difference between India and China in their approach to the problems of Communism lies in three factors. In China the district administration had broken down in 1911 after the revolution against the Manchus and, therefore, movements were allowed to grow up away from towns without either the Central Government being aware of what was happening or having the machinery to deal with them. In India, on the other hand, as the Cawnpore trials and the Meerut conspiracy case—apart from the regular arrests and convictions of Communist leaders—should show, the administration before 1942 was able to act effectively in the very early stages. An efficient district administration and a competent police service rendered the growth of a militant party practically impossible. Independent India has not only inherited but strengthened that system. Princely states, with weak administrations and autocratic regimes which tended to become breeding grounds of Communism in their last days—e.g. Telingana in Hyderabad and Vayalar in Travancore (Kerala)—were brought into line with the rest, thus eliminating the administrative weakness arising from different jurisdictions.

Another reason for the success of the Chinese revolution was the breakdown of the traditional social organization following thirty years of civil war. While in India during the 150 years of British power a reformation of society and religion had taken place, strengthening the bonds of society—in spite of many glaring weaknesses that remained—in China the 100 years of foreign influence and missionary propaganda had led to a loosening of social ties and the creation of a state of chaos. The revolution of 1911–12 and the political anarchy of war-lordism that followed hastened this process. 'Down with Confucius' was the main slogan of the May the Fourth movement, with which the social revolution in China originated. No wonder, therefore, that a new social doctrine, which claimed to be progressive, 'scientific' and promised heaven on earth found no difficulty in moving into the place vacated by religion and Confucian ethics. In India the transition from British rule to Independence involved no prolonged interregnum, or social or political anarchy providing an opportunity for the Communists to build up their strength. Further, though they had been given some guerilla training by the British in the period of the unnatural alliance between the two (see Rajbans Kishin's *Fragments from a Guerilla's Diary*) the British had withdrawn from this dangerous game before the Communists could gain real benefits from it. On the other hand, they left behind a highly disciplined and well-trained army loyal to the new government.

Finally, in China there was neither a system of democratic local government nor any attachment to civil liberties which could have provided resistance to a movement like Communism. The

Manchu empire vanished from the scene only at the end of 1911. It had created no modern institutions in the empire, nor allowed the growth of elementary popular rights like freedom of speech and assembly, independence of the judiciary and the rule of law. Till the last few days, the Son of Heaven continued to rule by the mandate from heaven and the citizens of the celestial empire enjoyed no political rights. The revolution was followed by a period of war-lord governments, the chief characteristic of which was that while a shadowy central government continued in Peking, subjected in turn to cajolery and blackmail by the Great Powers but afforded a patronizing protection in their own interest, the great provinces were under the autocratic military rule of usurping generals, each one a law unto himself. The 'governments' over which they presided were totalitarian dictatorships under which the people knew no rights. The Kuomintang government which in a measure restored the unity of the state was in itself a military regime and did not claim either to be democratic or liberal. It was only in its last days that the Kuomintang attempted even to promulgate a modern system of laws. Actually, Chiang's government never had a chance. From the beginning of its establishment as the national government of China in 1927 to the end of the Great War, the shadow of Japanese aggression forced the pace of its own militarization. Whatever the reason, the Chinese people under the Kuomintang had not been allowed to experience the advantages of personal freedom, supremacy of law and other civil rights.

It is a major fact which cannot be emphasized sufficiently that in societies which have had the experience of democratic life or where people have enjoyed freedom and civil liberties, Communist doctrine has failed to make any headway. In Britain after over forty years of existence the impact of the Communist party is negligible. In the northern democracies, Sweden, Norway and Denmark, the attractions of Communism seem to go unappreciated. Only in France and Italy has the Communist party been able to grow to national proportions but that, as is generally recognized, was the result of foreign occupation which provided the Communists with an opportunity to spearhead the movement of resistance and to raise the slogan of national liberation. But the Communist parties in these two great liberal states have not been able in the period following the war to improve their position, a fact which should amply prove that in spite of their great organizational strength and resources, in peaceful conditions Communist parties are unable to win the allegiance of the common people.

The difference between India and China in this respect is very marked. As we have noticed earlier, India has for over 100 years not only shared the liberal experience of the West but has to a large extent assimilated it in her tradition. Her national movement was itself liberal in its inspiration. From 1882, local self-government institutions were built up in India covering both municipal and rural areas. Gradually and no doubt by slow stages a democratic tradition has grown up through councils and assemblies. The position was far different in China. Neither at the district nor at the national level had China after the fall of the Manchus developed liberal or democratic institutions. Sun Yat Sen originally had visions of developing China into a great social democracy based on parliamentary institutions. But Yuan Shih Kai drove him out of power and the revolution that broke the Manchu power fizzled out into a system of war-lordism which divided China into reactionary satrapies. In short the breakdown of government which followed the Revolution of 1911–12 did not permit China to develop either political institutions or a democratic tradition, while all through the years of struggle with Britain, India had been able to develop the values of liberalism, enjoy civil liberties, and both in administration and in the national movement lay the foundations of democratic growth. Side by side with the growth of elected institutions under government, the Congress was also building up a massive democratic tradition. The Congress at all levels after the Gandhian reorganization in 1920 was an elective body based on a very wide franchise. It was federal in structure and the provincial committees which directed policy at their own level were elected bodies. In fact the Congress, under Mr Gandhi, took every care to develop a strong democratic tradition in the national struggle, while preserving its character as a mass movement under effective unified leadership at the centre. On the other hand, the Kuomintang which was originally conceived as a national party by Sun Yat Sen soon became militarized and had no democratic basis.

Thus from every point of view, the idea of India falling under the spell of Communism in the manner of China is based on a false analogy and a failure to appreciate the basic differences between the two countries. The success with which Burma was able to resist Communism, even when the administration was faced with a hundred troubles including a serious rebellion by one of its constituent nationalities (the Karens), by an appeal to nationalism and by the failure of Communism to capitalize on the cry of liberating the country from foreign domination, should prove conclusively that Communism as such has little chance in an Asian country unless it can identify itself with nationalism.

PART VI

THE PROFILE OF NEW INDIA

CHAPTER XIX

National Integration

Early in 1961 riots of a serious character broke out in certain districts of Assam. The dominant ethnic and linguistic group in the state had long felt that the Bengali minority was a privileged group which, under the shadow of British Imperialism, had expanded into their territory. The Bengalis, on the other hand, claimed that they were as much the residents of Assam and were entitled to the use of their language for official and other purposes, at least in areas where they were in a majority, on the same footing as Assamese. The tensions arising from these long-standing rivalries exploded into violent riots in which important personalities of both groups belonging to all political parties are said to have taken a leading part. Opinion in India was deeply stirred by the supporters of the Bengalis in Assam, while the Assamese felt that they were not receiving the sympathy of the rest of India in what they believed to be their legitimate claims.

Previous to these unfortunate incidents communal riots between Hindus and Muslims had taken place in Jabalpur and Bhopal. The immediate causes of these outbursts of communal fury need not concern us here. They were Hindu-Muslim riots in the genuine tradition of what had been a regular feature of Indian political life in the British period: but they created a deep impression as showing that communal bitterness was growing up again between Hindus and Muslims, and petty incidents arising from individual action were being looked upon and interpreted as communal acts which should be paid for by the community.

These incidents came as a shock to Mr Nehru and other political leaders of all parties who, in the moment of excitement, conjured up a vision of continuing communal troubles and jealousies between linguistic and regional groups. The cry was again raised that India was falling a prey to regionalism, linguism and other fissiparous tendencies and that the immediate need was for all parties to work for what was termed as the emotional integration of the people. A conference of the Chief Ministers of provinces and leaders of all non-communal parties (Congress, Praja Socialists, Communists, etc.) met under the chairmanship of Mr Jawaharlal Nehru and discussed the problem at length and also chalked out a programme of action in order to bring about greater integration.

But what is this national integration which India is said to lack? Is it an absence of a sense of loyalty to India, or of being an Indian: or is it that the different communities in India do not mix with each other and hold themselves aloof in social life? No one, I think, seriously holds that any considerable group in the country is disloyal to India. There may be a small section of Muslims who look towards Pakistan and feel a sense of divided loyalty. But no one denies that the vast majority of Indian Muslims are loyal to their mother country. The problem of integration is, therefore, basically, not one of breaking external ties, as it was in the case of the United States. If that were the case, it would have been simple. It is not that among the people of India there is no sense of Indianness. Even the most aggressive regionalists, outside the lunatic fringe of the great patriotic Tamil people in the South, emphasize their Indianness.

The fact is that regionalism, 'linguism' and communal tensions are problems of democracy everywhere. During the days of monarchical or autocratic power, it was a dominant group that exercised authority and integration meant only the solidarity of the dominant group. Actually, till the first Great War, nationality was determined by the composition of the governing, generally land-owning, classes. Even in India, this was the prevalent conception. Hyderabad and Bhopal were considered 'Muslim' states. Udaipur, Jaipur, Jodphur, Bikaner were considered Rajput states, though the Rajputs formed only a minority of the population in these states. In monarchical and autocratic states the problem of cohesion, until the growth of democracy, was solved by the cohesion of the classes exercising political power. With democracy, however, new problems came to the surface as equality and the equitable distribution of power are basic to a democratic structure.

The twentieth century is marked by the emergence of large multi-ethnical states. The United States which developed along these lines in the nineteenth century became the pattern of political development. Russia, after the great October Revolution, accepted the federal doctrine which had been tried so successfully in the United States and converted the old Czarist empire held together by military power and monarchical loyalties into a multi-racial multi-lingual state of more than continental proportions. Both of these great states demonstrated their political stability and their integration in relation to external powers in great and prolonged conflicts. And yet internally no one would say that their integration is even now perfect or that there are not regional and group tensions of a serious character in both the states. So far as the Soviets are concerned, the constant attacks on the 'Great Russian chauvinism' of their agents by the leaders in the Kremlin, and the known persistence of strong regional feelings in historic areas like the Ukraine, Georgia and Armenia, clearly establish that the monolithic unity that the Soviet Union presents to the outside world is not reflected in its internal relations. The tensions there are regional, ethnical and, in a way, nationalistic.

Nor is the case of the United States very different. As a largely emigrant society, the USA has had to take systematic steps to break the *external* loyalties of its different ethnic groups. That this was a serious problem became clear during the neutrality period of the first World War when large sections of the German-Americans —the hyphenated as they were called—openly professed a divided loyalty. In the second World War the Japanese-Americans were evacuated to less sensitive areas as their loyalty was suspect. The United States may thus be said to have successfully solved the problem of external loyalty of its emigrant ethnic groups—except of the Jews whose allegiance not to an external state but to a world-wide community remains strong as ever—through a determined educational policy, strengthened of course by the unparalleled economic prosperity and the broad-based political liberties in the new state to which they have emigrated.

Though the external loyalties—apart from the sympathies—of racial minorities have been extinguished, could it be said that national and emotional integration has taken place in the United States? The recurrent race riots, the resistance to the liberal racial policies of the federal government, residential segregation and widespread anti-Semitic feelings, these things which no one denies would clearly prove that national and emotional integration is by no means complete in a country which, apart from peoples of European origin, has large segments of Negroes, West Indians, Puerto Ricans, Chinese and Mexicans. But the loyalty of these groups to the United States no one would question now.

The problem in India arises not out of a lack of integration but of the plural nature of India's society. For the last 700 years India's society has consisted dominantly of two elements, Hindus and Muslims, functioning vertically, from the Himalayas to Cape Comorin, and socially operating in watertight compartments. Islam was an integrated community with the traditions of a ruling class and vague claims of being a conquering race. The Hindus were but imperfectly integrated over a long period but in the nineteenth century they became, as we have seen, a single community united by a reformed religion, culture and social organization, and claiming on the basis of their numbers and their new-found history to be the Indian people, with others constituting only racial and religious minorities. With the secession of the Muslim majority areas and their constitutions into the State of Pakistan, the Muslims in India became in effect a minority, though spread throughout India. The problem is the adjustment between the two, the acceptance by the Hindus of the Muslims as an integral part of Indian life, organized separately, possessing a culture of their own and constituting an important part of the Indian nation, though a minority: and equally the acceptance by the Muslims that in the new India the Hindus constitute not merely a majority but the dominant society and culture. The Hindus have to adjust themselves to the position that India is not merely Hindustan but a state where other communities have equal rights—in fact, accept the doctrine of the secular state as enshrined in the Constitution and forget the idea of a *Hindu pada padishahi*. The Muslims on their part, however much they may cherish their past, must discard the sense of superiority arising from their idea of being a conquering race who had ruled major portions of India for a long time and adjust themselves to the position of being a national minority, entitled to equal rights and privileges, but still as an organized group only a minority with its own culture and social structure.

The Hindu-Muslim relationship is the one major problem of

national integration, for the other minorities have no pretensions of being a conquering race with special historic rights. Nor do the Christians, Parsis, Sikhs and other communities stand face to face with Hindus all over India to constitute a national problem. Also they do not represent, broadly speaking, a separate culture.

There is one aspect of this question which neither leaders nor political analysts have dared to face frankly, and that is the relation of the Muslim community in India with Pakistan. There is no doubt that the vast majority of Muslims in India are loyal to the motherland. But there are groups whose allegiance is not so certain. People in India cannot easily forget that the agitation for separation—for Pakistan—was supported mainly by the Muslims of the Gangetic valley, especially the United Provinces, now Uttar Pradesh. The bitterness of communal feelings was also concentrated in this area, where the Muslims though a minority had been a ruling class, and were, from the social point of view, till Partition a dominant group. The UP Muslims, who were active supporters of Pakistan till August 1947, have in the main stayed on in India though most of their leaders have gone over to Pakistan. Is it to be assumed that overnight these followers of the two-nations theory, who had argued on the assumption that Hindus and Muslims could not co-exist peacefully as their principles of life were opposed to each other, became believers in a secular state and lost their attachment to the idea of Pakistan? The action of men like Chaudhari Khaliq-uz-Zaman from UP, and Hussein Imam from Bihar, who had stayed behind and as members of the Constituent Assembly taken the oath of allegiance and proclaimed their devotion to India, later surreptitiously going to Pakistan, would show that among certain sections of Muslims the pro-Pakistan feeling survived Partition. That with quite considerable groups the attachment to secularism is only nominal is frankly acknowledged by so eminent a Muslim as Col. B. H. Zaidi, Vice-Chancellor of the Aligarh University who, in his note on the report of the communal trouble in Aligarh, states: 'Since independence the University is gradually advancing towards secularism. But no institution with the history and outlook of the pre-independence era (when Aligarh was a citadel of pro-Pakistan and separatist feeling) could be transformed in the course of a few years, keeping in view the atmosphere of the country.' Later, in the same statement, Col. Zaidi says, 'the anti-national elements should be checked'.[1] What this means is that at the premier Muslim educational institution in India there survives to some extent at least the pre-independence pro-Pakistani ('anti-national') spirit.

The fact is that, while the overwhelming majority of Muslims in India are loyal Indian citizens, the agitation for Pakistan is too recent and provides emotional sustenance to sections of the Muslim intelligentsia in the Gangetic valley so that those who have stayed behind in India find it difficult to forget the past or to reconcile themselves to the concept of a secular India. Many Hindus (again mainly of the UP and Bihar), on the other hand, find it hard to accept the view that the Muslims who have remained in India, at least of their area, are not emotionally committed to Pakistan. They, therefore, find the doctrine of a secular state, at least so far as it relates to Muslims, a reflection of Hindu weakness which may endanger the security and future of the state.

The question may well be asked whether 'integration', emotional or social, between Hindus and Muslims, both separately integrated and with basically different social ideals, is necessary for our national unity. In a plural society what is required is an overriding loyalty to the State and a general tolerance of each other's ideals and not an assimilation of different groups. So far as the Muslims are concerned, that overall loyalty to India may be said to exist, though side by side with it a pro-Pakistan and pan-Islamic feeling may also survive in the minds of a small but diminishing group which with time may wholly disappear. So far as social and emotional integration is concerned, during the last 750 years, since Islam became a part of Indian life, in no sphere has such an integration taken place. Islam and Hinduism have influenced each other in marginal ways: for example in the formation of certain religious sects. An Indo-Islamic architecture developed but the architecture of the Hindus continued to evolve along its own lines. So far as art is concerned, the Moghul school was undoubtedly a variation of the Indo-Persian style as influenced by Hindu traditions, and yet it was never more than a court art. The Rajput and Pahari paintings, which were popular, mythological and religious, continued to develop all through this period on purely Hindu lines. Urdu may be cited as an example of the mingling of Hindu and Islamic cultural traits, and yet in its

[1] Statement in the *Hindustan Times* of November 26, 1961.

development, as different from its origin, it lost its character of synthesis and became predominantly Islamic in its background, culture and expression, drawing more and more on Persian than on Indian sources.

Thus, it will be obvious that while the Muslims will be an important section of the Indian people entitled to equality in all matters and also to the protection and encouragement of their religion and culture, any idea of their integration with the other communities should be considered as vain and meaningless. In fact the Muslim doctrine itself is one of an exclusive society, and so long as the community is loyal to the State and works in friendly collaboration with the rest and is not allowed to cherish grievances on the ground of lack of opportunities, no one could ask that the Muslims should merge their identity in a wider Indian community.

Another factor which, it is alleged, is standing in the way of India's complete integration is regionalism. No real democracy can function anywhere without a genuine and healthy sense of regionalism. Even quite small states like the Swiss Confederation are based on an acceptance of the value of regional feeling. It used to be said by a distinguished French statesman who represented the city of Le Havre that apart from questions affecting national security and the greatness of France, the most important national problem to him was the extension of the harbour facilities of his home town. Parliamentary representation, it will be conceded involves emphasis on local interests, subject of course to over-riding considerations of national policies. This is so even in unitary states, and nowhere is it considered as an element of weakness in the nation.

Federal constitutions are indeed meant to safeguard regional interests; that is the basis of a federal union. Naturally in a country like India where the constituent states are larger than many nations of Europe, and have histories and traditions which are of value and go back far into time, the feeling of regionalism is likely to be more emphasized than, say, in the United States, where many of the constituent units have no special historical identity. But in federations like Germany and the Soviet Union, regionalism is a well-marked and accepted characteristic so long as the primacy of national interests is recognized. In fact without a regional sense a federal system cannot work properly. It is the main factor which secures an equitable distribution of resources, a balanced development, and sees that there is no dominance by one area over another, and thus prevents the growth of separatist tendencies in the nation.

The great regions in India, with their developed languages, with their historic cultures, and continuous traditions are essential parts of the conception of India. No one can conceive of India except in terms of its great regions: Bengal, the Punjab, Gujarat, Maharastra, Andhra, Tamilnad, Kerala, Karnatak, the Gangetic valley, etc. Any other image of India would be something abstract, without flesh and blood. That these regions should feel proud of their tradition and history as parts of India and should emphasize their special contributions to India's culture is not a source of weakness but of national strength. In an autocracy, this feeling of regionalism could for a time at least be suppressed. Soon after the military junta took over in Pakistan, voices which had previously clamoured the interests of Bengal, Sindh, Punjab, etc., became silent, but it is too facile to conclude that overnight the regional feelings of these areas had disappeared. A democracy—especially a federal form of it—encourages such regional feeling, for not only does it help to safeguard local interests, but prevents dissatisfaction from taking root.

Regionalism in India has no doubt certain undesirable features; a sense of superiority over neighbouring groups, of uniqueness of contribution to the nation, of the special qualities of its people. These are inoffensive vanities, which may cause a temporary sense of jealousy but do not affect national interests. If the Bengalis feel that they have made a unique contribution to the growth of the national idea in India, and they are an exceptionally gifted race in matters of artistic creativeness, or if the Marathas feel that they are an imperial people, and the Punjabis that they are the sword-arm of India, these are aspects of a self-image that people have created which do not interfere with a nation's development.

Why then is there this talk of regionalism being a danger? Carefully analysed it would be seen to originate from areas and groups which enjoy at the present time more than their share of power. It is in fact essentially a cry of the vested interests who desire to safeguard the predominance they have achieved in the past. Industrially backward areas like Assam, Orissa and Kerala, clamouring for the creation in their states of major industries under central control, states which find that in the Central cabinet they are not adequately represented, governments which take special action to give them a start in economic development, these are generally denounced as encouraging regionalism.

Similar considerations apply in regard to languages. The regional languages of India are integrated with the life and culture of the areas in which they are spoken. In fact the Constitution recognizes this and these languages have been listed as national languages equally deserving protection and encouragement, though Hindi has been declared and accepted as the common language for federal purposes. The reorganization of the states broadly on the basis of linguistic unity has helped both to create a greater feeling of solidarity and integrity in the constituent states and to endow the regional languages with a sense of their own importance in national life. In many states they have been made the local official languages and in some places they have also been made the media of University education. Some of these actions may be considered unwise. It is a part of democratic political life to learn by mistakes: but it is difficult to see how this kind of enthusiasm, misplaced as it may be, weakens the nation or helps to develop separatist tendencies.

Rightly considered, it will be seen that India is no mere political federation: it is also a federation of cultures, involving different languages also. In such a federation there is a dominant Central Government under the protecting umbrella of which the units function and have their being. In the cultural federation also there is a dominant culture and society, but the other parallel cultures like the Islamic have their independent and guaranteed existence with equal encouragement from the nation. That is the type of integration that India has evolved and to attempt to force any other on her would be to go against the principles of India's historical evolution.

CHAPTER XX

The Political Profile

The age-old political tradition in India before Independence was that of an administering state. At all times, from the time of the Nandas in the fourth century BC, it was a vast bureaucracy that governed the country, collected its revenue, looked after the irrigation system and maintained law and order. Basically the British system was not different from that of the Mauryas or the Moghuls, except for the gradual introduction of elected representation and after 1919, of a form of limited democratic institutions. This, however, made no serious dent in the mighty administrative edifice that the British had raised on the earlier foundations which they had inherited.

The significant change that came over India during the last quarter of the century and became in the inter-war period a major factor in Indian life was the emergence of a political class. In Bengal, even during the first half of the nineteenth century, that is fifty years earlier than in other parts of India, the intelligentsia had turned its attention to political activities and had organized societies and associations and started journals and newspapers. In the other provinces this began only by 1870 and gained importance only with the foundation of the National Congress. In an administering state the politician who is ready with his criticism and liberal with his suggestions of improvement is not a welcome figure. He is an object of derision, a 'discontented babu' in the case of Indians and an interfering 'Paget MP' in the case even of British Members of Parliament who interested themselves in Indian affairs. This is not surprising. A politician becomes a central figure only in a democracy. Under an autocratic monarchy he is a seditionist; under a bureaucracy he is a nuisance. In British

India, which combined the characteristics of both, he was a seditionist and a nuisance. There was a further complication which also cannot be overlooked, and that was the racialist attitude of the British authorities. Till after the first Great War, the bureaucracy in India was almost wholly European. Though an Indian member was included in the Central and in each of the Provincial cabinets after 1909, the Government of India was and claimed to be a 'white' government. As the politicians were Western-educated Indians, it appeared to British administrators insufferable impertinence that the natives should presume to teach them how to administer India. Till the end of British rule in India, this sense of superiority of the civil servants and an attitude of barely concealed contempt towards the political classes continued to be a major factor of life in India.

If the attitude of the civil services towards the political classes was one of contempt, the common people in India, much to the disappointment of the European administrators, began to look upon them early as their champions. The early leaders of the Congress—Madan Mohan Malaviya, Surendranath Bannerji, Pheroze Shah Mehta, Gokhale and others—though not men of the people, were the heroes of the educated classes and were revered by the common people. This was not only because the people vaguely realized that they were fighting the country's cause at the risk of the anger of the rulers, and often at great sacrifice to themselves, but because the political leaders were in many respects the most representative minds of India at the time. Men like Malaviya and Gokhale were undoubtedly the cream of India's educated classes. Even the 'dumb masses', whose support the administrators claimed, realized that those leaders were their own kith and kin, but that the struggle they were engaged in was essentially in the interests of all Indians. The popular reaction to the arrest of Mr Tilak in the cosmopolitan city of Bombay long before the Congress movement became a mass struggle under Mahatma Gandhi's leadership, no less than the enthusiasm with which popular leaders were received in areas far away from their own province, provided evidence of the general public's attitude towards the political classes long before Mr Gandhi's advent into Indian politics. It is true that the ruling Princes, the landed aristocracy and certain specially favoured groups like the so-called 'martial classes' kept aloof from political parties and pretended to share the contempt of the Europeans for the educated classes. But it became evident with every year that passed that the new middle classes had become the determining factor in Indian life and had displaced the decrepit and decayed aristocracy to whom the British still continued to extend their patronage.

In the period between the end of the first war (1918) and the achievement of Independence political initiative definitely passed to these classes. The introduction of direct election to the provincial and central legislatures, the establishment of partial responsible government in the provinces and the creation of a central assembly with a non-official Indian majority—in short the beginnings of a democratic system—emphasized the special position of the middle classes represented by the National Congress. In spite of all efforts to set up factions and groups with the object of creating divisions in the national ranks, every election under the dyarchical system served only to prove the hold of the Congress on the electorate. The Congress tried successfully to combine the characteristics of a mass movement with the functions of a parliamentary party. It had thus even before Independence gained considerable experience of electoral organization and parliamentary control.

With Independence the political classes took charge of the country, and the politician became the central figure on the stage. Power lay with them; policies were decided by him. He represented the national will. The masses on whose support this power was based were organized, directed and controlled by the Indian National Congress which, in spite of Mahatma Gandhi's advice in favour of its abolition, was transformed from an organization for conducting the struggle for freedom into a political party for conducting elections and providing leadership for government. It is the Congress functioning as a party that made representative government possible in India. Its immense prestige, its organizational machinery and its nation-wide character with experienced leadership at all levels enabled the provisional government to conduct general elections based on adult franchise and secure in parliament and state assemblies large majorities belonging to the same party and functioning for common objectives under an accepted leadership. In this process of transforming itself from a broad-based national coalition, which it was in the days before Independence, into an effective political organization the National

Congress dropped segments of its supporters both on the Right and the Left, leaving it a centralist party with a socialist bias. It was a socialist group that left the Congress first. In 1946 they resigned in a body from the Congress and organized the Socialist party. In the period that followed Independence the conservative groups who had worked in co-operation with the Congress, recognizing the importance of contesting the general elections on their own platforms, shed their allegiance to the parent body. The parties of the Right were mainly at the State level and were limited to certain areas. A further secession of left-wing groups from the Congress took place in 1949 when an influential section felt that Congress policies were not radical enough and left the organization to form the Kisan Mazdoor Party. This was generally welcomed by the country as likely to provide an effective parliamentary opposition as the leadership of the new party both at the Centre and in the States was in the hands of widely respected political leaders like J. B. Kripalani who had been President of the Congress, T. Prakasam who, for more than a quarter of a century, had been the leading Congress personality in Andhra, and others of similar status in national political life. The Kisan Mazdoor Party, however, did not fare well at the general elections and consequently coalesced with the Socialists to form the Praja (people's) Socialist Party which constituted the main opposition to the Congress till the elections in 1962.

With the gradual elimination of conflicting elements within the party, the Congress was able to lay down the framework of a general policy within which it could chalk out a programme for the nation. Moving with cautious steps towards the left, the Congress at its annual session at Avadi (1956) defined its political objective as the creation of a 'socialistic pattern' of society. Later it came out more clearly in favour of a form of socialism which accepted neither class-struggle nor historical materialism as its dogmas. The socialism of the Congress emphasized the necessity for social equality, the ownership or control by the state of basic industries, co-operative agriculture and a tax system meant to ensure a more equitable distribution of wealth.

It was obvious from the beginning that the size and population of India, the regional feeling which is a characteristic of its history, and the federal structure of its government rendered the existence of strong national parties essential for the maintenance of India's unity. The emphasis on units which every federation involves has to be counter-balanced by a powerful cementing force which a political party with a national ideology alone can provide. From this point of view the service that the Indian National Congress has rendered after Independence is no less important than its services to the achievement of freedom. The state legislatures (with the exception of Kerala for a time) and the Central Parliament were able to function smoothly and carry out uniform policies all over India because the Congress as a national party was able to secure a workable majority at the Centre and in most states. It has also served as a national agency of communication, a transmission belt through which the policies and ideas of the Central Government were conveyed continuously to the people all over the country; and, conversely, transmitted to political leadership the reaction of the public to the acts and measures of government. The nation-wide organization of the Congress enabled the Government to keep in the closest touch with the people and to function as an effective democracy.

A democracy based on adult franchise functioning through elected members at all levels requires many thousands of representatives to run the machinery of popular government. Not only Parliament and assemblies, but municipal bodies, district boards, *zillah parishads*, village councils and other advisory bodies depend on elected personnel for their functioning. In the present circumstances it would be impossible for an individual of ordinary resources without an effective party organization behind him to canvass support, explain policies or to make himself known to the electorate. Thus, without organized parties, commanding resources and an army of volunteers elections would become the game of the wealthy. Without national parties with well-defined policies and organized support, parliamentary democracy would everywhere be a sham. The Congress and the other parties by functioning on a national basis have thus helped to strengthen democracy in India and have made the functioning of representative institutions easy.

A criticism is often voiced in India that the leviathan character of the Congress does not permit the growth of other parties and, therefore, in spite of the fact that there is a plethora of parties, there is no effective opposition in parliament. It is argued that as parliamentary democracy without the prospect of an alternative government is only a camouflaged one-party government—as the opposition remains only formal and nominal—parties which remain long in power without fear of being displaced become arbitrary, corrupt and tend to look upon all opposition as sedition. It is true that in parliament the opposition is weak and divided, and consequently the challenge of an alternative government is not there. The ineffectiveness of the opposition arises not from the fact that there is no chance of the Congress being displaced but the parties to the Left, which have so far constituted the opposition, lack alternative policies. With the objectives of the Congress, rapid industrialization, planning, social reforms, etc., they are in agreement. The policies that the Government follow, non-alignment in foreign relations, co-operation in commercial, cultural and industrial fields with all countries without reference to their political ideologies, meet with approval. The difference between the Congress and the opposition parties to the Left is one of emphasis and approach.

A root and branch opposition to the Congress and its policies could only have come from the Right. Its internal policies, the abolition of landlordism, racial social reform, systems of taxation which fall heavily on the richer classes, emphasis on the public sector in industry and its frankly egalitarian approach are naturally looked upon with alarm and anxiety by the orthodox conservative classes in the country. But no serious opposition developed from among them for a considerable time. The apparent indifference with which the conservative classes, the great landlords and jagirdars, the vested interests of religious and social orthodoxy, and the powerful capitalist groups accepted radical legislation affecting every aspect of their life, wealth, social status, religious practices and family land may seem surprising.

It was due to a number of factors, each one of them strong enough to weaken their position, but which collectively paralysed them from effective action. In the first place, these classes had been, generally speaking, supporters of the British in India. They had been the loyalists, the supplicants for titles, honours and dignities from the British, the people whom the foreign rulers always put forward as the real and genuine representatives of India. With the departure of the British they became demoralized for a time as the props on which they had leaned had been withdrawn from under them. Secondly, the happenings elsewhere in Asia, especially in China where the landlords and classes allied to them were being ruthlessly liquidated, made the policies of the Government of India seem moderate and liberal and there was the thankful feeling that moderate reforms in time might keep out the dangerous revolutionary trends which were making themselves evident in India also, e.g. Telingana. Determined opposition to reforms might, it was feared, lead to the growth of more radical movements in India. Thirdly, there was the immense prestige which the Congress leadership had acquired during the national struggle. To create an opposition out of scattered elements without popular support, considered at the best of times as stooges of the British, against the heroes of the struggle for independence, was altogether an impossible task at the time.

It is not that in special areas like the Punjab, Bengal or Orissa parties were not organized to oppose one or other aspect of Congress policy. The Jan Sangh in the Punjab and Western UP is a political organization representing a lower middle-class point of view which has shown considerable strength in its opposition to the Congress. In Orissa, about half of which had been under the authority of local princes till 1947, the dispossessed rulers allying themselves with the landed gentry organized a party known as the Ganatantra Parishad (Republican Party) which gave a stiff fight to the Congress in two elections.

An All-India conservative party was, however, slow to emerge, but when it came (1960) it was led by men who had long records of service in the Congress and whose political activities in the past had not been tainted by loyalism to the British Government, or by lack of sacrifice in the national cause. The founder leader of the Swatantra party was C. Rajagopalachari, who had not only been one of the prominent leaders of the non-co-operation movement from the earliest days but had held the highest offices under the Congress government. The chief Minister of Madras in the first Congress ministry (1937), Governor of Bengal, the first Indian Governor-General of India, Home Minister in the Central government and finally again Chief Minister of Madras, C. Rajagopalachari can claim that his record of national service is not inferior to that of anyone else. K. M. Munshi, another leading member of the party, was the Home Minister in the first Congress government of Bombay, Minister of Food and Agriculture in the Central Cabinet under Mr Nehru, Governor of UP till 1957. M. R. Masani, the Secretary-General of the party and its organizational chief, was once the Secretary of the Socialist group in the Congress and after Independence Ambassador to Brazil. The chairman of the party N. G. Ranga has also been till recently a prominent member of the Congress who had been many times to jail during the national struggle.

Thus the party leadership has a distinguished and unexceptionable background from the point of view of past service to the nation. No one could accuse the Swatantra leaders of being motivated by anything but the highest considerations. That is what gives the party such strength as it has been able to develop. The appeal of its policy tested at the 1962 General Election fell short of expectations. It met with but little success in major provinces like Madras, Bombay (Maharastra), Bengal, UP or the Punjab. In fact, except when it sailed under the colours of the former Ruling Princes as in Rajasthan or in Bihar where it was led by immensely rich zamindars, it made hardly any impact on the electorate. The national chairman of the party was defeated in his home constituency. The Secretary-General decided at the end to withdraw from the contest. The attempt to build up a nation-wide conservative opposition ended in failure. There was no doubt about what the party stood for. It was opposed root and branch to every aspect of Congress policy. In its election manifesto it had promised to abolish the planning commission. It made no secret of its opposition to the public sector in industry. It was all for free enterprise and capitalist industry. It was bitterly opposed to co-operative farming. In foreign policy it took its stand firmly on the side of the West and considered the policy of non-involvement as indirect support to Communism.

A significant feature of the Swatantra party from the beginning has been its association with high capital and with the feudal nobility. Some of the leading figures in its council like Sir Homi Modi and A. D. Shroff were quite recently directors of Tatas and are still associated with many corporations. Its leading support comes from the families of the former Ruling Princes one of whom, the Maharawal of Dungarpur, is an active worker in the party's interests. In Orissa the local party of princelings has merged with the Swatantra while Hindu communal parties, standing for the abolition of cow slaughter, the prohibition of beef and other old-world ideas have entered into electoral arrangements with them. In fact the hope of the Swatantra party has been to spearhead a grand alliance of reaction, a confederacy between the champions of orthodox Hinduism, the high priests of private enterprise and capitalist production, the feudal Princes and the landed nobility.

The emergence of the Swatantra party as a major right-wing opposition is important not so much as posing a direct challenge to the Congress, but as encouraging all the reactionary forces which had been in retreat after Independence to come together again. Thus the last two years have witnessed the revival of Muslim agitation under the old tattered flag of the Muslim League though it secured only an odd seat at the general election. The Akali agitation has taken new forms with the active encouragement of some of the leaders of the Swatantra party. The cow protectors are again vociferous in their demands. But it would be an exaggeration to conclude from this that the hold of the Congress has weakened or that in view of the right-wing agitation the ruling party will modify its policies. The popular support to the Congress and its policies has not been seriously affected, as has been conclusively proved by the 1962 General Elections which returned the Congress in a majority both at the Centre and in every one of the States. Even before the election Mr Masani had declared that he would be satisfied if the Swatantra could displace the Communists as the main opposition party to the Congress in Parliament. This they were not able to do. The Left remains the main opposition to the Congress.

One criticism, voiced not so much by national parties as by local organizations and parties functioning in the States, is that the Centre has aggrandized itself and is assuming more and more power at the expense of the States. The Indian Constitution is federal but, as we have already noticed, it is heavily weighted in favour of the Centre. But the progress of centralization has been much more rapid than anyone could have foreseen, and though it is not against the provisions of the Constitution, it may well be questioned whether it is in its spirit. To mention only two examples. Under the Constitution education, including universities outside those expressly declared federal, and public health are state subjects in which the States have full authority. But today, though the constitutional position remains unchanged, secondary education to some extent and university education as a whole have come under Central control. The expanding needs of the universities requires funds and the University Grants Commission, a central statutory body with federal funds at its disposal, is enabled by using the power of the purse to assume effective control of the policies and administration of the universities, displacing to a large extent the powers of the States. Every State desires, in view of pressure from the public, to establish new universities. Thus the States themselves become petitioners before the University Grants Commission for grants. Again, every State is an applicant for the favour of the Government of India for the establishment of regional engineering colleges, technological institutes and polytechnics. The result of all this is that the power of the States in respect of education has been greatly reduced.

It may be emphasized that the question is not whether in this particular case the expansion of central power is in national interests. It undoubtedly is. In the circumstances of India, especially in view of the feeling of regionalism, it is no doubt desirable and indeed necessary that University education should be controlled from the Centre: and further, in view of the integral connection between the university and the secondary school system the Centre should have a large voice in the shaping of secondary education also. These considerations are undoubtedly valid, but they cannot conceal the fact that the Constitution has been considerably tilted in favour of the Centre.

Another example no doubt of the legitimate extension of Central power relates to law and order which under the Constitution is reserved for the States. Clearly, apart from the local problems of enforcement of law and the maintenance of order, there is the wider problem of internal security for which the Central Government has the main responsibility. Besides, there are inter-state problems, like the prevalence of banditry in the Chambal ravines, affecting UP, Madhya Pradesh and Rajasthan, the activities of Pakistani agents, a semi-internal and semi-external problem, the revival of communal tensions, all of which require concerted action by the States and the Centre. Consequently, the power of the Centre in this sphere has also been expanding, with the connivance, if not the consent, of the States.

Broadly, it may be said that the political experience of the last fifteen years has disclosed a marked tendency towards the growth of federal power at the expense of the provinces in practically every sphere. The fact that the same party has been in power in all the States most of the time has no doubt helped in this process. But essentially the reasons for the growth of central power lie outside political considerations. The governmental tradition of the East India Company and the British Crown in India after the Regulating Act of 1773 was to centralize authority and weaken the provincial governments. Though the federal act elevated these provinces to States—endowing them with a notional sovereignty for the purposes of the federation—they were in fact only provinces and the long established tradition of their administration was to follow the directions of the Centre and this continued even after Independence. Besides, the steel frame of the Government was still the all-India services, especially the ICS, the Indian Audit and Accounts Services and the Indian Police, not only recruited on an all-India basis but forming an all-India cadre. When the question of the reorganization of the services came up, the Central Government led by the then Home Minister, V. J. Patel, was able, against the opposition of some of the major States, to keep the all-India services intact, agreeing only to a change in nomenclature from the Indian Civil Service to the Indian Administrative Service. The old system of deputation of civil servants from the provinces (now States) to the Centre and the reversion of officers after a period of service in Delhi to the provinces still continues and this helps the State administration to appreciate the all-India point of view while also conveying to the Centre the opinions and reactions of the States.

Apart from these administrative factors, there have been other major trends which have operated in favour of the growth of central power as against the power of the States. The financial resources left to the exclusive sphere of the States under the federation are inadequate even for normal progressive administration. A five-yearly financial settlement between the States and the Centre leaves the initiative even in the matter of the divisible sources of revenue with the Central Government. When it comes to development expenditure, every State is dependent on grants from the Centre. The external aid that is provided for major projects is necessarily with the Centre which has also a decisive voice in deciding the priorities of schemes. Thus every State has become a petitioner at the doorstep of the Central Government.

Even more important than the allotment of financial resources has been the influence of the Planning Commission in accelerating this policy of centralization of power. The Planning Commission is a Central body, and in drawing up schemes for development, it has to view India as a whole and allot priorities according to the Commission's judgment of the country's interests. While no doutb the plan is scrutinized by the National Development Council in which all the Chief Ministers are *ex-officio* members and the view of the States is urged there with vigour, these have inevitably to be subordinated to all-India considerations. Besides, the major development projects even in the States are centrally financed and controlled and often as in the case of the river valley projects they cover more than one State. The great industrial corporations owned and manned by the Central Government operate within the territories of States. Undertakings like steel plants, fertilizer factories, heavy electricals, locomotives, coach factories, ship-building corporations, which are situated in different States all over India are in fact projections of Central authority within the States in the economic sphere, as the machinery for the collection of income tax, central excises, are in the financial sphere. The growth of these leviathan undertakings no doubt eclipse the activities of the States. On the other hand, it should be remembered that they are helping to unite India in a more real sense than even the Constitution.

Other factors that have helped in the growth of Central authority are the intermediate bodies which came into existence for the purpose of co-ordination but which have in fact become the agencies of the Central Government. The University Grants Commission already alluded to is a very good example. The Central Water and Power Commission, the Oil and Natural Gas Commission, are other examples. The zonal councils of States which meet under the Chairmanship of the Central Home Minister to discuss common problems between neighbouring States also work effectively towards the increase of Central power based no doubt on discussion and consent. In fact a marked tendency has been for Central organization of this nature to spread out into the States.

The Constitution itself has created a kind of 'paramountcy' for the Centre by providing for the suspension of State governments and the imposition of 'President's rule' under certain conditions such as the breakdown of administration—a flexible phrase—financial bankruptcy, the pursuance of policies detrimental to India or the utilization of the State's executive power in such a way as to impinge upon the authority of the Centre. No doubt these are necessary provisions and have their origin in the vague claims of paramountcy which the British Government exercised in regard to the princely states of India. In the Government of India Act, 1935, a special clause had been introduced laying down that the executive authority of the units should not be used in such a was as to impinge on the authority of the federation. The necessity for this clause arose because the princely states insisted on claiming that as sovereign states the Centre should have no right of interference in their administrations, which claim the federation could accept only if they were prohibited from using their executive power against the authority of the Centre. This doctrine has been carried on to the new Constitution and extended so as to give to the Centre a positive power of interposing its authority through the President's rule in case of the breakdown of the State administration.

During the last fifteen years the Central Government has not been sparing in the use of this power of paramountcy. Generally speaking, where the Centre interposed its authority, there was adequate constitutional justification. But the case of Kerala stands on a different footing. The Communist party was in power in Kerala and the Congress was in opposition. There was no question that the Communists enjoyed the confidence of the legislature but the conflict in the legislature between the parties was carried into the country with the avowed object of bringing about an intervention by the Central Government. Without a breakdown such intervention would not be justified. So a breakdown had to be brought about. For this purpose organized direct action was resorted to. It was led by the Congress, under the authority of the Party High Command in Delhi, whose leaders continuously visited the state to give guidance to the agitation. That the Party High Command was in close association with the Central Government would hardly be denied. Having thus itself helped to create a political crisis in the State, the Central Government imposed the President's rule on the ground that there had been a breakdown of administration. The breakdown of administration was, if not created, at least promoted by the Central Government in order to enable it to give its intervention a legitimacy. In effect it was a reaffirmation of the doctrine of paramountcy.

As the government against which the power was evoked was Communist and had alienated certain powerful sections within the State, the constitutional aspect of this combined action of agitation by the party in power at the Centre and the use of constitutional authority by the government at the Centre was generally overlooked. But it has far-reaching implications as it has laid down a precedent for intervention in the States based on agitation supported from outside—in short the revival of the claim of the paramountcy of the Central power.

This paramountcy is further strengthened by the right which the President has for withholding approval of or referring back legislation which the Governor of a province may reserve for his consideration. The Governor himself is not only a nominee of the Central Government but its agent. So the approval of the Governor for legislative measures is in effect an approval of the Central Government. Conflicts may of course arise between a ministry enjoying the confidence of the legislature and a Governor who withholds his consent to legislation on his own or on advice from the Centre, but in view of the overwhelming authority of the federation such a conflict is unlikely. So long as the party in power at the Centre and in the States is the same, the Centre's authority will be supreme at both levels and no conflict need be expected: but where, as it happened in Kerala, the party in power in a State is in the opposition at the Centre, the Governor as representing the constitutional and the paramountcy powers of the federal government becomes an important political factor.

It is obvious that this tendency has grown not only because it is in the nature of things for the Central authority in a federation to gain strength at the expense of the States but because it responds to the need for national policies in many matters in the circumstances of today. Not only in respect of what may be called federal subjects, but also in areas within the sphere of State government like education, public health, industries, the necessity for united national policies would hardly be questioned. Besides, the large-scale industrialization under Central direction which India is trying to bring about requires fairly uniform standards in technical services, even where they are outside the scope of federal control. Irrigation, forestry, engineering—to mention only a few examples —clearly require all-India standards, and consequently the pressure from the Centre for all-India services in these matters has been mounting. The States Reorganization Committee also recommended the creation of other all-India services for the purpose of strengthening the administrative unity of India. Briefly, it may be said that Central organizations not only within the legitimate sphere of the federal government but in what may be called the large but undefined area of co-operation between the State and Centre are increasing in every direction.

This tendency is further strengthened by the industrial and labour organizations which during the British period had been built upon an all-India basis. The All-India Trade Union Congress and its affiliated organizations, the Employers' Federation, the All-India Manufacturers' Association, the Federation of Indian Chambers of Commerce and Industry and similar bodies which mould the opinion of large and influential classes, are organized on an all-India basis mainly to deal with the Central Government. The State governments hardly come into their calculation. The necessity for national policies in respect of industries, trade, labour problems—apart from the dominating influence of foreign exchange and import and export restrictions which are exclusively within the power of the Centre—gives increasing strength to the movement for centralization. The State governments, even when they resent it, are pushed along by these irresistible factors.

Has India developed no countervailing power to balance this trend? The existence of a strong sense of regionalism would normally have operated against the encroachments of the Centre. But actually such has not been the result in India. It cannot be emphasized too much that regional feeling in India has not been in relation to the Centre, except perhaps to a small degree in the State of Madras, but in a sense of rivalry *to other regions*. All are claimants for the patronage and bounty of the Centre. It is a kind of rivalry between the Tamils and the Andhras, the Gujeratis and the Marathas, the Bengalis and the Biharis, each desiring to go forward more rapidly than the other and each in a measure jealous of the other, that passes for regionalism in India. In many ways it is a very healthy feeling, but it does not create a countervailing power against the growing authority of the Centre. In fact it may even be claimed that this limited sense of regionalism strengthens the trends towards centralization, for each area looks to the Centre for greater assistance, more liberal treatment and more favoured allocation of industries and developmental activities.

If regionalism provides no countervailing power against centralization the new system of *panchayati raj*, or government based on village and block councils, provides even less. *Panchayati raj*, in which effective power in many fields is vested in primary units—village councils—is no doubt a revolutionary development in democratic practice. But what it does is to take away power from the State governments and entrust it to local bodies, thereby making the State governments even weaker in relation to the Centre. The village and block panchayats, while they may be effective instruments of local government, will be powerless against the Centre whose authority, while not directly touching them, will continue to grow unimpeded by any claims of state power.

Finally, it may be emphasized that great changes such as those which India has witnessed during the last fifteen years could only be stabilized by a new administrative system, centrally controlled, functioning as the instrument of national policies. Where a new system is radical in its implications, a new administrative machinery is required for its success. The growth of the civil services in India after Independence, working no doubt under political control, and handling problems with which the old ICS was unfamiliar—like the management of international trade, finance, banking and insurance, control of vast industrial concerns, supervision of large-scale welfare projects—is the reflection of the new society that India is building up. Necessarily it involves a continuing centralization of power, if not in respect of administration at least in respect of the formulation of policy and minimum control of standards of execution through financial assistance, the planning commission, advisory bodies and other similar institutions.

CHAPTER XXI

The Social Profile

We have seen in a previous chapter that a social revolution is being attempted in India through normal legislative processes. The personal laws of the Hindus which have come down from time immemorial are being changed. During the last fifteen years India has sought to effect radical changes in the laws relating to marriage, succession, women's right to property, etc., bringing the country on a level with modern societies in other parts of the world. The economics of the joint family which, even under the impact of modern capitalism-controlled industrial and financial growth in India has been to a large extent displaced by the overwhelming importance of the public sector in industries. The village societies on which life in India has been based in the past are being shaken up, welded together into larger social groups and communities and entrusted with political and economic initiative. The feudal influence of princes, talukdars, zamindars and large landowners has been liquidated. Classes and communities which have so far been among the under-privileged have been encouraged by political processes, no less than by economic policies, to assume greater importance in national life. From a status-dominated society India is gradually emerging as an egalitarian democratic community.

The most significant feature in Indian social life is the combination of what Max Lerner calls the metaphysic of secular promise with the desire for ultimate spiritual liberation. The secular promise is the outcome of the impact of the West, and is now shared broadly by all sections of the community. Even what used to be called the untouchable classes today look forward to better conditions of life. Education, medical services, higher wages and consequently better standards of comfort than they were ever accustomed to are being taken to their doorsteps. The awakening to this promise of a better life among the less privileged sections has been slow, but it is undoubtedly gaining momentum. Among the intervening classes, those between the middle strata of society and the depressed classes, the movement is more marked. All over the country castes, communities and classes who had long been neglected have suddenly realized the power vested in them by adult franchise, opportunities opened to them by the new education and by training in technical skills. Also, they have not been left unaffected by democratic conceptions. The trade unions, *kisan sabhas* (peasant associations) and other organizations have awakened them to their rights. Community development programmes, *panchayati raj* and other official programmes have shown the new generation in these classes that they are the masters. Consequently, there have been radical changes both in their social ideals and in their expectations.

If the metaphysic of secular promise has become a major factor with the common people, side by side with it one can see a strengthening of religious faith among all classes of people. There is undoubtedly growing up among limited circles—not confined to any particular class—a feeling of alienation from religion. It is a part of the secular movement. But as against this, all over India one can see the growth of a religious feeling, not dogmatic or sectarian but deeply moved by faith. This is the contradiction in India today. The first *kumbh mela*, a religious festival which takes place once in twelve years at Allahabad, after Independence became almost a demonstration of this revival of faith. More than 5,000,000 pilgrims gathered on the banks of the Ganges to have a dip in the sacred waters at the Sangam where the Jamuna joins the Ganges. Special trains had to be run to accommodate the rush of pilgrims. The police arrangements at Allahabad were strained almost to breaking-point. The frenzy which possessed the pilgrims was indescribable. The President of India and other high dignitaries were among the pilgrims. Nor is this to be considered an isolated display of religious fervour. Every place of pilgrimage, Badrinath and Kedarnath perched high in the Himalayas; Amarnath in Kashmir 13,000 feet above sea level; Gaya, Dwaraka, Puri, Tirupati, Rameswaram, to mention only the most important, bear witness not only to an ever-increasing number of pilgrims but to a strengthening of the religious spirit.

Another significant aspect of this development has been the influence of *gurus*, saints and holy personages, men and women, all over India. The first half of the twentieth century was particularly prolific in holy men who by their devotion, saintliness and presumably spiritual development were able to influence large sections of the community. They were not founders of sects or cults, but *gurus* who strengthened people's faith and gave guidance and comfort to their disciples. The most famous of these whose life and activities extended into the post-Independence period were Shri Ramana Maharshi, Shri Aurobindo, Anandamoyee Devi and Sivananda. Significantly enough it is a continuing phenomenon, and the disciples are in many cases not ordinary illiterate folk but people of education and intelligence. The demand for compulsory study of Sanskrit in schools, the enthusiasm for the rebuilding of temples destroyed by the Muslims in their iconoclastic zeal, demand for the prohibition of cow slaughter, are other significant features of this revival of faith.

Caste also continues to throw its shadow on the social scene. It is undoubtedly a diminishing factor in Indian life and yet the time has not come when we can say that it is merely a survival without an active hold on people's minds. The caste system has so long been a part of the process of life in India that it will take many generations before its baneful influence can be wholly exorcized from the spirit of India. Its legal basis, the prohibition of marriage outside caste, no longer exists. Other factors which helped it like the hierarchical view of society are also disappearing. Many castes which had been considered as low in rank have come up in the social scale, thereby rendering meaningless the traditional scales of caste. Numerous other factors are undoubtedly working towards not only the weakening but the elimination of caste as a social organization. And yet it would not be untrue to say that outside the sphere of politics and administration and to a considerable extent in the field of voluntary activity, the hold of caste though weakened continues to be a factor of importance. It is not the old system of exclusiveness, assumption of superiority, belief in the naturalness of the privilege of the higher classes—all these have undoubtedly gone. The Brahmins' superiority is not today accepted by anyone. Other communities have displaced the Kshatriyas in political power. Democracy by definition means government by the common people, while socialism to which the Congress is wedded and which is gradually being introduced not only as an economic but a social progress, means power in the hands of the working classes—the Sudras of the Hindu caste system. It is a Sudra government that is not merely the ideal but is gradually coming into existence in India. Consequently, though the caste processes are still a factor, it is not the caste system with its national assumption of the superiority of the higher castes that still continues to be in evidence.

One often hears of the prevalence of 'casteism', especially in politics. This accusation comes mainly from the higher castes whose privileged position in society, official life and politics, is being threatened by the awakening of the new classes. As in India caste relationships are best known and understood, this awakening of the lower classes is often expressed in caste terms. Thus the land workers in Madras who captured a considerable number of seats in the rural areas assumed a caste name and came to be known as *vahni kshatriyas*. In Rajasthan the displacement of the feudal Rajput jagirdars (land grantees) by the cultivating *jat* peasantry came to be interpreted in terms of the growing ascendancy of the *jat* castes. In this way the changes in social relationship and the acquisition of power by classes so long kept down or ignored appeared to the higher castes as a new form of caste struggle, though in truth they reflect the upheaval of democratic feeling among the lower classes of the past.

The rise of social democracy which is the major factor in Indian life after Independence is inevitably accompanied by large-scale changes in the social relationship between classes. Communities which as a result of long established land-owning (as in the case of the Nairs, Vellalas and Reddis, in the south and the Rajputs and others in the north) or through many generations of literacy and official traditions, as the Kayasthas in the north and Brahmins everywhere, enjoyed political power and social prestige find their position not only threatened but seriously encroached upon by others. The old classes, well-entrenched in power, fight bitter rear-guard actions and are able through their better educational attainments, political ability and social integration to gain time for themselves. But the pressure of democracy, leading to the transfer of political power, and the spread of education, bringing with it claims for employment, have inevitably caused the gradual displacement of classes which had for long enjoyed a near monopoly in power; and it is the rise of the new classes, clothed no doubt in caste formulae, which is often attacked by vested interests as 'casteism'.

The displacement of the traditional land-owning classes by the abolition of feudal tenures like jagirdari, talukdari and zamindari has also had important results in social relationships. This is specially true with regard to the Muslims. In Oudh, the majority of talukdars or feudal land-grantees were Muslims. They, together with their dependents, constituted the upper crust of Muslim society. To some extent this was true also of conditions in Hyderabad, Bhopal and other areas where Muslim rulers held authority. The abolition of these tenures had the result of impoverishing not only the small groups who considered themselves the aristocracy of the land but of rendering without means of livelihood or of employment large bodies of retainers and hangers-on who had never thought it right that they should have to work. It is this class which constituted the leisured classes in Muslim society. Finding themselves deprived of the support of the nawabs, talukdars and zamindars, they have added to the sense of helplessness which the Muslim community (outside Bombay and Madras where their main professions were trade and business) is feeling in the areas where they enjoyed social influence in the past.

The loss of the special official, social and political influence which the community had enjoyed under the British has been a source of discontent among a section of the Muslims who, finding it difficult to reconcile themselves to the position of a minority in a predominantly Hindu country, began to think in terms of a revival of communal politics. Remnants of the activists of the old pre-Partition Muslim League which had been quiescent began to come forward to claim communal leadership, especially at centres like the Aligarh Muslim University; incidents here and there gave them a fillip. The special conditions in Kerala which compelled the Congress into an opportunist alliance with the Muslim League gave the reactionary elements hope that they might be able to play a role elsewhere if they were organized on a communal basis.

The more intelligent leaders among them realize that the conditions today are totally different. In pre-Partition days the Muslims were in a majority in five provinces. Also, as rulers of important Indian States like Hyderabad and Bhopal and as a major land-owning community in UP they enjoyed special political importance. In fact, with elected political power in their hands in major provinces like the Punjab and Bengal, the Muslims before Partition were much more than a minority community. With the secession of Pakistan that position was irretrievably lost, for though the Muslims constitute no less than 45 million in India, nowhere are they in a majority or in a position of economic, political or social importance disproportionate to their numbers as previously in UP or Hyderabad. The aggressive section in the community, which dreams of organizing again along the lines of the old Muslim League, is forgetting the essential facts of the situation created by Partition and by the economic and social policies of the Indian Government during the last fifteen years.

Hindu communalism which is a parallel movement, is no less sinister. The dominance of Mahatma Gandhi in the political life of India for over twenty-five years had held in check the forces of Hindu communalism. With him Hindu-Muslim unity, which in effect meant the support of the claims of Muslims for special consideration, was a fundamental political principle. But with the approach of Independence those who claimed a dominant position for the Hindus and the creation of a Hindu state in India began to gain strength, especially as it became clear that the Muslims were determined to create a homeland for themselves. If Pakistan was to be created as a homeland for the Muslims of India, why should not the rest of India be converted into a Hindustan; so the argument ran. During the half-year preceding Partition, when there was an undeclared civil war in North India from Navakhali in East Bengal to Rawalpindi, the Hindu communal forces organized under the banner of the Rashtriya Swayam Sevak Sangh (the RSS) attained considerable popularity with the Hindus for their aggressive retaliation to Muslim attacks. In the months immediately following Partition, they posed a grave challenge to the Congress as they whipped up communal frenzy and became in effect a rival organization to the Congress, at least in North India. But they overplayed their hands. The assassination of Mahatma Gandhi by a Hindu fanatic, suspected to be inspired by, if not associated with this movement, led to a revulsion that drove underground the forces which wanted to transform India into a counterpart of Pakistan.

For a time the secular policy of the Congress had the field to itself. Hindu reaction had to be content with voicing opposition to 'cow killing', and to the social reform legislation of the Congress. But with the revival of Muslim agitation the old cries began again to be heard. The Hindu Maha Sabha and the Ram Rajya Parishad, the two political organizations which represent what may be called the fanatical Hindu view, both came forward to contest the general elections. Though they suffered total defeat at the elections, it is worth noting that frankly Hindu parties, with their programmes of a Hindu India, are in being and appealing to the public.

It would be a mistake to underestimate these forces. While there is no chance of a Hindu communalist party gaining influence to such an extent as to affect the secular character of the State, there is some danger that its opinions might find reflection in the activities of the rank and file of the Congress and at least in some areas might thus help to aggravate the fears of the Muslims, leading in its turn to the strengthening of Muslim communal organizations.

With the disappearance of feudalism based on princely privilege, hereditary landownership, assignment of revenue and land grants, the hierarchical character of Indian society underwent a change. The Maharajas, Nawabs and other titled nobility no longer claimed social leadership and were content to take a back seat. But a new danger seemed to loom large. The new millionaires with extensive industrial interests and vast patronage at their disposal seemed desirous to step into the place vacated by the nobility. The tradition in India had never been to accord place of pride to wealth. The caste system and the traditional aristocratic approach stood in the way of that. Even in the British period ICS officers, borrowing the snobbery of intellectualism and official power from the Hindus, looked upon businessmen as mere 'box wallahs'. But after Independence a determined effort was made by business tycoons to acquire political power as an adjunct to their financial empire. The control of the newspaper press passed into the hands not of 'newspaper barons' as in England but of industrial magnates. Some of them even began building up political connections with party leaders. The social aspects of this new development were checked by Government by its system of taxation. A crippling super-tax at higher levels of income, an expenditure tax, a wealth tax, succession duties, gift tax and other legal methods of 'soaking the rich', together with a stricter administration of company laws, nipped in the bud the tendency of a developing capitalism to concentrate wealth in a few hands and thereby create a new social class in which values were based on incomes. The feudal seignorage attempted by people like Ramkrishna Dalmia and the predatory financial empire-building of men like Mundhra were resented by the common people of India. The socialist-biased government allied to the caste-biased people put an early stop to the growth of such tendencies.

Finally, we may consider the change that has come over the position of women after Independence. We have noticed in an earlier chapter how the non-cooperation movement led to the rapid emancipation of women by their participation in the political struggle. The Constitution gave them equal political rights and opened up avenues of employment. Socially, however, the position underwent a change only with the new legislation. The social code which took the place of the traditional personal laws of Hindus effected a revolutionary change in the position of women. Marriage was made a civil contract; polygamy was abolished. Divorce was permitted under certain well-defined conditions. Caste restrictions in respect of marriage were abolished. Also a uniform marriage law was enacted for all Hindus. The law of succession was changed so as to give women the right to inherit a share in the family property. Briefly, a far-reaching revolution in respect of women's rights has taken place.

Though the legal rights of Indian women are now on a par with those in the most advanced societies, the social temper has not changed sufficiently to reflect these trends. Marriages are still, generally speaking, even in the case of educated families, arranged by parents. Also, they take place generally within the broad framework of caste, though the insistence on the same or similarly grouped sub-castes has practically disappeared. No doubt in the higher circles of society there are numerous cases of marriages outside caste. This is not now—as it was in the past—frowned upon by society or disowned by relatives.

In the field of employment also, the pattern is on the whole conservative. Though a few exceptionally brilliant women compete for the administrative and foreign services, the majority of educated women limit themselves to the professions of teaching and medicine. A few choose law, and increasing numbers are now seeking employment in business firms as secretaries and clerks.

Politics attract a few, and a number of them have achieved distinction in parliamentary, social welfare and other spheres of public work.

Women in industry have not had the same social impact as in the West. Mostly they are uneducated, but with the spread of education women employed in industries may in time come to have greater influence in bringing about social changes. The cinema industry and the newly popular career of classical dancing have opened up fresh fields of activity for women. India has the second biggest motion picture industry in the world and it provides employment for a large number of educated women. In the earlier years of the cinema the class of women who took to it as a career came mostly from among professional dancers, a community which at all times had specialized in dance and music. But soon educated women from good families began to come forward. Devika Rani, a relative of the poet Tagore, Enakshi Rama Rao, Durga Khote and others who were the pioneers in this field braved public opinion when they chose the cinema as a career, and their success opened the way for many others. The cinema actress with large income and unorthodox ways of life, popular with the general public, has naturally had a considerable impact on society. No less significant had been the influence of classical dancing. Indian classical dancing had lost favour with the educated public in the nineteenth century through its association with dancing girls attached to temples among Hindus and with women of loose morals among Muslims. The social reformers who were puritanical in their opinions and who dominated social thinking in the second half of the nineteenth century considered dancing to be a degenerate and immoral art. It was only at the beginning of the century that opinion began to change. Through the efforts of Rabindranath Tagore at Santiniketan, Rukmini Devi in Madras and the poet Vallathol in Kerala, classical dancing began slowly to gain social prestige and popular approval.

Broadly speaking, however, in spite of these new trends, Indian womanhood has remained conservative. Women have obtained equal rights and economic independence; social freedom has come to them; and yet they remain conservative in their approach to life, accepting the traditional ways of life and resisting the impact of changing ideas.

CHAPTER XXII

Conclusion

It will be seen from what has been said in the foregoing pages that India today is the scene of a great experiment. What her leaders are seeking to do is to create a new civilization which absorbs and assimilates important elements from the rest of the world but builds on her own historical foundations. It is more than a process of modernization. It is an attempt to extend the bases of her own life by the acceptance of ideas like freedom, equality, government by consent with the participation of all sections, which were alien to her inherited social conceptions. It also seeks to build on the foundations of modern science, technology and large-scale industrial production. A welfare state which enables its members to live a materially good life, provides them with the goods and services which will make their lives easier, better and less subjected to the strain of poverty, illness and other avoidable hardships, while at the same time cultivating her own ethical and spiritual values, is the ideal for which India is working today. In some ways it is a unique experiment, for though in China a similar experiment is being conducted on a larger scale, what is being attempted in India has added significance because of the democratic processes of persuasion, consent and co-operation through which the ideal is sought to be realized. It is without doubt the greatest attempt in democracy that has ever been made. More, it is unique in the sense that it is the first revolution consciously undertaken through democratic processes. Its success or failure will affect not only India but the other non-Communist states in Asia whose problems are of a similar character.

The immensity of India's population, the unbroken continuity of her history, the special characteristics of her culture, these entitle her to a place as a major unit in the family of nations. Culturally, she represents a world of her own; standing apart from but in close relations with the Islamic world, the new Communist world, the world of Europe and America. Her transformation into a modern society utilizing to the fullest possible extent her human, material and spiritual resources for the welfare of mankind is, therefore, something which is of general significance. It is a process of transformation that India is engaged on now.

No doubt much that was considered picturesque and characteristic of India will be lost in this process of transformation. Caste, so long considered the identifying feature of Indian life, will certainly disappear, though its dying pangs may still cause pain and misery. The famed handicrafts of India will no doubt continue as luxury products, but they will play but little part in the economy of the country. The great difference between the rich and the poor, which marked the life of India in the past, will give place to a better distribution of national wealth. The most significant change will no doubt be in the attitude of the people towards work. The caste society emphasized the importance of intellectual life and the manual labourer was relegated to the position of a Sudra while skilled workers like blacksmiths, carpenters and weavers were classified among sub-castes belonging to the lower rungs of the caste hierarchy. In an industrial society, labour gains in importance while technicians rise in social scale and become elevated into a new semi-Brahminhood. This change which is taking place before our eyes will bring about a transformation such as has never been attempted in India.

The real question which will determine the importance of the Indian Revolution in world history is the durability of the change now taking place in India. The birth of a new civilization, an attempted synthesis of the East and the West, a co-mingling of the two producing a new way of life with a distinct individuality, this is what India today stands for. While retaining its Indian character and strengthening its spiritual foundations, New India has sought to assimilate the social purposes, the political conceptions and the economic organization of the West. If this synthesis proves to be durable and the institutions through which it is expressed gain vigour and strength through normal growth, then India will be the forerunner of a new movement, which by incorporating the ancient societies of Asia into the world-order may effect a historic transformation in our own lifetime. If either it fails or its growth is stunted, then Asia will again fall back in the march of time. But the danger is not of failure or of stunted growth; nor is it of a denial of the foundations on which she has so far built up her life and an acceptance of a rival doctrine of world organization, based not on continuity but on a complete breach with the past; but there is a danger of the development being warped and modified midway by the loss of dynamism or by the traditional forces donning the raiments of progress, assuming control and changing the direction of growth. The Communist danger, though undoubtedly there, is not serious; but the danger of old India with its appeal to the common people reasserting herself when the revolutionary enthusiasm of the present generation weakens, or when there is a setback to its programmes through causes beyond control, is there.

The battle is joined as at Kurukshetra, but only the future can say on which side the victory will be.

INDEX